China Tomorrow

Demain la Chine
Démocratie ou Dictature?

China Tomorrow

Democracy or Dictatorship?

Jean-Pierre Cabestan

Translated by N. Jayaram

ROWMAN & LITTLEFIELD
Lanham • Boulder • New York • London

Published by Rowman & Littlefield
An imprint of The Rowman & Littlefield Publishing Group, Inc.
4501 Forbes Boulevard, Suite 200, Lanham, Maryland 20706
https://rowman.com

6 Tinworth Street, London SE11 5AL, United Kingdom

British Library Cataloguing in Publication Information Available

Library of Congress Cataloging-in-Publication Data

Names: Cabestan, Jean-Pierre, author. | Jayaram, N., 1955– translator.
Title: China tomorrow : democracy or dictatorship? / Jean-Pierre Cabestan ; translated by N. Jayaram.
Other titles: Demain la Chine. English
Description: Lanham : Rowman & Littlefield, [2019] | Includes bibliographical references and index.
Identifiers: LCCN 2019003467 (print) | LCCN 2019019976 (ebook) | ISBN 9781538129593 (electronic) | ISBN 9781538129579 (cloth : alk. paper) | ISBN 9781538129586 (pbk. : alk. paper)
Subjects: LCSH: One-party systems—China. | Political culture—China. | Authoritarianism—China. | Democratization—China. | China—Politics and government—2002– | China—Politics and government—Forecasting.
Classification: LCC JQ1519.A45 (ebook) | LCC JQ1519.A45 C3313 2019 (print) | DDC 320.951—dc23
LC record available at https://lccn.loc.gov/2019003467

For Shu-tsui and Lucien Bianco,
who encouraged me to write this book

Contents

Introduction

The Chinese Political Regime's Future: A Resurgent Debate

This book is a reflection on the current state of China's political regime and its future. It aims to contribute to debate on this important issue and stimulate a discussion not only among experts but also with all knowledgeable people interested in the country.

Some commentators, especially Americans, predict the collapse in the near term of the Chinese political system, corroded by corruption and increasingly losing control over the society it governs. I contend, however, that the regime will find sustenance through its capacity for adaptation and modernization, using not only all repressive measures but also economic and financial ones at its disposal, and because of the support it enjoys among the largest section of elites and Chinese society as well as the main aspirations of this society and the weakness of democratic urges within it.

STRENGTHS AND WEAKNESSES OF PREVIOUS ANALYSES

Analyses predicting the Chinese regime's meltdown are based on two separate presumptions. Some, like that of Gordon Chang in *The Coming Collapse of China* (2001), see the current economic model as headed for ruin. Others hold that without democracy and the rule of law, China will be unable to sustain economic development and especially innovation.[1] The prognoses published by David Shambaugh and Minxin Pei in 2016 stem from this second school of thought.[2]

In Gordon Chang's view, the state enterprises' weak finances, accumulation of nonperforming debts, the opening to foreign competition imposed by China's accession to the World Trade Organization (WTO) in 2001, rising unemployment, the countryside's relative impoverishment, an unprecedented rise in corruption, and irreparable damage to the environment are all factors that will sooner or later lead the economy and consequently the political system to ruin. At that time (2001) Chang gave the regime installed by Mao Zedong in 1949 another five or at most ten years.

Obviously things have not turned out that way. Drawing on its WTO membership advantage, China has emerged as the world's second largest economy. Some public enterprises continue to lose money, but Zhu Rongji as premier dismantled many of them between 1998 and 2003, letting thirty to forty million public sector workers go; since then many public companies that survived have prospered on the back of the country's economic growth and internationalization, a number of them becoming true global behemoths. In parallel, the private sector has grown rapidly, currently representing 60 percent of gross domestic product (GDP) and becoming the main jobs provider (80 percent of urban jobs). And while the financial system has several weaknesses, they have mostly been fixed since the 2008 financial crisis and are being managed with greater prudence. The government has internationalized the yuan without making it convertible or permitting complete liberalization of capital flows; these rebooting plans, introduced beginning in 2008, boosted nonproductive investments, at the same time aggravating the indebtedness of local governments and also state enterprises. It was the astute conservatism of the People's Bank of China, the central bank, and its governor from 2002 to 2017, Zhou Xiaochuan, that indirectly benefited the shadow banking sector, with all the risks it posed for both sellers of financial products and investors, entrepreneurs, and members of the new middle classes.[3]

These new weaknesses gave rise to new and more sophisticated analyses, which one way or another predicted that the Chinese economy would get caught in a *middle-income trap,* in which comparative advantages recede (wages rise, return on investments and competitiveness of products and services fall, and economic growth slows) while the cost of any further upgrading (research and development, attracting talent and innovation) becomes prohibitive. Some analyses link this double difficulty of attracting talent and innovating with the constraints that the authoritarian political system imposes on society; they may thus be aligned with the second school of "Cassandras."

In fact, after the end of the Cold War, and strongly influenced by events and Francis Fukuyama's thesis about the definitive victory of democracy over not only Soviet totalitarianism but all other forms of government,[4] many Westerners believed that the future of the People's Republic of China (PRC) now stood compromised. The magnitude of the 1989 Chinese democratic movement and its violent repression on June 4 on Tiananmen Square, Beijing's political and geographical heart, contributed to consolidating this view. But this post–Tiananmen massacre optimism did not last. China's economic success and the political stability it has enjoyed since 1989 have evidently weakened this argument and prediction until quite recently. Quickly challenged by Samuel Huntington and others, who argued that since the end of the Cold War conflicts of civilization have replaced ideological ones, Fukuyama's thesis was more radically eclipsed by the events of September 11, 2001, and the surge of radical Islamism.[5] The gradual rehabilitation by the Chinese Communist Party (CCP) of traditional political values and culture has in a way confirmed Samuel Huntington's analysis.[6]

Early in the first decade of the twenty-first century, many agreed with Andrew Nathan in acknowledging the Chinese regime's resilience and thus its ability to forestall until a distant future all political change.[7] In 2006 Minxin Pei published a work highlighting the limits of the authoritarian development model.[8] He asserted that China's economic development model would not usher in democracy; that the neoauthoritarian state would continue to play a key role in the country's rise; and that the CCP's gradualist strategy with regard to reforms had thrown up new challenges, including an unprecedented increase in corruption and the appropriation of the economy by local party elites, who were mainly responsible for an insurmountable "governance deficit" and were also mounting resistance to all political change. Meanwhile, Nathan began to refine his verdict, invoking Chinese authoritarianism's "impermanence," the erosion of its political legitimacy, and a possible transition provoked by a new Tiananmen.[9] But then most China experts, including David Shambaugh, held that the CCP's ability to adapt was stronger than its propensity to decline, or what they called risks of atrophy. Shambaugh offered as proof the setting up by Jiang Zemin and then Hu Jintao of a form of "soft authoritarianism" ready to adopt political reforms.[10] I revisit later this highly contestable observation, which explains the optimism of numerous analysts regarding the CCP's capacity to continue overseeing economic development.

So what unleashed a new wave of skepticism about China's future? Three main causes stand out: economic slowdown and the rising specter of the middle-income trap; fragmentation and the weakening of authority under Hu, as well as the major scale of apparently uncontrollable corruption in the political system;[11] and the stubborn refusal of the CCP leadership to introduce any political reform, on the contrary being willing to consolidate the party's monopoly power and since 2012 to recentralize it around its chief, Xi Jinping. Further, the Bo Xilai affair in 2012 and what it revealed about the practices and privileges of the party's higher nomenklatura and the struggles among them might also have triggered some observers' change of mind.[12]

In *China's Future*, after establishing a useful link among the country's economic, social, political, and international situations, Shambaugh traces back to the 2007 speech by Premier Wen Jiabao at the National People's Congress the beginning of specific problems, or rather Chinese authorities' awareness of their magnitude.[13] Then, Wen declared that China's economic development was characterized by four evils: instability, imbalances, absence of coordination, and lack of sustainability. His successor, Li Keqiang, did not deviate from this, calling in 2015 for a change in the growth model, from development drawing on investment and exports to one based on consumption and services, while also curbing overcapacity in industry and strengthening agriculture. This is precisely the task Xi and his government have undertaken since the CCP unveiled in 2013 an ambitious plan for economic and institutional reforms; henceforth the market would play a "decisive" role in the economy.

Shambaugh now reckons that if the regime persists with what he calls "hard authoritarianism" — that is, the path Xi favors — Chinese authorities will not be able to achieve this delicate metamorphosis. He envisages three other options for the future: at one extreme, the installation of a neoauthoritarianism that in his view would inevitably lead the Chinese regime to regression, atrophy, and finally collapse; at the other extreme, the regime's evolution toward a semidemocracy, simply put, Singapore-style, which alone can help it achieve the reforms and transition to a market economy and new growth model that the CCP has promised; and between these, apart from the maintenance of Xi's hard authoritarianism, a return to the soft authoritarianism of the years 1998–2008.[14] While the first type of authoritarianism would condemn China to stagnation and decline, the second can only lead to a partial success of its reforms and limited transition toward a market economy. Shambaugh has suggested that probably after the 19th CCP Congress (which took place in October 2017), a milder authoritarianism would take shape for a while, if only in order to reactivate reforms the economy needs, but that the authorities would be condemned, because of resistance from the party nomenklatura, which would fear its interests being upset, to return to hard authoritarianism, leading in fine to the current regime's collapse.[15] Shambaugh is careful not to set a time frame, merely indicating that the regime's endgame is afoot.[16]

For his part, Minxin Pei focuses on the corruption phenomenon; he holds that it is structural, meaning at the heart of the system, and the crony capitalism that the CCP has adopted can only lead to its ruin. The current campaign against corruption is aimed at demonstrating to society that the party intends to stem the rot and also at consolidating the authority of Xi and his allies. But basically, given the interlocking of political authorities and occasions for personal enrichment—which some economists call "economic rent"—as well as the lasting importance of the public sector (which controls assets representing more than 50 percent of GDP), the CCP has a stake in continuing to tolerate a high level of corruption and not attacking the phenomenon's deep-rooted causes. Deemed at the start of reforms to be a stimulant to development, corruption has increasingly turned predatory and thus is an obstacle to growth and a factor in the party-state's putrefaction. It could trigger failure of reforms and eventually regime collapse. Pei acknowledges that the decline process could take several years, slightly correcting his earlier predictions, which conditioned regime stability on its economic success and the effectiveness of its repression mechanisms.[17] He also links democratization to the economic development level attained[18] and further takes as a yardstick the life of the Soviet Union (seventy-four years), thus fixing the Chinese regime's end at around 2023.[19] Continuing his comparison to Vladimir Putin's Russia, Pei sounds pessimistic regarding the nature of political transition and the type of regime that might take shape in China.[20] But like Shambaugh, he believes that the People's Republic is in an advanced state of decline, to be eventually replaced by another type of regime.[21]

It was in 2012–2013, after the Bo Xilai affair, that the consensus on the regime's stability and longevity began to crumble. Nathan wrote in January 2013 that "the consensus is stronger than at any time since the 1989 Tiananmen crisis that the resilience of the authoritarian regime in the People's Republic of China (PRC) is approaching its limits."[22] Some Chinese dissident intellectuals, such as Zhao Hui, backed this rather optimistic analysis, while remaining circumspect about the duration of the decline, which they feared would be "protracted, highly unstable and unsettled."[23] The publication of Charter 08 by Liu Xiaobo, a document signed by more than eight thousand intellectuals, academics, lawyers, and businesspeople just after the 2008 Beijing Olympics, played a role in this change of perceptions, some Chinese commentators foreseeing the irreversible nature of the country's democratization.[24] Witness the Arab Spring and the rapid rise in China of the cost of social stability (*weiwen*), the mix of repression, surveillance, and micromanagement of conflicts.[25] In other words, before Shambaugh and Pei, a body of work had already prepared the ground for their analyses.

More analyses of China's political future have been published since 2016. Here I mention just two of them: Carl Minzner's *End of an Era* and Sebastian Heilmann's *Red Swan*.[26] As the former's full title indicates, China's "authoritarian revival" and lack of institutionalization are jeopardizing not only its reform process but also its empowerment. Minzner disagrees with Shambaugh, in the sense that for him "the trends and practices that have sustained the engine of China's reform era have been steadily grinding down since the early 2000s. And in the absence of fundamental political reform, things are beginning to break loose. China is starting to slide."[27] Heilmann's study, on the contrary, underscores the party-state's resilience and in particular its capacity to centrally guide economic development while at the same time accepting a degree of decentralization that communist regimes usually refuse to grant. However, in his epilogue, taking 2012 also as a turning point, Heilmann shows how Xi's "top-level design" and inclination to adopt what he calls a "crisis mode of governance" have increased China's systemic risks and weakened the government's legitimacy.[28]

However stimulating they may be, these analyses contain many weaknesses. On the one hand, they are particularly fixed in time; for instance, they deplore the dysfunction and drift that Xi has rightly tried to correct, such as the weakness and splits among central authorities and the unchecked explosion of corruption. Conversely, they see in Xi's power concentration a source of political uncertainty or go as far as holding him responsible for decisions, such as killing political reforms and undermining the party-state's institutionalization, that go back to 1989 and are clearly linked to the perpetuation of one-party rule. On the other hand, while the vulnerabilities present in the Chinese regime highlighted by these authors are recognized, are they strong enough to endanger it? The accelerated flight of elites and capital from China; intensification of the repressive, even paranoid character of Xi's regime; corruption's systemic persistence; risks posed by economic slowdown; the growing indebtedness of public enterprises and of local administrations; and difficulties in changing the growth model constitute issues observers are now obsessing over. However, to believe that these difficulties could by themselves trip up the regime underestimates the solidity of the unwritten social — and probably unequal and unfair — contract that the CCP has entered into with Chinese society, or rather imposed on it.

IS CHINA'S REGIME REALLY IN DANGER?

This book intends to show that Chinese authorities are well aware of all the risks discussed heretofore; that until now they have succeeded in their efforts at political, administrative, juridical, and economic adaptation, gradually transforming and modernizing the official ideology as well as the multiple institutions on which they rely to ensure the country's development and its integration in the world economy without, however, disturbing the bases of the one-party regime installed in 1949; and that the CCP has the ability to continue adapting and presiding over China's destiny for much longer, given its control of the situation and success in rallying large segments of society to the idea that it must retain forever the monopoly over political power.

I am not alone in advancing this hypothesis. Among recent works that have arrived at the same conclusion, Bruce Dickson's *The Dictator's Dilemma* stands out. Based on several series of detailed opinion surveys that I discuss in chapter 3, Dickson shows how the CCP, relying on successive reforms, has boosted its political legitimacy and overcome much of the discontent in society.[29] Although in *Populist Authoritarianism* Wenfang Tang's argument and his methodology are less convincing, exploring in depth China's political culture, he reaches similar conclusions about the regime's popular support and sustainability.[30]

Clearly the PRC is not eternal, nor are, for instance, the Soviet Union, North Korea, and Taiwan's authoritarian martial law regime (1949–1987). In the long term, the People's Republic is doubtless bound to cede place to another political system; the CCP is condemned to disappear or to transform itself and to agree to compete for power with other political forces in a more open and hopefully pluralistic framework. Nonetheless, for multiple reasons—historic, ideological, and structural—that are explained in this book, this democratic transition has a good chance of being delayed, chaotic, and incomplete.

Numerous forces and constraints block such an evolution. I list them briefly here: the immensity and diversity of the territory and population; the long Chinese bureaucratic tradition, meant precisely to manage this size and diversity; the impressive might of the Communist Party institution and the political culture and practices largely imported from the Soviet Union that it imposed on Chinese society beginning in 1949; acquired political and economic interests (or rent) of the Communist nomenklatura and their families; private entrepreneurs' heavy dependence on political authorities; weak democratic values, a weakness that the CCP and Soviet habitus (an internalized pattern of behavior) have not only perpetuated but also aggravated; the as yet embryonic nature of civil society; the might of repressive institutions; the isolation and vulnerability of forces agitating for democracy; and finally the support from economic elites and large segments of the middle classes for the current regime, due both to their dependence on the CCP and their fear of any instability and return to past chaos.

In view of these reasons, my hypothesis is that the CCP has installed what I have elsewhere described as a "new authoritarian equilibrium," which should help with maintaining its dictatorship for a long time.[31] How long is a long time? It is impossible to tell, so numerous are the internal and external factors influencing any evolution or fate of the current political regime: say twenty years, but thirty years too sounds credible. The real questions are what type of political system the People's Republic will cede place to and what forms this metamorphosis could take. On those issues, I am more pessimistic; for reasons that I develop presently, the CCP would rather be a regime that is still largely authoritarian, elitist, paternalist, imperial, and doubtless dictatorial and could most probably perpetuate itself in China, and in the long term, the transformation of this regime has strong chances of turning out to be chaotic, marked by profound political fractures, aborted attempts at democratization, conservative reverses, and militarist tendencies, aimed at preserving, in case of a political void, the country's unity and stability.

Evidently it is important to locate this reflection in the long term or François Braudel's *longue durée* and to bear in mind that each national trajectory is by definition different from those witnessed thus far, especially since the end of the Cold War. Chinese history and culture have their importance, weighing as they do on reality but more so—being constantly revisited, deconstructed, and reconstructed by the elites of the moment—on the mentalities and state of mind of society. However, in my view, more fundamental is the rupture constituted by the installation of a Soviet- and thus Leninist-inspired regime on the Chinese mainland in 1949. I try to highlight wherever possible the major linguistic, ideological, and organizational differences as well as those in terms of political and moral values that this break has caused and has nurtured until now despite the PRC's reforms and opening to the outside world since 1979. Similarly, in this book I have tried to think beyond the Xi Jinping era, a sequence in the PRC history that can extend for another one or two decades but can also abruptly come to an end at any time.

China has modernized over nearly forty years in an environment quite different from that of the former Soviet Union. East Asia is a region earlier dominated by Japan's economic development and globalization, then the eruption in the 1960s and afterward of the Four Dragons (South Korea, Hong Kong, Singapore, and Taiwan), a region that has also gradually democratized, first Japan post-1945 thanks to US occupation, then the currents that spread in the 1980s to Southeast Asia. Known as the "third wave of democratization," dear to Huntington, it saw the Philippines, Taiwan, and South Korea bail out of the "authoritarian development" model that had helped them in the early phase to modernize and to establish in a non-European cultural environment—Confucian in the last two—political institutions inspired by European Enlightenment. East Asia is ultimately a zone heavily marked by Cold War divisions and whose security, despite the rise of China's might and increasingly because of this rise, is still largely guaranteed by the United States and the system of US bilateral alliances (especially with Japan, South Korea, the Philippines, and Thailand) that took shape after the end of World War II.

It is thus necessary to see the Chinese authoritarian development model alongside other Asian experiences; it would then be possible to tease out the similarities, thereby relativizing the originality of the "Chinese path" and differences among them, refocusing attention on the Beijing regime's Leninist baggage.

Finally, it is also imperative to take into account and try to evaluate the possible future role of the Chinese economy's gradual globalization, but also, albeit more slowly and partially, the role of Chinese society in any future evolution of the PRC political system. Contrary to liberal ideologues' optimistic hypotheses, this role is far from being necessarily positive: the economic and even diplomatic interconnectedness between China and other major or emerging powers can also end up diminishing any external transformative or destabilizing force.

What conclusions should democracies draw from the Chinese regime's solidity and its ability not only to adapt to globalization of its economy but also to influence others? This question too cannot be evaded.

But before speculating on China's possible political futures, it is necessary to understand the bases of the current regime, its differences with previous Chinese dispensations, and the forces presently at play.

NOTES

1. Gordon G. Chang, *The Coming Collapse of China* (London: Random House, 2001).

2. David Shambaugh, *China's Future* (Cambridge, UK, and Malden, MA: Polity, 2016); and Minxin Pei, *China's Crony Capitalism: The Dynamics of Regime Decay* (Cambridge, MA: Harvard University Press, 2016).

3. Disagreements about the size of China's middle classes abound, including about the use of the plural, which I find more appropriate. In 2012 the Chinese middle classes already included 420 million people, though they experienced very different standards of living; see China Power, "How Well Off Is China's Middle Class?," https://chinapower.csis.org/china-middle-class/. As Jean-Louis Rocca and others have argued, the middle class is as much a social construct as a reality; Jean-Louis Rocca, *The Making of the Chinese Middle Class: Small Comfort and Great Expectations* (Basingstoke, UK, and New York: Palgrave Macmillan, 2017).

4. Francis Fukuyama, *The End of History and the Last Man* (New York: Avon Books, 1992).

5. Samuel Huntington, *The Clash of Civilizations and the Remaking of World Order* (New York: Simon & Schuster Paperbacks, 1996).

6. Suisheng Zhao, ed., *China and Democracy: Reconsidering the Prospect for a Democratic China* (New York and London: Routledge, 2000).

7. Andrew Nathan, "Authoritarian Resilience," *Journal of Democracy* 14, no. 1 (January 2003): 6–17.

8. Minxin Pei, *China's Trapped Transition: The Limits of Developmental Autocracy* (Cambridge, MA: Harvard University Press, 2006).

9. Andrew Nathan, "Authoritarian Impermanence," *Journal of Democracy* 20, no. 3 (July 2009): 37–40.

10. David Shambaugh, *China's Communist Party: Atrophy and Adaptation* (Berkeley: University of California Press, 2007).

11. Cheng Li, "The End of the CCP's Resilient Authoritarianism? A Tripartite Assessment of Shifting Power in China," *The China Quarterly*, no. 211 (September 2012): 599–602.

12. François Godement, *Contemporary China: Between Mao and Market* (Lanham, MD: Rowman & Littlefield, 2016). Son of former elder CCP leader Bo Yibo, Bo Xilai came to prominence when he was promoted to CCP Politburo member and Chongqing municipality party secretary in 2007. There, he supported harsh anti-organized-crime policies and adopted a neo-Maoist style, hoping to be part of Hu Jintao's succession. However, his wife's decision in late 2011 to poison a British businessman with whom she had had a dispute precipitated his fall and expulsion from the party in 2012. Accused of abuse of power and corruption, he was sentenced to life imprisonment a year later.

13. Shambaugh, *China's Future*, 1.

14. Shambaugh, *China's Future*, 124–136.

15. Shambaugh, *China's Future*, 136.

16. In "The Coming Chinese Crackup," *Wall Street Journal*, March 6, 2015, on which *China's Future* is based, Shambaugh sounded much more peremptory and less nuanced, provoking diverse reactions.

17. Minxin Pei, "Is CCP Rule Fragile or Resilient?," *Journal of Democracy* 23, no. 1 (January 2012): 27–41.

18. Minxin Pei, "The Twilight of Communist Party Rule in China," *The American Interest* 11, no. 15 (November 12, 2015), https://www.the-american-interest.com/2015/11/12/the-twilight-of-communist-party-rule-in-china/.

19. Minxin Pei, "Is China's Communist Party Doomed?," *The Diplomat*, October 1, 2012, http://thediplomat.com/2012/10/is-chinas-communist-party-doomed/; and more recently, "The Beginning of the End," *The Washington Quarterly* 39, no. 3 (Autumn 2016): 131–142.

20. Pei, *China's Crony Capitalism*, 266.

21. See also Pei's interview in *Le Monde*, February 19–20, 2017, 13.

22. Andrew Nathan, "China at the Tipping Point: Foreseeing the Unforeseeable," *Journal of Democracy* 24, no. 1 (January 2013): 20.

23. Mo Zhixu (penname of Zhao Hui), "China's Future: Unstable and Unsettled," *China Change*, April 6, 2016, https://chinachange.org/2016/04/06/chinas-future-unstable-and-unsettled/. See also Zhenhua Su, Hui Zhao, and Jingkai He, "China at the Tipping Point: Authoritarianism and Contestation," *Journal of Democracy* 24, no. 1 (January 2013): 26–40.

24. Yu Liu and Dingding Chen, "Why China Will Democratize," *Washington Quarterly* 35 (Winter 2012): 41–63; and Jean-Philippe Béja, Fu Hualing, and Eva Pils, eds., *Liu Xiaobo, Charter 08, and the Challenges of Political Reform in China* (Hong Kong: Hong Kong University Press, 2012).

25. It was in 2010 that the *weiwen* budget overtook that of the People's Liberation Army, prompting several analyses that deemed it unsustainable in the long term. See Xi Chen, "The Rising Cost of Stability," *Journal of Democracy* 24, no. 1 (January 2013): 57–64.

26. Carl Minzner, *End of an Era: How China's Authoritarian Revival is Undermining Its Rise* (Oxford and New York: Oxford University Press, 2018); and Sebastian Heilmann, *Red Swan: How Unorthodox Policy Making Facilitated China's Rise* (Hong Kong: The Chinese University of Hong Kong, 2018).

27. Minzner, *End of an Era*, 165.

28. Heilmann, *Red Swan*, 201–211.

29. Bruce J. Dickson, *The Dictator's Dilemma: The Chinese Communist Party's Strategy for Survival* (Oxford: Oxford University Press, 2016); more generally on the Xi era, see Elizabeth C. Economy's excellent book *The Third Revolution: Xi Jinping and the New Chinese State* (New York: Oxford University Press, 2018).

30. Gathered for the most part in 2008, 2010, and 2012, Tang's data, however, do not tell us much about the Xi Jinping era. Wenfang Tang, *Populist Authoritarianism: Chinese Political Culture and Regime Sustainability* (New York and Oxford: Oxford University Press, 2016).

31. Jean-Pierre Cabestan, *Le système politique chinois: Un nouvel équilibre autoritaire* [The Chinese political system: A new authoritarian equilibrium] (Paris: Presses de Sciences-Po, 2014).

ONE

China's Current Political System

A Strong, Sustainable, Authoritarian Equilibrium

It is difficult to describe in a few pages the current Chinese political system, its strengths and weaknesses, and just as important, its relationship with the Chinese economy and society. I have elsewhere done so in detail, and the Francophone reader may consult that work for further information on the functioning of institutions and mechanisms organizing the relations between the regime and society.[1] At the risk of oversimplifying, it may be noted that since the start of reforms and opening of the country in 1979, its political system has not been totalitarian but authoritarian; although led by a single party, this political regime has overseen unprecedented economic development and increase in the country's international might. The CCP has itself undergone a profound transformation: it has modified its ideology, improved cadre training, loosened its command structures, modernized its functioning, and crucially, focused its activities on the economy. At the same time, it has stoked unprecedented corruption and given rise to a new plutocratic managerial class that displays nepotistic and mafia-like tendencies.

Nevertheless, the CCP faces no risk of an early death; since 1989, drawing lessons from the Soviet Union's collapse, it has on the whole managed to fashion a new economic and social environment without at the same time weakening its monopoly control of political life. It has also succeeded in containing corruption and criminal tendencies to the extent it considers acceptable. Moreover, the CCP has maintained tight control over the military and other security forces, and no other credible political entity threatens its future. In other words, the CCP's authoritarian, developmentalist, and nationalist project has every chance of anchoring it in power for a long time to come.

CHINESE PARTY-STATE:
A PARADOXICAL INSTITUTIONAL REALITY

The CCP and the state it established in 1949, the PRC, constitute an impressive but paradoxical system. This complex institutional architecture, which I call the party-state, given the fusion between these two institutions, is in many respects solid, flexible, and sustainable. It adopted all the political, economic, and social transformations imposed by Mao and his comrades in the 1950s. It withstood the turmoil of the Mao era, especially the Great Leap Forward (1958–1961) and the Cultural Revolution (1966–1968). And it rebuilt itself after 1968, when the People's Liberation Army (PLA) disarmed and repressed the Red Guards and restored order. After Mao's death in 1976 the party-state, taken over by Deng Xiaoping and his allies, set to work on the reform and opening policy. It ordered the PLA to use force to end the 1989 democracy movement and presided over economic development and globalization, a process that over thirty years lifted China to rank number two in the world for GDP and doubtless topmost in purchasing power parity terms.

This quick description of well-known phases in the PRC's history is meant to refocus attention on its impressive organizational capacity and its equally remarkable ability to adapt.[2] This aptitude and nimbleness, elasticity even, is mostly ideological and structural but also, above all, required by the need to extricate society from poverty and the ambition to transform China into a great power capable of rivaling the United States.

Obviously China's economic development was the result of multiple individual decisions and private initiatives on society's part. The role Deng and other reformers played was mainly ordering the party-state to give a free rein to economic actors, at first rural with the dismantling of the people's communes, completed by 1984, and then foreign and urban ones. By 1979 China had begun attracting external investments (to begin with from Hong Kong and then Taiwan), established special economic zones, and started scrapping state monopoly in a growing number of industrial and service sectors.

However, the CCP has never wanted to share power with other political forces or to withdraw completely from control of the economy. In this regard, elements of ideological and institutional continuity as well as political strategy between the Mao era and the reform period should never be underestimated.[3] The system still functions on the back of politico-administrative institutions established in the 1950s. And while the party's objectives have clearly changed, the official language in daily use has hardly evolved. It remains a Soviet-inspired jargon in bad Chinese—and since 1958 in simplified characters, a veritable cultural castration of traditional ideograms—that anyone outside the party apparatus strains to comprehend. The CCP has been advancing shrewdly, relying when needed on "guerrilla tactics" that Mao used in another context to impose reforms. It proceeds as much on the strength of campaigns—such as those Xi Jinping launched against corruption in 2013—and directives put out by the party as on that of laws and regulations. The discretionary power enjoyed by party leaders at various levels and in the party-state's various bureaucracies continues to be the main plank of its modus operandi, its ability to adapt, its successes and failures, and its drift toward corruption. Besides, all land still belongs to the state; "collective" in rural areas, it is managed by local governments or village leadership or both, a source of endless quarrels. In urban areas it is public property, with local administrators enjoying the power to dispose of it with quasi-discretion. In general, although the market now is expected—to use a formula adopted by the CCP Central Committee Plenum in 2013—to play a "decisive role" in the economy, the party-state intends to retain ownership and control of enterprises it deems strategic. Placed under the aegis of the State-owned Assets Supervision and Administration Commission (SASAC) and provincial SASACs and gradually consolidated, these major enterprises (ninety-six national-level ones in 2019) are also sources of rent for the Chinese ruling class.

In fact, as a promoter of development and economic liberalization, the party nomenklatura has directly and liberally taken advantage of both the rent-seeking situations offered by the maintenance of a powerful state sector and the incestuous relations of interdependence with private economic actors, enriching its leading cadres and their families and thus fostering the emergence within it of a plutocratic new privileged class with nepotistic tendencies. Right from the 1980s, children of leaders, commonly known as "princelings" (*Taizidang*), have jumped into "the sea of business" (*xiahai*). For instance, Li Peng's children invested in energy, Jiang Zemin's offspring in electronics, and Deng Xiaoping's descendants in armament.[4] At local levels, the still largely informal nature of rules and the systematic exploitation of the well-known "personal relations" (*guanxi*) have facilitated the rise of "red" family progeny (*hong'erdai*) and CCP cadres' children (*guan'erdai*) and, in some regions, more worryingly, a "mafia-ization" of the bureaucracy.[5]

That is why the CCP—with almost 90 million members (89.6 million in 2018), with about 30 million cadres out of a total of nearly 70 million state cadres in the larger sense (administration, enterprises, public establishments, and the PLA) and about 10 million leading cadres, including 650,000 at the departmental level and above (*chuji yishang*)—constitutes in many respects a contradictory and paradoxical reality.[6]

Far from being a political party in the sense understood in the West, the CCP, in the conception of both its leaders and members, is not only the dictator (as in "dictatorship of the proletariat") and organizer of the state but also, it might be said, its "life force" (its *qi* in Daoist terms), without which it would wilt and die.[7]

A Modernized and Sprawling Government System

This immense organization's most modernized and convincing aspect is its state façade. The State Council and its multiple organs (ministries, commissions, bureaus, central bank, etc.) marshal an impressive capital of economic intellect, administrative competence, and regulatory capacity. As everywhere, bureaucratic rivalries and coordination deficiencies are rife. Moreover, procedures are vague, change constantly, and command scant respect. Errors in management or economic and financial communication abound; the 2015 stock market crash was one of the most recent instances, the government having given the wrong impression to shareholders that their assets could only appreciate. At the top of the vast bureaucratic pyramid, the premier and his team often struggle to prevail, with the four layers of local party committees and governments enjoying, despite the party's centralizing role, large although uneven powers of interpretation and adaptation of central decisions to local conditions. They wield greater real powers than do decentralized entities of many federal states. Given the average Chinese province's size—comparable to a European country with populations five to six times larger—is it any wonder?

But on the whole this administrative machine works and in general works well, even increasingly so, when compared with the last years of the Mao era.[8] Commanding bigger means, lodged in more modern and vaster buildings, and with better trained and better paid personnel, Chinese governmental organs resemble more and more those of other developed Asian countries. Directives and instructions reach far corners of the land. Although still very decentralized yet subject to constant reform, the fiscal system fills state coffers satisfactorily. In guiding the economy and benefiting from a high growth rate, the party-state has constantly shown itself to be attentive and prudent, even conservative, preempting risks, avoiding crises, and ensuring social stability through a mix of material incentives and targeted repression. The strategy of gradual internationalization of the yuan or *renminbi*, the Chinese currency, without however making it fully convertible, perfectly illustrates this prudence; Beijing clearly intends to keep control of capital flows and avoid, in prevailing circumstances, too quick an appreciation or depreciation of its currency. And relations between Beijing and local governments have struck a balance that on the whole satisfies the various administrative levels, with crucial issues centralized (budget, security, propaganda) and the rest decentralized, especially matters of local economic development.

Facilitating this modernization, relations between the administration and society have in general improved; services are being provided more promptly (residence permits, identity cards, passports, business registrations, etc.). Local officials' functions are clearer, more transparent, and rule based, except when it comes to dealing with those taking on the regime head-on. Further, the successors of imperial China's "grievance drums," bureaus for letters and visits (*xinfang bangongshi*), were reactivated and their powers strengthened in the first decade of the twenty-first century; each day they receive and transmit to relevant services numerous complaints and reparation demands submitted by individuals.[9]

The judicial system has professionalized and modernized. Albeit under the aegis of the CCP and its powerful political and legal affairs commissions, judges, prosecutors, and lawyers are now real jurists trained, like elsewhere, in law schools. I examine in chapter 4 the extent to which major limitations persist, especially when it comes to the right to a defense and any matter with a political color, and to what extent the party remains above the law.[10] Also, "local judicial protectionism" remains a major problem, and it is unclear whether reforms introduced in 2014 aimed at autonomizing and recentralizing the judicial institution could eradicate it. Nevertheless, Chinese laws continue to expand in influence, gradually facilitating the establishment of—though not genuine rule *of* law, in which the government would be just another entity before the law—at least rule *by* law, with laws playing a certain normative role. More and more disputes and complaints are being settled in courts rather than through administrative mediation or by the bureaus for letters and visits.[11] Finally, although poorly controlled and enjoying powers that are still mostly discretionary, the penitentiary system is also being modernized, urban prisons having mostly replaced labor camps set up in remote rural or inhospitable mountainous areas.

The reform of the cadres' management system has facilitated the modernization of China's administration in the larger sense (courts included); recruited through competitive examinations and henceforth "public servants," these cadres seem to embody the perpetuation or rather restoration of the imperial era merit system. Their careers, especially those of "public servants in leading posts," proceed in line with their achievements, successes, and failures; while the growth rate of their sector or area of activity remains an essential factor for promotion, the maintenance of social stability, environmental improvements, and even their physical appearance have been playing a bigger role.[12] Some commentators, such as Daniel Bell, reflecting official Beijing discourse, go even further, arguing that the party-state has adopted a system for selecting elites more effective than that in pluralistic democracies.[13]

Finally, albeit under the harsh gaze of the authorities, the media are getting better at informing society. Taboo subjects are shrinking. The government can still block sensitive information, and it has intensified crackdowns on "rumors," expanding punitive measures against presumed authors. It has also to contend with increasingly rapid diffusion of information online and across international borders (see chapter 4). The CCP intends to rely considerably on the media to control local cadres' machinations and curb corruption.[14] Such is the case when central authorities protect or even sometimes encourage journalists investigating some scandal that may have propaganda uses, even if such means confront both local resistance as well as political limits set on all media authorities.

An Opaque, Omnipotent, and Poorly Institutionalized Party

But there is another side, which is more opaque, darker, plutocratic, even mafia-like, and in many cases barely institutionalized in the Chinese regime, mainly centered in the party apparatus, security services, state enterprises, and also to some extent in the armed forces. Make no mistake: the distinction commonly made between party and state is illusory. The party controls the state and the armed forces through leaders who occupy leadership functions in both the distinct structures. Thus, the CCP general secretary and Politburo Standing Committee number one, currently Xi Jinping, is also head of state (president of the PRC) and of the armed forces (chairman of the Central Military Commission of both the party and the state); the number two of the Chinese leadership's holy of holies, which since 2012 has seven members and probably meets weekly, is the premier, currently Li Keqiang. The number three heads the National People's Congress (NPC), China's parliament (Li Zhanshu since March 2018). And so forth. The leaders of the CCP's major central departments, topmost government leaders, the two top PLA generals, and heads of the biggest municipalities and provinces belong to the Politburo, a collective of twenty-five members (with just one woman since 2017, but two earlier) that meets about once a month. Almost all ministers of the State Council and heads of provinces have places in the Party Central Committee, the assemblage consisting of about two hundred of the country's most powerful leading cadres and holding its plenum each year (nearly four hundred attend, including alternate members without the right to vote).[15]

What characterizes the party is its opacity, its refusal to make public the real processes (not merely formal ones) of leaders' selection and of decision making as well as political differences that could divide the leadership, not to mention the wealth the leaders and their families have amassed. The vital role of the Party Central Committee's "leading small groups" at the national level—of structures that had long remained secret coordinating essential government activities (finance and economy, agriculture, foreign affairs, Taiwan, etc.) and for the most part now headed by Xi—testifies to this deliberate willingness to maintain opacity. The elevation of some of these leading small groups (finance and economy, reforms, foreign affairs, and cybersecurity) to commissions in March 2018 has not really increased their transparency.

As in most traditionally nondemocratic entities (family, enterprise), the promotion of the CCP's and the state's cadres is based on the principle of co-optation. Applying the long-in-use Leninist- and Soviet-inspired nomenklatura system, the CCP's leading organs draw up at each administrative level and in each sector lists of candidates for leading posts. The system is quite decentralized, with the center overseeing the career of just about five thousand leading cadres and the others appointed by party organs at lower levels. Prepared by powerful organization departments of the CCP, promotions within the party, as within the state structures, are in principle decided collectively, following elaborate consultations, by leading organs at superior levels. In reality the top leader of the relevant CCP committee (*yibashou*) decides.

At the national level, the CCP Congress of more than 2,300 delegates—elected in principle but in reality chosen by various party constituencies such as provincial committees and further vetted by the national leadership with the help of the Central Committee Organization Department—meets once every five years. It approves the general secretary's report and elects the Central Committee, choosing candidates from a list on which they number less than 10 percent more than the number of posts to be filled. This list is drawn up centrally following a consultation in the form of a poll of a sample of CCP members, which since 1997 has been expanded, to 33,500 in 2007.[16] The Central Committee in turn elects the highest party bodies (Politburo and its Standing Committee, Central Military Commission [CMC], etc.) according to an as yet largely opaque procedure. This has also evolved since 2002, facilitated by Hu Jintao's initiative to nurture intraparty democracy (*dangnei minzhu*). In 2007 Central Committee members were asked to choose future Politburo members from a list, again compiled centrally, of two hundred senior cadres of ministerial rank. In 2012 they were also able to choose members of the Politburo Standing Committee. However, this practice was called into question in 2017; before the 19th Party Congress that took place in October, Xi preferred to have face-to-face consultation with 57 current or retired leaders and seek the opinion of 258 other officials of ministerial rank, including a certain number of generals. Consequently, he fully restored the principle of co-optation by the topmost leadership. The reason cited was the temptation in 2012 of some ambitious candidates such as Sun Zhengcai, who was close to Hu and later became Chongqing's party secretary and one of Xi's potential successors, to buy votes and rig the election.[17] In July 2017 Sun was dismissed from all his posts, expelled from the party, and jailed. Be that as it may, the practice Hu introduced had its limits; it was the incumbent authorities who put together the candidate list, and consultations resembled opinion polls rather than a binding vote. In fact, the leadership in place has always retained the option of ignoring the results. Procedural opacity has helped greatly.

In reality, the choice of holders of the highest leadership posts has always followed secret and complicated trade-offs among leading party heavyweights. Their election is thus a mere formality. More important, co-optation of leading cadres reintroduces political, factional, and personal variables that contradict the meritocracy principle. Of course, as of now most of the leaders chosen are competent and well educated. But as in any other political organization, it would be naïve to think that their selection is not also influenced by other considerations. The long hold of Zhou Yongkang, a former security chief (2007—2012) who is now in prison, over the energy sector where he built most of his career and then over the security services, shows the extent of party leaders' discretionary powers. Similarly, Xi's tendency since 2012 to promote leaders who had worked with him in Fujian and Zhejiang, where he spent several years, highlights the key role that links of allegiance play in the careers of party cadres. Thus, a great majority of Politburo members emerging from the 19th Party Congress are from Xi's camp. Conversely, the way in which Bo Xilai in 2012 and his indirect Chongqing successor Sun Zhengcai in 2017 were dismissed and jailed shows how paltry the institutionalization of CCP's functioning has been despite the convening at regular intervals of national congresses and central committee plenums.

Given the opacity surrounding each nomination, at the top, at intermediary levels, or even at the grassroots, it is impossible to know with certitude the power equations present and the way in which new promotees are chosen. Consequently, outside observers have to strain to identify work relations that newly promoted leaders have developed with their seniors, and they draw therefrom often unreliable conclusions about the allegiances each has managed to build and the new relations among the so-called factions within the CCP leadership. While clientelism seems to be the main factor in promotion, once elevated, leaders' interests evolve based on multiple factors. For example, although chosen by Jiang and not Hu, who favored Li Keqiang, once in power Xi Jinping turned against the "Shanghai clique" led by Jiang. Moreover, the term "faction" is itself debatable, especially when applied to leading cadres who have spent most of their careers in a single institution such as the

Communist Youth League (CYL) or to as loose a grouping as the "prince-lings" (*Taizidang*) or children of the party's pioneer leaders. In fact, the Youth League, the "nursery" of the CCP's future leaders, is far from having only trained allies of Hu Jintao, its former leader; Xi Zhongxun's son Xi Jinping saw Bo Xilai, son of Bo Yibo, less as an ally than as a dangerous rival whose fall he ensured in 2012.

Be that as it may, these discussions find no place in the official media and appear only sporadically online because of censorship. Moreover, the major corruption scandals that have broken out since 2012 and the Bo Xilai affair have run a somber but predictable course: they have been increasingly presented as matters of political indiscipline and even "plots" and "coup d'état" attempts, thereby confirming a posteriori ru-mors swirling online over several years but also raising more complex and insoluble questions regarding succession mechanisms and even the issue of regime stability.[18] I return to this issue later.

Ordinary party members' political lives are better known but much less significant. Soon after they become members, they join a cell or com-mittee that requires regular meetings and adherence to strict rules of confidentiality about discussions conducted or documents distributed. As they rise in the hierarchy, becoming cadres and then leading cadres, these rules too get stricter.

It could well be said that the CCP is the world's largest secret society, one that operates according to its own rules, placing itself outside, and often above, the law. The party only lets out information that can help consolidate its hegemony and legitimacy and take the sting out of any discourse or forces of a pernicious kind.

The party has the means to maintain this exceptional status. It contin-ues to command a vast network of branches (4.6 million in 2018 com-pared to 3.8 million in 2005). It closely controls the state sector; 10 million of the 40 million state enterprises' employees are party members and are grouped in 800,000 committees.[19] The party has adapted to the new so-cioeconomic reality, progressively investing in the private sector and so-cial groups; in 2018 about 1.9 million "non-state enterprises" or officially 73 percent, and 303,000 "social organizations" or nongovernmental or-ganizations (NGOs) (62 percent) had a party committee.[20] However, these figures need to be treated with caution given the reported total numbers of private enterprises (27 million in late 2017) and unregistered NGOs (2 to 3 million) (see chapter 4). In reality, tallying diverse data available, it may be estimated that in 2018 just 20 percent of private enterprises (against 11 percent in 2012) and 10 percent of foreign-funded enterprises had party committees.[21]

The CCP is a highly hierarchical and segmented organization. Ordinary members play a marginal role, their main mission being to propagate party news and policies; while some join out of ambition, mainly because they want to pursue a career in the administration or the state sector (public enterprises or establishments), most are approached by the organization in view of their sociological and intellectual profiles. Students and private entrepreneurs are now the party's favorites.

Cadres are more immersed in the party's political life but have little role in decision making, which remains the monopoly of leading cadres (*lingdao ganbu*), a bureaucratic category particularly important in China, as in all socialist countries. They constitute so to speak the Chinese political system's vertebral column.

From time to time, official media reflect the more or less muffled debates among the leadership, such discussions and differences in general concerning public policy issues, such as economic policy. Thus in 2016 an "authoritative person," no doubt Liu He, economic adviser to Xi, issued direct criticism of Premier Li's stimulus measures, advocating instead steps to clean up public enterprises' and local governments' debts.

The publication of these debates draws attention to the absence of divergence on the regime's fundamentals: the one-party system, organization of powers, repression of dissidents, and censorship. Above all is the fierce determination to snuff out disagreements and hide them, letting rumors circulate instead, as they are by nature unverifiable. In this regard, Hong Kong serves as a sounding board.

For leaders of the CCP this omertà, founded on security considerations, is vital for stability and regime survival. Beijing's furious reaction in 2012 against the *New York Times* for publishing a report on the fortune amassed by then premier Wen Jiabao's family or against *Bloomberg* for its investigation into the wealth accumulated by Xi Jinping's brothers and sisters shows how sensitive such issues are. Some Chinese people eventually gained access to these articles, in English and then in translation, but what mattered for the authorities was to punish the media outlets (the *New York Times* is now censored in China) so as to dissuade as many foreign journalists as possible from following their path.

The Legitimizing Role of Formal and Local State Institutions

Turning again to state structures, they consist not merely of able administrators but also of a slew of representative institutions I call "formal," in the sense that they are largely powerless but participate in the regime's political legitimization and democratic pretentions. These are, to start with, people's congresses, chosen directly by electors at the township (*xiang*) and county (*xian*) levels and indirectly at higher levels, with the NPC at the top. At each of these congresses, the CCP selects the candidates, introducing, at least on paper, a relative incertitude (30 percent of normal candidates, i.e., those who are not leading cadres, will not be elected) but ensuring that about two-thirds of deputies are party members. The party's objective is to see that congresses include representatives of local elites (private entrepreneurs, cadres, doctors, and teachers). A similar procedure governs the selection (not election) of Chinese People's Political Consultative Conferences (CPPCC) members from the county level to the national one, in all of which, however, two-thirds of members do not belong to the CCP but are drawn from new elites (including intellectuals, artists, and sports figures). In view of the status, legal protection, and high-level access that such memberships confer, many entrepreneurs and nouveaux riches buy election or nomination to such bodies.

This evolution is significant, as it broadens the process of consulting new elites without ceding any power whatsoever. Decision making is retained by central or local party organs and executed by corresponding-level government services. While the governor or mayor of an administrative constituency is in principle chosen by the respective people's congress, the person is always number two in the party committee, behind its secretary. In case of personal rivalries, rarely do congresses rebel against party committees, preferring preemptive bargaining with them behind closed doors.

This extent of exposure of the political system could be interpreted as a factor in the regime's evolution and eventual democratization. But for the moment, the totality of political and administrative power rests with the party-state, ceding to the congresses and to consultative conferences a limited right to examine local decisions—especially regulations that need to be approved by congresses—and nominations of local leading cadres (apart from government officials, others elected in principle but chosen by the CCP in reality are judges and prosecutors).

At the grassroots level, villagers' and urban residents' committees are mostly elected. These elections have led to democratic or, more often, local pluralism experiments. At times they seem like challenges that activists seek to seize. But here too, in most cases the candidates are preselected and approved by higher level governments such as of the county or township, and therefore by the party. In 2016 at Wukan, a rebel village in Guangdong, the party showed it was capable of forestalling any upsets that could lead to its losing control; the mayor elected in 2012 is now imprisoned for corruption.

The party-state has put in place, especially at local levels, more or less formal processes of consultation with society. Opinion polls, often organized on the sly, help keep the most unpopular officials out of leading posts (party secretary, mayor, or governor). Moreover, major administrative decisions are subject to public discussion, often organized by the local people's congress. But the party-state remains the arbiter of these debates, generally using them to justify measures it has chosen.

In sum, as some observers have noted, the Chinese political system has established a form of "consultative Leninism" or more generally, "consultative authoritarianism."[22] In other words—and this is a term I have used previously—after Tiananmen, the system established a "new authoritarian equilibrium" that has demonstrated solidity and resilience thus far.

In this brief presentation several specific realities contributing to reducing China's political sphere and thereby strengthening regime stability stand out: (1) the official political system is limited to the party-state, despite the—largely CCP-guided—election processes; (2) the country is run like a company without shareholders and thus is particularly opaque, whose chairman-managing director or chief executive officer is the party number one; (3) political life is but administrative life; (4) politics is the monopoly of a highly hierarchical secret society, the CCP, which despite its large membership (6.5 percent of the population) remains dominated by an elite of co-opted leading cadres, predominantly male; and (5) Chinese society is not invited, much less incited, to take interest in public affairs or to participate in political life except by joining the party and mouthing its official discourse. As I demonstrate here, despite the emergence of an embryonic civil society, an efficient system of repression dissuades most Chinese from taking part in politics.

This "depoliticization" of Chinese society is part of a deliberate political project. Political matters are the monopoly of the party-state and above all its leading cadres. Whoever ventures into this sphere without express invitation—for example to study "Xi Jinping thought"—faces risks and dangers. Thus, there is a strong inclination on the part of CCP propaganda organs to denounce "politicization" of any issue through external criticism, a term understood as pejorative in the eyes of these organs. This propensity has rubbed off on Hong Kong, where the establishment has exhibited such an "allergy," sometimes wittingly and at others unknowingly, to politicization. It is just a tool meant to consolidate the CCP's monopolistic hold on politics and boost the regime's chances of survival.

LESSONS FROM THE SOVIET UNION'S COLLAPSE

Right after Tiananmen, on Deng Xiaoping's advice the CCP drew its own lessons from the Soviet Union's collapse. After two years of strict control, in January 1992 Deng toured Shenzhen, China's first special economic zone, established in 1979, and announced the relaunch of reforms, once again setting development at all costs and attainment of a moderately prosperous society (*xiaokang shehui*) as the party's primary goals. This was in his view the only way China could avoid the "tragic" fate of Lenin's land: the CCP's fractionalization, atrophy, and eventual loss of power.

There was another side to this new strategy, no less crucial and much studied by Shambaugh and others: prepare the party for the new task and the new economic environment thus created.[23] Without precedent, this adaptation required a transformation of the ideology, organization, and training of the party-state's cadres.

Among the most significant ideological innovations was that of the party's "three represents" (*sange daibiao*), jargon coined by Jiang Zemin in 2001, mainly aimed at letting private entrepreneurs join the CCP. As a consequence, the CCP was becoming a "Party of the whole people" (*quanmindang*), as some Chinese observers then claimed, more a nationalist than a communist organization. While the "scientific outlook on development" dear to Jiang's successor Hu Jintao and enshrined in 2007 has not quite caught the popular imagination, it contained the idea that the CCP was henceforth a ruling party (*zhizhengdang*), no longer a revolution-ary one, and must therefore focus on a gradual improvement of the country's governance (*zhizheng*). This objective, mooted in 2004 by Jiang's former adviser Zeng Qinghong, remains one of the party's major priorities, even more so as the Xi-led CCP is keen to show that Chinese-style one-party rule is far more efficient and suited to the country's needs than Western-style governance, permanently stymied and challenged by electoral upsets, opposition parties, and public opinion.[24]

With Xi this ideological evolution has been buttressed; the "Chinese dream" is not just a nationalist power quest. It also envisages attaining by 2021, that is, the CCP's centenary, the "moderate prosperity" that Deng conceived of and making the People's Republic into a "strong, prosperous, democratic, civilized, harmonious and beautiful" "modern socialist country" by 2049, its own centenary. Enshrined during the 19th Party Congress, all these ideas were integrated into what is termed "Xi Jinping thought on socialism with Chinese characteristics for a new era."[25]

In order to ensure success, Xi launched an extraordinary anticorruption campaign (discussed below) and unveiled a series of new economic and institutional reforms. All these measures were motivated by a gnawing disquiet on the part of Xi and perhaps the entire party leadership caused by the specter of the Soviet collapse. In fact, soon after taking charge Xi reactivated discussions on the lessons to be drawn from that fatality. In December 2012 he made an internal speech that was distributed a month later to all party members, identifying two main causes for the disintegration of the Communist Party of the Soviet Union (CPSU) and the Soviet Union itself: (1) the challenging of socialist "ideals and beliefs" (*lixiang xinnian*) and the negation of Lenin and Stalin, replaced by a veritable "historical nihilism" (*lishi xuwuzhuyi*); and (2) the "depoliticization" (*feizhengzhihua*) and "stratification/nationalization" (*guojiahua*) of the army and thus its "separation from the party" (*feidanghua*).[26] Xi concluded his speech with this infamous sexist remark: "Finally, Gorbachev announced the disbandment of the Soviet Communist Party in a blithe statement. A big Party was gone just like that. Proportionally, the Soviet Communist Party had more members than we do, but nobody was man enough to stand up and resist" (*dan jingwu yi ren shi nan'er, mei sheme ren chulai kangzheng*).[27]

This denunciation of dangers stemming from "bourgeois liberalization" is hardly new; it goes back to the immediate post-Tiananmen period and even the 1979 arrest of Wei Jingsheng, who first advocated the "fifth modernization"—that is, democracy—in the aftermath of Mao's death. Criticism of Mikhail Gorbachev, deemed a "traitor to socialism," has been constant since 1991. Hu Jintao, succeeding Jiang in 2004 as chairman of the Central Military Commission of the Party, declared: "Because of the openness and pluralism he championed, Gorbachev caused confusion among the Soviet Communist Party and the people of the Soviet Union. The Party and the Union fell apart under the impact of 'Westernization' and 'bourgeois liberalism' that he implemented."[28]

Under Xi repressive measures aimed at preventing any "peaceful evolution" toward democracy have proliferated. In 2013 the CCP put out an internal circular (meant to have remained secret), the famous "Document No. 9," which directly attacked Western political values such as constitutional democracy, universal suffrage, an independent judiciary, a "nationalized" army, the separation of powers, press freedom, and a multiparty system.[29] I discuss later the extent to which Xi tightened the party's hold over the PLA. But what was striking in his speech was his nervousness over the ease with which the Soviet regime had disappeared. Was one to believe the CCP was teetering on the edge of a precipice? Most probably the then-new general secretary wished to alert his colleagues and persuade them of the need to fight more seriously against corruption and to relaunch reforms, without however weakening the one-party system. Hence his fierce and relentless repression of the constitutionalist movement, which right from early 2013 had sought to take advantage of Xi's plan to put the party's "power within the cage of regulations." Hence also, and even more so, his opposition to any political reform worth the name; only administrative reforms to strengthen government efficiency and judicial reforms to modernize the legal system have been introduced since 2013. Hence also his move to concentrate in his hands far greater powers than his predecessors, to inscribe his "thought" in the CCP statutes, to promote a personality cult that had been denounced after Mao's death, and in March 2018, to lift any time limit on his term in office.

In any case, Xi's views on the defunct USSR and their continuity with those of his predecessors explain, if that was necessary, the CCP leaders' relentless opposition to any turning back on the one-party system and the essential aims of decisions and reforms introduced since 2012: consolidate the current political regime to guarantee its long-term survival.

XI JINPING'S ANTICORRUPTION CAMPAIGN

It is in this context that Xi's campaign against corruption must be understood. It is said to be unprecedented in the sense that it has targeted both "tigers" and "mice"—that is, high officials as well as subaltern ones implicated in this "crime."[30] With this aim, the CCP has greatly boosted the powers and the vertical answerability of the principal institution charged with accomplishing the task: the party's discipline inspection commissions network. Headed by Wang Qishan from 2012 to 2017 and since then by Zhao Leji—both Xi confidants—the Central Commission for Discipline Inspection of the CCP has multiplied its inspection missions in provinces and government departments, state enterprises, and public establishments. Moreover, since 2012 local commissions fall mainly under the discipline commission of the higher level and no longer the party committee of the same level, an organizational pattern that had previously stymied the commissions' work.

Results of the campaign were not long in coming; official statistics published since 2013 attest to a steep rise in the number of cadres incriminated. Between 2012 and 2017 as many as 1.53 million party members faced disciplinary action for corruption, contrasted with 670,000 over the previous five years (2007–2012). Little by little, as Xi consolidated his power, several heads long considered beyond reach began to tumble; besides Zhou Yongkang they included two freshly retired senior PLA generals, Guo Boxiong and Xu Caihou, as well as Hu Jintao's former right-hand man, Ling Jihua (equivalent to chief of staff). Coming on the heels of the Bo Xilai affair, which had revealed to most ordinary Chinese people the extent of privileges party leaders enjoyed, the campaign quickly proved popular, especially among the urban middle classes, greatly magnifying Xi's image.

However, being structural, corruption is likely to persist. As of now, it is certainly less visible: external signs of wealth accumulated by officials have disappeared; banquets and foreign trips have been reduced to a minimum; and the risks cadres run if caught for passive corruption have become much greater. One might well say that Xi's campaign has to some extent brought down petty corruption, which directly affected Chinese society.

At the same time, the party-state has retained the most crucial of its discretionary powers, in allocation and regulation of land, mining permits, starting new enterprises, and so forth. No outside or independent oversight confronts these powers; the party's discipline inspection commissions only intervene when ordered to do so, and the press has remained largely muzzled on corruption cases, except when a national newspaper takes it upon itself, and not without risks for its journalists, to investigate a local scandal. While the judicial system is more professional and predictable than before, it does not constitute a path for viable and credible recourse in case of a dispute with the administration. It is impossible for any private entrepreneur to float a business without negotiating terms with the authorities. If the anticorruption drive has had any consequence for those needing government services, it is in substantially raising the contents of "red envelopes" given to the bureaucrats who can help.[31] Moreover, published information seems impressive, but looking at the mass of cadres and officials and the endemic nature of corrupt practices, the campaign appears to be meant more to stoke fear than to really punish. In fact, a mere 58,000 (or 3.5 percent) of the 1.53 million party members disciplined for corruption between 2012 and 2017 were prosecuted, highlighting the persistent leniency with regard to the CCP's "black sheep."

Most of all, Xi's anticorruption campaign has in no way made a dent in the rent phenomenon that has benefited both the members of the party nomenklatura and their families.[32] For instance, although Xi at first sought to cap the salaries of officials at state enterprises and banks, he swiftly abandoned the plan, facing resistance from them and the stubborn obstruction they put up through retaliatory measures to public sector reforms. Further, the campaign hardly stemmed the mafia phenomenon observed in numerous localities.[33] Such localities became lawless zones, or rather those where the law of the strongest prevailed; local authorities backed by musclemen imposed their rules for wealth extraction, terrorizing the mass of people.[34]

Evidently the other crucial restriction facing Xi's anticorruption campaign has been the party-state apparatus. It has shown little desire to apply the many measures approved by the three major Central Committee plenums following the 18th Party Congress (2013, 2014, and 2015). In other words, though all powerful in Beijing, the CCP general secretary is less so away from the capital.

This is why from 2015 onward the campaign took on more of a political turn. Xi's opponents, or rather those found to have paid insufficient allegiance to him, henceforth became the main victims, with Wang Qi-shan regularly exhorting respect for the party's "political discipline." For example, as previously mentioned, in July 2017, three months before the 19th Party Congress, Sun Zhengcai was dismissed as party secretary of Chongqing, which until 2012 had been Bo Xilai's fief. Sun, replaced by Xi confidant Chen Min'er, was a representative of the sixth generation of communists initially promoted by Hu Jintao to succeed Xi or Li Keqiang. More important, Sun was expelled from the party and jailed, at first for corruption and then, following an investigation by the Central Commission for Discipline Inspection, for "conspiracy" and "cheating" in internal party elections.[35]

What is most striking in this campaign is the traditional, even Stalin-ist, methods used by the party's discipline commissions. Once declared corruption suspects, CCP officials are detained and interrogated outside the judicial system, for instance in some hotel or obscure rural residence, with no legal safeguards. The proliferation of protests among the no-menklatura against such treatment led the CCP to introduce some re-forms, but of a marginal nature; thus, before the transfer of the case to judicial organs, the suspect has no access to a lawyer's services.

More interesting, and also worrying for our study, is the quasi-absence of criticism, among the public, of these methods used by the party's inspection organs. It is understandable that society at large does not feel affected by such methods, which in any case seem to be effective. Few analyses in China have examined the deep-rooted causes of the cor-ruption cases made public; for instance, how was General Guo Boxiong able over ten long years (2002–2012) to sell promotions within the PLA and get rich with such impunity? These silences, as well as Xi's popular-ity, tell us much about the still-pervasive, dominant political culture in China and about the regime's life expectancy (see chapter 3).

In sum, the ongoing anticorruption campaign has a good chance of persevering. No doubt other campaigns will follow. They are part of the party-state's mechanisms for self-regulation and legitimization and thus are much needed. Nevertheless, they refrain from attacking corruption's systemic sources, because if they did that, they would weaken the very foundations of the CCP's monopolistic power and thus militate against the dominant class interests they serve.

CONTROL OF SOCIETY AND REPRESSION OF DISSIDENTS

Much has been said about intensified repression against dissidents, acti-vists, and NGOs since Xi took power. I do not contest this judgment; various security-related decisions, laws, and regulations adopted since 2012 constitute efforts to more effectively prevent the emergence of any opposition to the CCP, to nip in the bud any political challenge. These measures include the creation in 2013 of a Xi-led National Security Com-mission and adoption of laws on national security, protection of state secrets, and foreign NGOs, as well as the arrest in July 2015 of more than two hundred human rights lawyers, most of whom have been released since but kept under strict surveillance.

However, there is greater continuity than generally perceived in this repressive policy; again, it can be traced back to Tiananmen and even 1979, that is to say, to the suppression of the "democracy wall" and the arrest of Wei Jingsheng. Since then the CCP and its security services have closely watched all dissident activity. In 1998 Jiang ordered the disman-tling of the China Democratic Party and the arrest of all its leaders. A year later he banned the Falungong, a Buddhist religious organization popu-lar among sections of the military and the elderly, which practiced the Chinese exercise *qigong* and which had long sought to be legalized na-tionwide. There was some hope of political reforms after Hu Jintao took the helm in 2002, but that evaporated fast. In 2008 Hu had Liu Xiaobo arrested just before the release of Charter 08, which called for gradual democratization and was initially signed by more than three hundred Chinese scholars. A year later Liu was sentenced to eleven years in pris-on, where he stayed for nearly nine years, being hospitalized with termi-nal cancer just a month before his death in July 2017. In October 2010 the Chinese government vigorously condemned the awarding of the Nobel Peace Prize to Liu, imposing severe economic sanctions on Norway.

Nevertheless, some observers attributed to Xi's predecessors a genu-ine desire for reform and political opening.[36] I believe they harbored no such desire. The priority Jiang accorded, starting in 1996, to establishing a "socialist rule of law state" never implied the setting up of courts inde-pendent of the party or leniency toward those challenging the regime. Similarly, Hu's plan for fostering intraparty democracy, besides its super-ficial character, was in no way conceived of as the first stage of a gradual democratization of the People's Republic, nor did the repression against those who sought such an evolution end. Between 2003 and 2013 Premier Wen Jiabao issued several calls for relaunching "political reforms," letting it be understood that village-level elections could be extended to higher administrations (townships and counties). But these turned out to be more invocations meant to burnish the country's image abroad than any concrete reform plans. And when Wen did get to introducing some sort of political reform, the misunderstanding of the concept's meaning was never dispelled; in fact, promoted by Deng himself since 1986, "political structural reform" (*zhengzhi tizhi gaige*) remains a set of measures aimed at improving, modernizing, and consolidating the party-state's leadership over society as well as the style of governance, not a process for ending the one-party system. To cite a well-known expression, these are reforms within the party-state system (*tizhinei*) that anyone finding themselves outside the system (*tizhiwai*) would be powerless to influence.

In other words, the CCP has always been watchful. With Xi, it has simply become more vigilant and sophisticated. That said, is it really threatened?

In fact, many have questioned how well-founded the regime's apparent paranoia is. In my view, this paranoia stems more from a perceived need on the part of Xi and his team to better manage risks than from any eagerness to fight against a hard-to-find, organized opposition. I return later to reform and democratic movement or movements, bearing in mind that such movements are weak, divided, and most important, unknown to the great majority of Chinese society.

AN ARMY UNDER PARTY CONTROL

The PLA has always been a political army, under strict party control through the Army's General Political Department, the network of political commissars—who as in all Soviet-type countries double as unit commanders from company level onward—and CCP committees within the forces. It should be noted that almost all officers are party members, this allegiance constituting an essential factor in promotion.

Like his predecessors, Xi has ceaselessly reminded those in uniform of their supreme duty: obedience to the party, before defense of the nation. Some say he has been even more insistent. They are probably right, but two motifs explain this desire to boost party control over the PLA. First is the spread of corruption within the forces in the 2000s, and not only in the services in charge of logistics (and thus of the army's vast real estate) or weapons acquisition. As noted previously, as occurred in the civil administration, most senior military officers sold promotions hand over fist. The second motif is more important and in some ways more worrying: the PLA's growing autonomy in terms of political power under Hu's charge. Hu had a weak hold on the army and paid little attention to its day-to-day management. He also contributed to the fragmentation of the party's political leadership (the Politburo and its Standing Committee), letting leaders such as Zhou Yongkang set up a veritable "independent kingdom," and to some extent gave free rein to the military. That his predecessor Jiang stayed put as chairman of the CMC until 2004 did not help either.

Quite simply, Xi had to correct a situation that had become worrying in the PLA. He did so in two ways: on the one hand by successfully extending the anticorruption campaign to the armed forces, wherein some fifty odd generals were arrested, and on the other by recentralizing within the CMC, starting in late 2015, all the major PLA departments, including of course the General Political Department but also the Commission for Discipline Inspection of the Party inside the armed forces; in April 2016 he granted himself the title "commander-in-chief" (*zongzhihui*) of the CMC "Joint Operations Command Centre." He also imposed on the PLA a reorganization of its functioning and creation of joint structures that have a good chance of engaging top generals for at least another decade, without, however, disturbing the specificities and egoisms of each wing, an enduring fragmentation that in reality protects the party against any political rebellion among the forces.

Many issues arose from the Hu-era drift, including the risk of Chinese forces' "Third-Worldization." However, this phenomenon should not be exaggerated. During the same period, China's military machine rapidly developed and modernized. The PLA boasts a great power navy, increasingly present not only in maritime domains that Beijing claims (Paracels, Spratlys, Senkaku) but also in the Western Pacific, the Indian Ocean, and the Gulf of Aden; equipped with fourth-generation aircraft, its air force has become a high performer, while the largely mechanized territorial army has had its personnel reduced to about 1 million (from 1.3 million in 2012). Internal order is secured by several police forces (including the urban police's *Chengguan*) and by the Armed Police (which has increased from 660,000 to 1.2 million), a distinct force under the exclusive direction of the CMC since January 2018 (before it reported to both the CMC and the State Council's Ministry of Public Security).

In other words, as a volunteer army now, the PLA is more powerful as well as more professional, mainly mobilized by the ambitious external objectives that the CCP has assigned to it. At the same time, it remains as political as it was earlier. The PLA's everyday operations, as well as its close relationship with the party, have remained opaque as well. But except during major political or social crises, the PLA has little reason or chance to distance itself from the political authorities and a fortiori rebel or take charge of the country's future (see chapter 6).

CONCLUSION

China's political system is solid and in rude health. It has sustained several transformations, mostly decided by the CCP leadership and implemented through the diverse institutions it controls. The system does suffer from some tensions and dysfunction. Xi Jinping's moves to set himself above his equals and personalize supreme power have had the objective of overcoming these weaknesses, strengthening central authorities' actions, reversing fragmentation of authority, combating indiscipline at the periphery, and thus consolidating the political regime. While such concentration of power in the hands of one individual poses obvious risks, one cannot but be struck by the Chinese political system's vigor, its gradual modernization, and its capacity for ideological and organizational adaptation not only to the economic and social environment it has created but also to the new globalized international environment in which the country has been affirming its might.

This system has also been demonstrating its consistent prowess in managing and, importantly, preventing risks: the appearance of organized political dissidence, the uncontrolled spread of corruption, and of course any autonomization of the military. And all this has been done without the party's submitting to laws or accepting any limitation on its powers. The maintenance of constraining dependence links between the party-state on the one hand and private entrepreneurs and society at large on the other, the pervasive attractiveness of party membership, and the effectiveness of repressive organs explain this solidity, which is greater than previous Chinese regimes enjoyed (see chapters 4 and 5).[37]

As discussed later in this book, other factors contribute to extending the current regime's life expectancy: the present state and very slow evolution of political culture that still dominates Chinese society (chapter 3), the party's tight control of civil society and the weakness of the democratic movement (chapter 4), and elites' conservatism (chapter 5). But it is important to highlight at the outset the strength and the resilience of the new authoritarian equilibrium established post-Tiananmen within the political system established in 1949. And in my view, this system's ability to adapt continues to clearly outweigh the risks of atrophy and disintegration it could run.

NOTES

1. Jean-Pierre Cabestan, *Le système politique chinois: Un nouvel équilibre autoritaire* [The Chinese political system: A new authoritarian equilibrium] (Paris: Presses de Sciences-Po, 2014).

2. Vivienne Shue and Patricia M. Thornton, eds., *To Govern China: Evolving Practices of Power* (Cambridge, UK: Cambridge University Press, 2017).

3. Sebastian Heilmann and Elizabeth J. Perry, eds., *Mao's Invisible Hand: The Political Foundations of Adaptive Governance in China* (Cambridge, MA: Harvard University Press, 2012).

4. Jean-Luc Domenach, *Les fils de princes: Une génération au pouvoir en Chine* [Princelings: A generation in power in China] (Paris: Fayard, 2015); and Stéphanie Balme, *Entre soi: L'élite du pouvoir dans la Chine contemporaine* [Among themselves: The power elite in contemporary China] (Paris: Fayard, 2004).

5. Minxin Pei, *China's Crony Capitalism: The Dynamics of Regime Decay* (Cambridge, MA: Harvard University Press, 2016).

6. "2017nian Zhongguo gongchandang dandnei tongji gongbao" [Internal statistical report of China's Communist Party 2017], *Xinhua*, June 30, 2018, http://www.gov.cn/shuju/2018-06/30/content_5302456.htm; and Lea Shih, "Centralised Leadership, Heterogeneous Party Base: Changes in the Membership Structure of the Chinese Communist Party," *Merics China Monitor*, August 16, 2017, 6, https://www.merics.org/sites/default/files/2017-09/China%20Monitor_40_FTZ_EN.pdf.

7. Zheng Yongnian, *The Chinese Communist Party as Organizational Emperor* (London and New York: Routledge, 2010).

8. Dali L. Yang, *Remaking the Chinese Leviathan: Market Transition and the Politics of Governance in China* (Stanford, CA: Stanford University Press, 2004).

9. Isabelle Thireau and Hua Linshan, *Les ruses de la démocratie: Protester en Chine* [The ruses of democracy: Protest in China] (Paris: Seuil, 2010).

10. Sida Liu and Terence C. Halliday, *Criminal Defense in China: The Politics of Lawyers at Work* (Cambridge, UK, and New York: Cambridge University Press, 2016).

11. Stéphanie Balme, *Chine, les visages de la justice ordinaire* [China, the faces of everyday justice] (Paris: Presses de Sciences Po, 2016).

12. Leng Ling, Danglun Luo, and Guoman She, "Judging a Book by Its Cover: The Influence of Physical Attractiveness on the Promotion of Regional Leaders," SSRN,

September 7, 2016 (last revised December 8, 2018), https://ssrn.com/abstract=2834626 or http://dx.doi.org/10.2139/ssrn.2834626.

13. Daniel A. Bell, *The China Model: Political Meritocracy and the Limits of Democracy* (Princeton, NJ: Princeton University Press, 2015).

14. Yongshun Cai, *State and Agents in China: Disciplining Government Officials* (Stanford, CA: Stanford University Press, 2015), esp. 137–143.

15. There have been 204 members and 172 alternate members since 2017, including only 10 and 20 women, respectively.

16. Wang Xiangwei, "How Xi Jinping Revived Old Methods by Abandoning Intraparty Democracy," *South China Morning Post* (hereafter *SCMP*), November 5, 2017 (updated July 20, 2018), https://www.scmp.com/week-asia/opinion/article/2118352/analysis-how-xi-jinping-revived-old-methods-abandoning-intraparty. See also Joe Fewsmith, "The 19th Party Congress: Ringing in Xi Jinping's New Age," *China Leadership Monitor*, no. 55 (Winter 2018), 16–17, https://www.hoover.org/sites/default/files/research/docs/clm55-jf-final.pdf.

17. Jun Mai, "Three Disgraced Chinese Communist Party Officials Accused of Trying to Rig Elections," *SCMP*, October 27, 2017 (updated July 20, 2018), https://www.scmp.com/news/china/policies-politics/article/2117190/three-disgraced-chinese-communist-party-officials.

18. On the relationship between these rumors and the Bo Xilai affair, see Ho Ping and Huang Wenguang, *A Death in the Lucky Holiday Hotel: Murder, Money, and an Epic Power Struggle in China* (Philadelphia, PA: Public Affairs, 2013).

19. Wendy Wu, "How the Communist Party Controls China's State-Owned Industrial Titans," *SCMP*, June 17, 2017, https://www.scmp.com/news/china/economy/article/2098755/how-communist-party-controls-chinas-state-owned-industrial-titans.

20. "2017nian Zhongguo gongchandang dandnei tongji gongbao."

21. Cabestan, *Le système politique chinois*, 97; and "Woguo minqi 2700 wanjia minying jingji caizheng shouru zhan bi chao 50%" [China's 27 million private enterprises account for more than 50% of the private economy's fiscal revenue], *Renmin Ribao, Haiwaiban* [People's daily, overseas ed.], May 1, 2018, http://www.xinhuanet.com/fortune/2018-05/01/c_1122767077.htm.

22. Steve Tsang, "Consultative Leninism: China's New Political Framework," *Journal of Contemporary China* 18, no. 62 (November 2009): 865–880; and Jessica C. Teets, *Civil Society Under Authoritarianism: The China Model* (New York: Cambridge University Press, 2014).

23. David Shambaugh, *China's Communist Party: Atrophy and Adaptation* (Berkeley: University of California Press, 2007).

24. Deng Zhenglai and Sujian Guo, eds., *China's Search for Good Governance* (New York: Palgrave Macmillan, 2011). See especially the chapter by the official CCP intellectual Yu Keping, "Good Governance and Legitimacy," 15–21.

25. "Xi Jinping's Report at 19th CPC National Congress," *Xinhua*, October 18, 2017, http://www.xinhuanet.com/english/download/Xi_Jinping's_report_at_19th_CPC_National_Congress.pdf.

26. It may be noted that unlike society at large, the PLA is expected to remain politicized.

27. Gao Yu, "Beijing Observation: Xi Jinping the Man," *China Change*, January 26, 2013, https://chinachange.org/2013/01/26/beijing-observation-xi-jinping-the-man-by-gao-yu/ (Chinese version: http://www.dw.com/zh/男儿近平/a-16549520?&zhongwen=simp).

28. Gao, "Beijing Observation."

29. "Document 9: A ChinaFile Translation," November 8, 2013, http://www.chinafile.com/document-9-chinafile-translation. See also Elizabeth C. Economy, *The Third Revolution: Xi Jinping and the New Chinese State* (New York: Oxford University Press, 2018).

30. China's criminal law does not distinguish between crimes and misdemeanors but does between serious crimes and minor ones.

31. In China, traditionally "red envelopes" (*hongbao*) are handed out to younger members of the family or dependent staff on the occasion of the Spring Festival. By extension they have become a convenient way to bribe officials.

32. Pei, *China's Crony Capitalism.*

33. Pei, *China's Crony Capitalism.*

34. One of the best illustrations of this "mafia-ward" drift is available in Graeme Smith, "Political Machinations in a Rural County," *The China Journal* 62 (2009): 29–59.

35. Jun Mai, "Three Disgraced Chinese Communist Party Officials Accused of Trying to Rig Elections."

36. David Shambaugh, *China's Future* (Cambridge, UK, and Malden, MA: Polity, 2016).

37. Bruce J. Dickson, *The Dictator's Dilemma: The Chinese Communist Party's Strategy for Survival* (Oxford: Oxford University Press, 2016).

TWO

Bureaucratic Tradition and the Soviet Model

Patterns of State Hegemony

In the West as well as in China, there is often a tendency to represent the current political system in the People's Republic as a direct successor of the two-millennia-old imperial system that long ensured the country's unity. Of course elements of continuity between the imperial bureaucratic tradition and the current politico-administrative organization are evident, prominent among them, as is widely known, being the selection of officials through competitive examinations. In fact, the CCP often cites this tradition to defend the unprecedented system of control over society and individuals it has set up. People in China are used to the state's hegemony over their lives, which they have largely internalized.

Nevertheless, the differences between the imperial bureaucratic tradition and the Leninist system introduced in 1949 and still in place are fundamental and too often underestimated, including by PRC Chinese, as much in terms of institutions and organization as in those of ideology and political culture. These differences explain to a large extent the solidity of the CCP's power and its strong capacity to adapt, as well as its much better chance of survival than the imperial system had, which after a long period of decadence that started near the end of the Qianlong reign in the eighteenth century quite naturally crumbled in 1911.

Further, the comparisons made between the two systems often disregard the evolution of ideas in China and numerous attempts at reform toward the end of the Manchu dynasty (1644–1911) and in the republican era (1912–1949)—that is to say, during the century between the First Opium War (1840) and the establishment of the People's Republic.

ELEMENTS OF CONTINUITY

Yet one cannot give short shrift to the elements of continuity between the Chinese bureaucratic tradition and more generally the imperial system on the one hand and institutions of the People's Republic on the other. Since the late 1970s, Maoism's burial, the launch of reforms, and a return to more stable and predictable administrative practices have narrowed the gap between the two models. The CCP's instrumentalization of nationalism and the rehabilitation of the imperial (and even republican) past also helped reinforce the perception of such a continuity, in China at first and then abroad.

It should be clear at the outset that even when it was divided, China has always been an administered land. Qin Shihuang's unification of the empire in 221 BCE is often cited as the bureaucratic tradition's founding moment. In reality, beginning with the Zhou dynasty (1066–221 BCE), the politico-geographical entity later named China (a term that came from Qin) was administered, albeit highly decentralized and later fragmented into rival entities (the famous "Warring States"). It was in the Warring States era (475–221 BCE) that Chinese thinkers on politics and administration emerged, led by Confucius and his disciples but also the Legalist school (Han Feizi, Shang Yang, etc.), whose fierce but effective governance methods were later used by Qin Shihuang, as they were by many of his successors, albeit often without acknowledging their source.

Intellectual and political disputes between Confucians and Legalists were foundational, as they advanced two opposing approaches to governing people that remain more complementary than contradictory in practice today: government by "superiors" or "gentlemen" (*junzi*), competent people concerned not with personal interest—which is the lot of the "petty people" (*xiaoren*), that is, the uneducated sectors—but rather with the quest for common good on the one hand and government by law (hence the school of laws, *fajia*, or Legalists), to be understood as criminal law (*xingfa*) or punishment, on the other.

From Han to Manchu (Qing), Tang to Song, Yuan to Ming, all the emperors promoted the government of superiors, who later came to be called scholar-officials or literati. In this sense, Qin Shihuang constituted a traumatizing exception: he went down in history as the sovereign who buried alive a large number of lettered Confucians. At the same time, imperial governments always kept criminal law within easy reach, so to speak, invoking it unhesitatingly to deal with popular uprisings, insubordination, intrigue or corruption on a mandarin's part, and any other infringement of what they deemed harmony under heaven (*Tianxia*).

This opposition between Confucians and Legalists remains crucial to this day and has been the subject of a body of analyses by sinologists such as Lucien Pye.[1] Mao, a great admirer of Qin Shihuang, favored his Legalist-inspired methods to suppress all opposition, ensure obedience from the party-state bureaucracy, and maintain cadres' rectitude and, crucially, their allegiance. He was a sort of modern symbol of the violent dictator (*baojun*). An example is the intensity with which Mao opposed Confucian thought, agreeing to launch in 1974, at the far end of his life, the "Criticize Lin (Biao), Criticize Confucius" (*Pi Lin Pi Kong*) campaign instigated by his wife, Jiang Qing, and other radical leaders of the Cultural Revolution. It was surely paradoxical to link the sage to the marshal who had most ardently backed Mao in this latest venture and had reestablished order with the army's help, suppressing with a very legalist ferocity the Red Guards his leader had earlier mobilized, unwisely arming them against the regime's top bureaucrats, including party member number two, Liu Shaoqi. But Qin Shihuang and Legalism continued to be honored until the death in September 1976 of the founder of the People's Republic and the fall a month later of his political allies, the infamous "Gang of Four." Thus, under Mao socialist law had been reduced essentially to criminal law, breaking with the Soviet tradition of drafting civil and commercial codes and transferring to party cadres the power to resolve disputes through mediation or more often through unchallengeable administrative decisions.

In contrast, Zhou Enlai, Mao's indispensable but servile premier (from 1949 until Zhou's death in January 1976), and his indirect successor, Deng Xiaoping, were often considered Confucians. Zhou strove to safeguard the stability and functioning of government machinery during a period jolted by numerous mass movements and catastrophes, including the Great Leap Forward (1958–1961) and Cultural Revolution in the narrower sense of the term (1966–1968), and Deng restored socialist (and Soviet) administrative and judicial institutions abused by Mao, then modernized them so as to make them serve economic development and reforms.

However, as in the imperial era, neither Mao nor Zhou nor Deng entirely neglected the other side of the bureaucratic tradition. Mao left to Zhou the jobs of leading the government, the State Council, even at the height of the Cultural Revolution, and then gradually rebuilding the country's institutions with the help of Deng, rehabilitated in 1973 before being dismissed again in January 1976; Zhou and Deng and their successors never hesitated to use punishment to suppress all political challenges and keep opponents at bay as well as to stem officials' corruption.

With Xi Jinping, it might well be said that the scale has again tilted toward Legalism; although he increasingly invokes Confucianism, the CCP chief has also openly reinstalled Mao's ideas, insisting, even while initiating his own era, upon the continuity between the beginnings of the People's Republic and of the reform period, exhibiting a deep distrust of—inescapably wrong—human nature, and displaying an obvious penchant for repression.[2]

Apart from this opposition between Confucians and Legalists, two elements of the "celestial bureaucracy" so well analyzed by Etienne Balazs have in a way survived to this day: the emperor and the administration.[3] An entire school of Chinese historians, represented for example by Wang Yanan,[4] and a Sinological tradition abroad, headed by well-known experts such as Léon Vandermeersch, Tu Weiming, and Philip Kuhn, stress the continuity between institutions of the empire and those of successor regimes, including of the People's Republic.[5] Their argument is similar to that of Alexis de Tocqueville, who showed in *L'Ancien régime et la Révolution* (*The Ancien Régime and the Revolution*) how the French government's deep-rooted centralizing tendencies transcended the political upheavals of the late eighteenth century.

In fact, the temptation to compare any contemporary Chinese strongman to emperors of yore is ever present. The inevitable concentration of civil and military powers in the party and state number one, the intimidating protocol surrounding all his activities at home and abroad, the supposed extent of his discretionary powers, and the opacity that marks the exercise of his prerogatives encourage such comparison. Further, Xi's inclination since 2012 and especially since 2017 to call into question the "collective leadership" principle at the CCP's top level, and to raise himself above his equals in the Politburo and its Standing Committee by promoting his "thought' (*sixiang*), reactivating the personality cult, and perpetuating his reign beyond the ten-year limit, contribute to supporting in China and abroad the comparisons not only between Xi and Mao but also between the Xi era and the periods officially deemed flourishing ones, when powerful and respected emperors ruled, such as Tang Taizhong or Qianlong. Sino-centrist diplomatic theories of *Tianxia*, according to which the whole world gravitates around a glorious China with its rediscovered power, are now finding an impressive echo, especially within the People's Republic.[6] Also, most diplomatic meetings in Beijing with the current Chinese strongman are readily interpreted as prostrations by representatives of humble tributary kingdoms before the most august personage of the imperial communist court.

From this flows a well-known paradox: it is in socialist countries whose official ideology promotes the idea, or rather myth, that people make history that not only are powers highly concentrated in small numbers of hands but society has the most belief in the determining role of major personalities or "great men." I discuss later the admiration many Chinese have for strong leaders, most prominent of them being no doubt Vladimir Putin and Donald Trump, and consequently for the personal role Xi has been playing, particularly in the anticorruption drive and on the international scene. It suffices here to note the popular backing for the installation of a powerful central authority capable of imposing its decisions on a local bureaucracy that is too often autonomous or corrupt. Such support generally reflects and perpetuates the belief firmly embedded in Chinese society that the emperor is irreproachable and that he is sometimes poorly advised and more important, misled by subordinates. Surveys invariably show that dissatisfied Chinese people heap their criticism generally on officials they directly deal with and rarely target intermediate levels of the administration and even less the central authorities and the topmost leader (see chapter 3).

Such perceptions reflect a monist (*yiyuanhua*) or holistic conception of authority: for the CCP, as in Confucian thought, a "good government" is one that does not limit its own powers but rather uses all its power to symbolize imperial sovereignty in the best way possible. In Theodore de Bary's formulation, "moral restraints . . . are intended not to make (the prince) less of a king but to help him be a king."[7] Conversely, in Confucian perspective, as in that of the CCP now, bad government reflects a moral decadence among elites rather than institutional rigidities or dysfunction.

China's long bureaucratic tradition has also been a highly pervasive and serious element of continuity. The country has for long been governed by a complex and hierarchical administration that guaranteed numerous services of public and economic interest such as major irrigation works, maintaining granaries, regulating markets, and managing famines.[8] The empire's requirements in economic, hydraulic, and ecological terms spawned the well-known theories of Marx's "oriental mode of production" and Karl Wittfogel's "oriental despotism."[9]

Created by the Han in the second century BCE, the *xian* (county) remains the country's basic administrative division. The organization of the central government in six major ministries goes back to the Sui dynasty, which in the seventh century was the immediate predecessor of the Tang, and that arrangement lasted practically until the empire's fall in 1911, instituting administrative bodies that have survived, such as finance, civil service, army, and justice. The famous mandarin system, the class of scholar-bureaucrats expected to be impartial and chosen through competitive examinations since the Song (tenth century), introduced a meritocratic ideal (*xiancheng*) which, after having been challenged and abandoned by Mao, has been fully restored since the early 1990s. Whereas the PRC's founder preferred promoting party and state cadres who were "red" before being "expert," their recruitment since the late 1970s has been based on both their competence and their allegiance to the regime. Since 1993 officials have been systematically selected through examinations, reconnecting with a tradition the West has borrowed from China since the nineteenth century, first in the British Empire (Indian Civil Service), then in Britain itself (Royal Civil Service) and elsewhere in Europe. This continuity led Tu Weiming to conclude: "The Confucian scholar-official still functions in the psycho-cultural construct of East Asian societies."[10]

Among the characteristics specific to Chinese bureaucratic tradition that the CCP inherited are, first, elitism as a direct consequence of the system, which was in principle meritocratic and particularly demanding in the selection of imperial era administrative elites. The concepts of elites (*jingying*) and elitism (*jingyingzhuyi*), banished under Mao, have regained a privileged place in the PRC's political vocabulary with disconcerting ease and no real critical ethos, especially among official intellectuals.

The second element of continuity is the concentration of power in the head of each locality or public organization (*yibashou*), the introduction of work divisions among administrations, the absence of separation of executive and judicial powers, and finally the adoption of an autonomous system of vetting officials known in the imperial era as the Censorate. Regarding the latter, it should be noted that Mao was an exception, stripping all real powers from the party's control commissions and dismantling them at the start of the Cultural Revolution. It was only at the beginning of the reform era that a control system of CCP and state cadres was restored, with the institution in 1978 of the party's discipline inspection commissions. And as has been noted, it was not until Xi launched the anticorruption campaign in 2013 that these commissions became more powerful and independent of CCP committees at the same level, to which, however, they still continue to report, thus connecting more closely with the Tang and Ming censors' tradition (*yushi*).

The traditional recourse permitted against administrative authorities constitutes another element of continuity; in fact, today's petitioners greatly resemble those of yore, taking to the same forms of protest against injustices suffered (*yuan*, the classical character for injustice that is still regularly used) by flocking to the headquarters of the local government or, if it remains deaf, to Beijing.[11]

It would be tempting to take the comparison between the imperial and communist bureaucracies further and add the adherence to written procedures, importance of seals, ritualism, opacity, and a cult of hierarchy, even a passion for it. Forms of ritualism have evidently changed and are dominated now by the official workings of the party, punctuated by its Congress and the annual Central Committee plenary sessions, as well as the state apparatus, marked each year in March by the "two sessions" (*lianghui*) of the NPC and the CPPCC. Meanwhile, the protocol and etiquette around these activities, and even the reception of foreign guests, seem like rightful continuations from the "Immobile Empire" dear to Lord Macartney, the first British envoy to China in 1793, and to Alain Peyrefitte.[12]

Alongside this opacity is a governance system that clouds issues and misleads observers about the real seats of power. Just as the dowager empress Cixi preferred to "oversee politics from behind the curtain" (*chuilian tingzheng*)—that is, make decisions after spying on ministers and advisers—the CCP rarely arrives at decisions in public, and the leaders who have the greatest influence are not necessarily those occupying the most prominent official positions. For example, Premier Li Keqiang is only the nominal head of government, his powers with regard to economic policy in reality being largely usurped by a party-leading small group (and now commission) presided over by Xi and overseen on a daily basis by Liu He, a close presidential adviser and since 2017 a Politburo member. Therefore one needs to be wary of formal rules declared by the state and even the party; they are religiously invoked, but rarely respected, such being the vast discretionary power of the number one at each level.

What is most striking in China is the cult of hierarchy and the passion for organization and administrative titles. The hierarchical principle is, of course, the basis of all administration, not only of the legal-rational bureaucracy so well analyzed by Max Weber. However, inscribed as it was in the Book of Rites (*Liji*) and anchored in the empire's ideological and political history, this administrative principle in China reflects a Confucian conception that makes hierarchy the key for harmonious familial and thus social life. This hierarchy obsession becomes the model for all organized activity. Thus, heads of public enterprises receive an administrative-equivalent rank in line with the importance of the entity they manage, for instance vice minister for heads of major national behemoths. Armed with such titles and ranks, the heads of these state companies are powerful enough to thumb their noses at provincial authorities and a fortiori Chinese embassies in countries where they operate.

In *The Origins of Political Order* (2011), Francis Fukuyama saw in China the first modern state that largely attributed its establishment to the key role played by the class of scholar-bureaucrats recruited over a millennium based on merit.[13] Obviously state building in China is rooted in more than two millennia of history. However, did imperial China, like the contemporary one, stand on "three pillars" of stable political order as Fukuyama defines it: effective state, rule of law, and an accountable government? That is doubtful. The imperial legal tradition was above all penal and only secondarily administrative; the resurrection of laws since the launch of reforms is far from having helped the People's Republic acquire the rule of law. Like the emperors, the CCP's supreme leaders are only accountable to themselves, except of course in the case of a revolution and, needless to say, on the off chance it succeeds.

FUNDAMENTAL DIVERGENCES

Despite these similarities, the imperial bureaucratic tradition and the political system set up in 1949 diverge in fundamental ways. The similarities presented here are like rosy images or caricatures, which mostly fall apart under closer analysis of ideological, political, and institutional realities past and present. There is a tendency to forget that 1949 constituted a radical rupture, and for many Chinese a traumatic one, that CCP leaders may not challenge or "revisit" without endangering the regime's bases.

The most basic of these divergences, from which flow many other political and organizational differences, is ideological. The current Chinese regime's Marxism-Leninism and what I would call "Sovietism" appear to be toned down.[14] The communist ideal's transformative strength has obviously disappeared. Meanwhile Sovietism—including the study of Stalin's works—remains the ideological, organizational, and legitimizing basis of a party at once managerial and militant and whose missions, despite the reforms introduced since 1979, have always been and still remain more important and numerous than those of imperial bureaucracy. Xi and the 19th Party Congress have merely confirmed this significant reality.

Among the party's missions, pride of place goes to economic development and direct management of a host of state enterprises, which despite the rise of the private economy continue to control key industry sectors (energy, heavy industries, and infrastructure) and services (transport and telecommunications), or what has often been called the "commanding heights of the economy."[15] Its other undertakings include direct surveillance of the population; neutralization of any political, social, or religious force capable of challenging the ruling party; and more generally, unrelenting action against all external and internal enemies. During the imperial era, control of society was more restrained, variable, and erratic, especially in religious matters. And it was wielded mostly indirectly via local elites, the gentry, often jointly responsible for maintaining public order. Thus, the communists replaced a "semi-managerial order" with a "total managerial order." While this observation by Wittfogel is less true of the economic domain now, it remains fully applicable in the political arena.[16]

Several crucial institutional characteristics stem from the CCP's ideological precepts. First is the transformation of the state into a party-state or, to be more accurate, the establishment of state institutions managed by the CCP and fused with it. Such fusion, copied from the Soviet Union, has been fully incorporated; thus, the current seven Politburo Standing Committee members share the topmost posts of the party and the state. In this institutional framework, the armed forces fall under the CCP and its supreme head and not under the government.

Second is the creation of a Leninist- and Soviet-inspired nomenklatura system, which confers on the party a monopoly over promotions to leading posts in all the organizations depending on the party-state. Since the introduction in 1993 of public servants' selection through examinations, this has evidently evolved; these administrative professionals are the main—though not the only—candidates for future CCP leading cadres. However, it is party membership and political loyalty, not mere merit or impartiality and much less neutrality, that determine their selection and promotion. Thus, while the CCP has tried since the start of reforms to select more competent cadres, their careers continue to be subject to political and especially clientelist criteria. Consequently, the administration is a political entity subservient to party interests. This is not to say that in imperial China, as in any other bureaucratic system, political or practical factors such as the venality of offices did not play a role in the promotion of mandarins (*guan*).[17] But any allegiance to a faction (*dang*, in the original and very negative connotation of the word "party" in Chinese) was forbidden. The proliferation of factions toward the end of the Ming is often considered a crucial factor leading to the dynasty's decline and defeat by the Manchu armies.

Whereas the imperial avoidance system (*huibi zhidu*) ensured that officials could not serve in their province of origin, this rule was abandoned under Mao and has hardly been applied systematically since the beginning of the reforms. In the imperial era, the number of officials selected through examinations and put in charge of major public jobs was quite low: twenty thousand civil officials and twenty thousand military officers during the late Qing.

This leads to the third major difference: imperial era bureaucracy was in reality quite restrained. On the one hand, apart from official functionaries, it included about 1.5 million auxiliaries chosen by the former and taking care of most day-to-day administrative chores; on the other, the administration's grassroots level was the *xian* or county, the gentry exercising the intermediary role with family clans and village communities.[18] But the bureaucracy the CCP established in 1949 has been a sprawling one despite reforms and several simplifications introduced since 1979. It is present in each township (*xiang*), town (*zhen*), and, in a form more participative and democratic in principle, each village (*cun*) or urban community (*shequ*). As noted previously, with ten million government officials (seven million of them recruited through examinations), the bureaucracy has a total of nearly seventy million cadres, including those in the party apparatus, state enterprises, and institutions, as well as official mass organizations. Even adjusted for population size, these figures are striking, highlighting the multiple missions the CCP and its ruling ideology demand of the state. And there is no question of the party either relaxing its tight grip on public industrial groups deemed strategic or relying on private entrepreneurs—modern equivalents, mutatis mutandis, of imperial era rural gentry—to collect taxes and maintain social stability. Rather, they are increasingly often under surveillance from party organizations that they are required to host in their business precincts.

Finally—and this stems directly from the CCP's ideological project and ambition to stay in power forever—China now commands an immense machinery for surveillance of the population and any organized activity. To facilitate the economic development and supplementary financial means the regime needs, this surveillance apparatus has been modernized and on the whole rapidly deployed, helping nip in the bud any dissident political activity, strictly controlling the Internet, and registering only those NGOs that will not hurt the regime's stability (see chapter 4). In 2010 the state budget earmarked for safeguarding stability (*weiwen*), that is, internal security, began to overtake that of the PLA. This gap has persisted since then ($160 billion compared to $150 billion in 2016).

In sum, the People's Republic and the party-state established in 1949 are more inheritors of the Soviet governance model established by Lenin and Stalin than of the celestial bureaucracy of the imperial epoch. Also, the latter comparison is even more misleading, as it fails to take into account the fundamental transformations of the Chinese state at the end of the Manchu era and in the republican period.

REPUBLICAN CONTINUITIES AND RUPTURES

Any reflection on the future of the Chinese political regime must take into consideration reforms introduced at the end of the empire and during the republican era. At present, in an attempt to legitimize the current regime by invoking the supposed glory of imperial dynasties, conservative forces are seeking to minimize the profound political changes of the late imperial and the republican periods, concentrating on the humiliations inflicted by the West and Japan. Obviously this narrative and historical reconstruction overlooks several historical realities. The humiliation the Chinese suffered in that period was mainly caused by the Manchu, who dominated the political system, imposing the synarchy principle (one Manchu, one Han, the first having precedence over the second) for all key posts in the bureaucracy, meanwhile proving incapable of lifting the country out of poverty. This led to the Taiping Rebellion (1850–1864), which left twenty million dead and accelerated the empire's inexorable weakening, as well as to the rise among nationalist movements of a current favoring restoration of the Ming dynasty. This also fed a predominantly racial approach to nationalism (*minzuzhuyi*), the Chinese nation (*Zhonghua minzu*) representing the Han majority, with the other ethnicities called upon to merge and mix with this majority.[19]

For a great majority of Chinese elites in the second half of the nineteenth century, more important than opposition to invaders and Manchu tutelage was learning from the West and taking aboard diverse currents of thought they believed could help modernize China. The success of Japan's Meiji restoration (1868) and China's military defeat by the Japanese army in 1895 sped up this process. While the Marxist and Leninist currents eventually prevailed with the CCP's military victory over the Nationalist Party or Kuomintang (KMT), it was the liberal ideas in matters economic as well as political that spread most quickly and dominated the entire period. These ideas were introduced by famous scholars and intellectuals such as Yan Fu, Kang Youwei, Liang Qichao, and Hu Shi.

This is why Chinese reformers have always had a great interest in the movement of ideas and institutional transformations of the last years of the Qing and the period after the Republic of China (ROC) was born in 1912. This interest has grown since early in the twenty-first century among Chinese intellectuals, especially given the KMT regime's democratization in Taiwan and the resumption of cross-Strait relations.

Chinese elites have always been divided over the solutions for challenges facing their country at any given moment. Some Qing officials such as Zhang Zhidong wished to import just the "Western techniques" while keeping the political system's "Chinese substance," in line with the well-known *Zhongxue wei ti, Xixue wei yong* formula.[20] Others, such as Kang Youwei and Liang Qichao, artisans of the timid and ill-fated 1898 Hundred Days' Reform, wished to modify governance methods (*bianfa*) but failed in their efforts when faced with powerful resistance to any political change. Unlike Japan, which in 1889 had established a constitutional monarchy with a Diet partly elected through restrictive suffrage (based on the amount of property tax paid), China merely set up an education ministry; on a constitution, elections, or parliament, there was silence. Moreover, numerous tentative reforms that the Manchu court finally approved after the crisis—and warning—of the Boxer Rebellion (1900) were motivated by a political instrumentalist approach; for China it was all about acquiring the same institutional arms as the West and, importantly, modernizing and strengthening the state in the face of menacing foreign powers, although to the detriment of citizens' individual rights.[21]

Of course the political transformations in China even before the fall of the empire and the 1911 revolution testify to the awareness among the elites starting in the latter part of the nineteenth century of the decadence and irrelevance of their system of government as well as the influence of Western and liberal ideologies. In 1905, as no public jobs could be found for all those who passed the exams, imperial examinations were abolished. Around the same time, Shen Jiaben introduced major reforms of the criminal code, banning among other things the cruelest punishments.[22]

Toward the end of Cixi's reign (1908) the first drafts of a constitution betrayed the pervasive preoccupation, even obsession, with strengthening the state and more generally building a modern one. The same was true of the plan for the gradual introduction of a constitutional government, unveiled toward the end of his life by Sun Yat-sen, the first provisional president of the ROC (1912); it aimed to prepare Chinese society, which was rather backward and rural, for the exercise of democratic rights. After a period of military government, in order to reunify China under the republican banner (*junzheng*), the KMT—the party that had led the revolution—was expected to exercise its tutelage (*xunzheng ou dang-*

zheng) over the political system. The plan was to first set up a veritable party-state, or rather hand over power to a party capable of forming a modern state (*yidang jianguo*).[23] This plan was executed by Chiang Kai-shek, who succeeded Sun as head of the KMT and of the nationalist army formed in Canton (now Guangzhou). Having rallied most of the warlords to his side during the famous Northern Expedition (*beifa*), Chiang set up the central government of the Republic of China in Nanjing, the country's new capital, in 1927–1928.

Nonetheless, in Sun's as well as the KMT's view, a constitutional and democratic regime (*xianzheng*) was meant to eventually take shape. Initially intended to end in 1935, after the encirclement campaigns against communist guerrillas, the tutelage continued because of Chiang's conservatism and the Sino-Japanese War (1937–1945) until 1947, when the constitution adopted the previous year came into force. Although national elections were organized in 1947–1948 in all the regions under nationalist administration, a constitutional regime never took shape owing to the resumption of civil war with the CCP and the KMT's flight to Taiwan in 1949. The continuation of the state of war with the communists was Chiang's reason for freezing all application of the Constitution of the Republic of China while in Taiwan until his death in 1975. It was his son and successor, Chiang Ching-kuo, who in 1987, a year before his death, lifted martial law and introduced the first democratic reforms. Whereas the KMT's tutelage as well as the martial law imposed on Taiwan from 1950 were conceived of as provisional, the CCP's domination over the People's Republic is deemed to be perpetual. In this regard, it is worth noting that the constitutionalist movement that sprouted in China from 2008 has in fact demanded that the CCP give up tutelage over the state and accept the principle of a constitutional regime (*xianzheng*), which alone would have allowed a real implementation of the constitution adopted in 1982.

Sun Yat-sen's political and institutional ideas also presented elements of continuity with imperial tradition. In the institutional project he initiated, which was picked up by the KMT and enshrined in the Constitution of the Republic of China in 1946, Sun envisaged the establishment of not three but five distinct authorities or councils (*yuan*) that could act as checks and balances on each other: the Executive Council, Legislative Council, Judicial Council, Control Council, and Examination Council. Directly inspired by the most "modern" institutions of the imperial tradition, the last two councils were created to respectively oversee officials and organize their recruitment through examinations. Despite eventual transformations (today the Control Yuan is not elected but appointed by the president with the approval of the Legislative Yuan, or parliament), this separation of five powers remains in force in Taiwan where, since its democratization, they function more or less as Sun had visualized. The institution of recruitment of officials through examinations has been modernized and is no longer based on the assimilation of Confucian classics but on the grasp of administrative, judicial, and economic knowledge.

In general, Sun and the KMT were inspired by the liberal ideas of the Enlightenment and especially of Montesquieu. Sun's Three Principles of the People—nationalism, democracy, and people's well-being—offer a modern and "Sinicized" synthesis of an ideology of Western origin. Sun's objectives were to transform the Chinese empire—in which following the fall of the Ming in 1644, the Manchus, Mongols, and Tibetans held a privileged institutional and religious position—into a modern and multiethnic nation; create institutions for a constitutional and pluralist democracy; and offer minimum social guarantees for a population still largely impoverished.

The May 4th movement of 1919 confirmed this domination of liberal ideas among Chinese elites. Provoked by the Treaty of Versailles, which handed Japan the German possessions in China, the demonstrators of May 4th highlighted the famous calls for "Mister Science and Mister Democracy," conceived of and internalized as two inseparable facets of any modernization of the country.

Among the May 4th actors, some Marxist intellectuals, such as Chen Duxiu, one of the CCP's founders, became spokesmen for a "scientific and instrumentalist" approach to democracy, which can be considered the ideological breeding ground of the Leninist regime installed in 1949. More generally, the influence of socialism and the young Soviet Union was perceptible in the political ideas Sun developed toward the end of his life (he died in 1925); that was the case with his third principle, "people's well-being" (*minsheng*), the foundation of the KMT's social policy, his opposition to imperialism, his rapprochement with the Bolshevik regime, and the decision to enter into an alliance with the CCP, founded in 1921.

All the same, the May 4th phenomenon consolidated the predominance of liberal and democratic ideas. These were represented by many groups, the most famous of them being the New Youth (*Xin Qingnian*) movement, intellectuals such as Hu Shi and Cai Yuanpei, and writers such as Lu Xun and Wen Yiduo.[24] More generally, the KMT's ideology was largely based on liberal principles. Of course Leninism directly influenced the Nationalist Party's organizational pattern. But the KMT never acquired the level of quasi-military discipline or opacity of the CCP, a weakness that contributed to its defeat by Mao's army in 1948–1949. Chiang had briefly been seduced by the European authoritarian and totalitarian regimes of the 1930s, such as fascist Italy and then Nazi Germany, which had helped modernize his army in Nanjing. Further, from 1931 Chiang and a majority of KMT chiefs imposed a conservative course, seeking much more to reconnect with Confucian tradition and run a strong government than to spread Sun's democratic ideals, political pluralism, and respect for people's liberties.[25] In the economic domain, the advent of the Nanjing regime slowed down the development of private enterprise, especially family capitalism, which had enjoyed unprecedented growth in the early twentieth century, in favor of crony capitalism and the state sector.[26] These are evolutions not without ramifications and continuations in the People's Republic now.[27]

However, the KMT could never completely turn its back on its liberal ideology, which was the basis of both the 1911 revolution and the close relations the ROC had developed with the United States and other democratic countries, nor totally suppress political opposition to its government.[28] These relations were not merely diplomatic and military, although during the Sino-Japanese War, and especially after the United States entered World War II against Japan in 1941, such links were mostly augmented. They were also economic, social, academic, and religious. The role of Western and particularly American religious congregations and missionaries in republican China was enormous, notably in education, contributing to the spread of liberal and democratic ideas. For instance, American philosopher and educator John Dewey, who was much attached to democracy and was a friend of Hu Shi, the translator of many of his conferences during his two years in China (1919–1921), exerted a large influence on Chinese elites.[29]

In other words, as Frank Dikötter says, the republican era was an "age of openness," a theater of much drama, vicissitudes, and authoritarian tendencies but also of real economic development, a flowering of ideas, multiple experiences of modernization, and most crucially a readiness to draw inspiration from outside and appropriate democratic principles from the West.[30] Contrary to CCP propaganda, republican China was not synonymous with decadence and with an inability to modernize the country. In fact, it was a veritable laboratory for ideas and reforms in all domains: economy, agriculture, education, culture, judiciary, military, and even politics. Without the Sino-Japanese War, as Mao himself admitted (and thanked the Japanese for), the CCP would never have come to power, and the KMT could well have achieved its task of economic and then political modernization.

Three examples of ROC accomplishments suffice. First, the six codes of the ROC (*Liufa Quanshu*) that the KMT promulgated between 1928 and 1935 constitute an impressive body of work, which has not only served as the basis of laws in force in Taiwan today but also deeply influenced the judicial reforms Deng introduced after 1979. Second, in the international arena, it was Chiang and not Mao who in 1943 abolished foreign concessions or extraterritorial zones, which accorded numerous legal privileges and guarantees to expatriates in China. It was Nanjing and not Beijing, as a founder member of the United Nations (UN), that contributed to the drafting of the Universal Declaration of Human Rights in 1948. And third, many historical and diplomatic documents of the immediate postwar period show that had Chiang succeeded in retaining his regime in Nanjing after 1949, he would have compelled Britain to return Hong Kong much earlier than the CCP managed to do. In other words, when it comes to the former British colony, the People's Republic prolonged rather than shortened the "humiliation" the "Chinese people" suffered.

Finally, the republican era was also the only time in modern Chinese history when genuinely pluralistic national and local elections were organized; first were the legislative elections of 1913, which the KMT won. It would have been in power with Song Jiaoren as prime minister had he not been assassinated at the behest of the then strongman Yuan Shikai. Second were the 1947–1948 elections, whose democratic character was much more debatable but which in the context of the renewed civil war between the KMT and the CCP were the last real national elections organized in China before Mao took power.

CONCLUSION

Clearly there is need for caution regarding the discourse from the PRC authorities and official historians on the country's past. What occurred in 1949 was less a fundamental rupture with the imperial period than with the ideas that had spread and the reforms introduced in a China that was effervescent, open to the outside world, even cosmopolitan, during the late Qing and the republican eras.

If there is an essential element of continuity between the imperial and republican traditions on the one hand and the PRC on the other, it is what Etienne Balazs called "statism" and the overwhelming role the bureaucracy and officials play.[31] This statism stems largely from the Confucian ideology and the monist conception of political power it offers. It also is attributable to the vastness of the territory to be administered and central authorities' ever-present need to depend on reliable representatives capable of maintaining local societies' stability and the country's unity. Mention may also be made of the key role the state has played in China's development strategy in both the republican and current periods. More generally, in Confucianized East Asian countries such as Japan, Taiwan, and South Korea, the state, while letting a particularly dynamic familial capitalism prosper, is not only a regulator but also an organizer of development, education, and social services.

Nevertheless, CCP cadres seeking to eulogize and idealize the scholar-officials of yore and to imitate their impartiality or at least to assume the appearance of their dignity have stood out from their models because of their very ideology, mission, competences, and practices.[32] Also, unlike the KMT, which espoused a liberal ideology and considered its tutelage over the state to be provisional, the CCP has always considered leadership of the state as its right forever and itself as the immanent representative of the "people." Moreover, in contrast to the KMT and all previous regimes, the CCP exercises total domination over the state and hegemony over society, maintaining a level of surveillance and repression never seen before, which modern means at its disposal also render more effective. These are differences that make any transition of the current regime toward democracy much more difficult.

That being said, the question arises whether in the context of modernization, privatization, urbanization, and globalization of China's economy, the administration could still exercise the "absolute power" that Balazs attributed to it in the 1960s. Although private entrepreneurs remain highly dependent on the party-state, as discussed later, such dependence is reciprocal and contributes to undercutting the bureaucracy's omnipotence.

Consequently, while continuing to administer a substantial part of the economy and strictly control society, the party-state of the PRC is on the whole advancing on a path leading away from the one it chose in 1949. It is this new orientation that is in fact leading the CCP to invoke tradition and restore Confucianism. The destination and the culmination of this itinerary are of interest next.

NOTES

1. Lucian W. Pye, *The Mandarin and the Cadre: China's Political Cultures* (Ann Arbor: Center for Chinese Studies, The University of Michigan, 1988).

2. See François Bougon, *Dans la tête de Xi Jinping* [On Xi Jinping's mind] (Arles, France: Solin/Actes Sud, 2017).

3. Etienne Balazs, *Chinese Civilization and Bureaucracy: Variations on a Theme*, trans. H. M. Wright, ed. Arthur F. Wright (New Haven, CT, and London: Yale University Press, 1964).

4. Wang Yanan, *Zhongguo guanliao zhengzhi yanjiu* [A study of Chinese bureaucratic politics] (Taipei: Sufeng chubanshe, 1987). The book's first edition was published in 1948, before the advent of the People's Republic.

5. Kuhn tried to show the elements of continuity in the Chinese state's efforts to adapt and modernize since the mid-nineteenth century: establishing a clear fiscal base and strengthening central authorities. Philip A. Kuhn, *Origins of the Modern Chinese State* (Stanford, CA: Stanford University Press, 2002), viii.

6. See "Historical Perspectives on the Rise of China: Chinese Order, Great Harmony, and Tianxia," special issue, *Journal of Contemporary China* 24, no. 96 (2015).

7. Theodore de Bary, "Chinese Despotism and the Confucian Ideal: A Seventeenth-Century View," in *Chinese Thought and Institutions*, ed. John K. Fairbank (Chicago: University of Chicago Press, 1967), 195.

8. Pierre-Etienne Will, *Bureaucratie et famine en Chine au XVIIIe siècle* [Bureaucracy and famine in China in the eighteenth century] (Paris-La Haye: Mouton/EHESS, 1980).

9. Karl Wittfogel, *Oriental Despotism: A Comparative Study of Total Power* (New Haven, CT, and London: Yale University Press, 1957).

10. Tu Weiming, ed., *Confucian Traditions in East Asian Modernity: Moral Education and Economic Culture in Japan and the Four Mini-Dragons* (Cambridge, MA: Harvard University Press, 1996).

11. Isabelle Thireau and Hua Linshan, *Les ruses de la démocratie: Protester en Chine* [The ruses of democracy: Protest in China] (Paris: Seuil, 2010).

12. Alain Peyrefitte, *The Immobile Empire* (New York: Knopf, 1992). On ritualism, see Léon Vandermeersch, *Les deux raisons de la pensée chinoise: Divination et idéographie* [Two characteristics of Chinese thought: Divination and ideography] (Paris: Gallimard, 2013), 168–187.

13. Francis Fukuyama, *The Origins of Political Order: From Prehuman Times to the French Revolution* (London: Profile Books, 2011).

14. On the Soviet Union's influence over China, see Lucien Bianco, *Stalin and Mao: A Comparison of the Russian and Chinese Revolutions* (Hong Kong: The Chinese University Press, 2018); Thomas P. Bernstein and Hua-yu Li, eds., *China Learns from the Soviet Union, 1949–Present* (Lanham, MD: Lexington Books, 2010).

15. The expression was coined by the Soviet economist Yevgeni Preobrazhensky (1886–1937).

16. Wittfogel, *Oriental Despotism*, 441.

17. Lawrence Lok Cheung Zhang, "Power for a Price: Office Purchase, Elites Families, and Status Maintenance in Qing China" (PhD diss., Harvard University Press, 2010).

18. For an illustration of the scale and tasks of imperial era local administration, see Michel Cartier, *Une réforme locale en Chine au XVIème siècle: Hai Rui à Chun'an, 1558–1562* [Local reform in sixteenth-century China: Hai Rui in Chun'an, 1558–1562] (Paris-La Haye: Mouton, EPHE, 1973).

19. John Fitzgerald, *Awakening China: Politics, Culture, and Class in the Nationalist Revolution* (Stanford, CA: Stanford University Press, 1996), 120–122.

20. "Chinese knowledge as substance, Western knowledge as instrument."

21. Andrew J. Nathan, *Chinese Democracy* (Berkeley: University of California Press, 1986).

22. Jérôme Bourgon, "Shen Jiaben et le droit chinois à la fin des Qing" [Shen Jiaben and the late Qing legal reform] (PhD diss., Ecole des Hautes Etudes en Sciences Sociales, Paris, 1994).

23. Fitzgerald, *Awakening China*, 185–186.

24. Sebastian Veg, "Quelle science pour quelle démocratie? Lu Xun et la littérature de fiction dans le mouvement du 4 mai" [What sort of science for what sort of democracy? Lu Xun and literary fiction in the May Fourth movement], *Annales: Histoire, Sciences Sociales*, no. 2 (2010): 345–374. See also Sebastian Veg, "New Readings of Lu Xun: Critic of Modernity and Re-inventor of Heterodoxy," *China Perspectives*, no. 3 (2014): 49–56.

25. Lloyd E. Eastman, *The Abortive Revolution: China Under Nationalist Rule, 1927–1937* (Cambridge, MA: Harvard University Asia Center, 1990).

26. Marie-Claire Bergère, *The Golden Age of the Chinese Bourgeoisie, 1911–1937* (Cambridge, UK: Cambridge University Press, 2009).

27. Alain Roux, *Chiang Kaï-shek: Le grand rival de Mao* [Chiang Kai-shek: Mao's great rival] (Paris: Payot, 2016).

28. Edmund S. K. Feng, *In Search of Chinese Democracy: Civil Opposition in Nationalist China* (Cambridge, UK: Cambridge University Press, 2000).

29. Jessica Ching Tze Wang, *John Dewey in China: To Teach and to Learn* (Albany: State University of New York Press, 2012).

30. Frank Dikötter, *The Age of Openness: China Before Mao* (Hong Kong: University of Hong Kong Press, 2008). However, note that Dikötter often pushes the argument rather too far.

31. Balazs, *Chinese Civilization and Bureaucracy*, 317.

32. Even under the Qing, more than 90 percent of the population lacking education was excluded from the imperial examinations. See Benjamin Elman, *A Cultural History of Civil Examinations in Late Imperial China* (Berkeley: University of California Press, 2000).

THREE

Democratic Culture

Repressed, Fragile, and Distorted

This chapter intends to show that the PRC's dominant political culture remains largely antidemocratic, shaped by a mix of traditional Confucian values and Leninist principles instilled into society through more than seventy years of one-party rule and communist propaganda.[1] It also demonstrates that this dominant culture, though unsettled, acts as a damper on any willingness to pursue democratization.

To be sure, democratic ideas never completely disappeared in the PRC after 1949. As will be seen, their influence has only grown because of economic growth, urbanization, globalization, and the rise of vast middle classes.[2] But these ideas have been consistently smothered or repressed each time they emerged in public, for instance during the Hundred Flowers campaign (1957), toward the end of the Mao era (April 1976 demonstrations), at the beginning of the reform era (1978–1979 democratic movement), and in the late 1980s (1989 spring), blocking their spread and strengthening the hand of the authorities. They face daily assaults by a CCP engaged in an unrelenting frontal combat against what it calls "Western democracy" or "bourgeois democracy" and against the universality of human rights. The CCP has instead promoted "socialist democracy and legality," increasingly "with Chinese characteristics" but always under its own absolute leadership. Thanks to advances in modern technologies and the increase in its financial resources, the party-state has buttressed its ability to "format" political values to which the majority of

Chinese society adheres and thus to slow down the emergence of democratic ideas or distort their content. Be that as it may, as I discuss later, the fear of chaos or simply uncertainty continues to persuade most Chinese people to support the current regime.

Many analysts are inclined to minimize the role of dominant political values in any future transformation of the regime, either because they believe that only elites' opinions matter or because they hold that other evolutionary forces, much more structural or social, such as the rise of educated and urbanized middle classes, modify situations quasi-mechanically.[3] But it seems to me that Chinese society's current state of mind and its approach to politics constitute, at least in the medium term, major factors of resistance against any challenge to the one-party system.[4]

By political culture I mean not only a set of unconscious and conscious political attitudes but also a corpus of civic values developed from normative principles and political rules flowing from a certain conception of the world and of society.[5] Opinion polls throw light on Chinese people's political culture even though their results stem from a larger systemic environment and must therefore be contextualized. Although at present some questions can still not be directly posed during surveys, these opinion polls inform us about Chinese society's political priorities and aspirations.[6]

WHAT THE CHINESE THINK

In general, Chinese people support the PRC political system and recognize the legitimacy of its established institutions: the party, the government, the NPC, and the PLA. They trust and identify with these institutions as well as with their symbols, such as the national flag that the CCP introduced in 1949; approve (or do not question) their mission; and in most cases the policies those institutions set.

As several studies show, the level of satisfaction with the party and government is the direct result of the Chinese economy's unprecedented growth, a large majority's growing affluence, improved access to health care, and a general amelioration of society's standard of living. As with the CCP's administrative capacities discussed in chapter 1, a majority of Chinese people, aware of the successes of their country as well as the failures and weaknesses of other countries, especially their Asian neighbors, appreciate the gradual improvement in quality of governance. Chinese society's high level of satisfaction is the direct consequence of the PRC's rise, showing how much the priority accorded by the party since 1989 to stoking nationalism has paid off.[7]

Since the 1990s, for Chinese people stability and development have taken precedence over democracy, professional success over extension of individual freedom, and economic and social rights over political ones.[8]

More surprisingly for a Westerner, from this satisfaction stems a peculiar and, to my mind, distorted vision of democracy that generally appropriates the CCP discourse on "socialist democracy," such as that defined by a 2005 White Paper—that is, of a "people's democracy" not only led but entirely administered by the party.[9] Midway through the 2000s, 84 percent of Chinese considered their country to be already democratic, and 66 percent thought this democracy would continue to deepen.[10] These results have been confirmed by more recent studies, notably a most convincing one by Bruce Dickson: in 2014, as in 2010, a majority of urban Chinese people were satisfied with the quality of the current "democratic system." But by "democracy" those questioned did not mean a system in which "everyone votes" or even "majority rule"; they understood democracy as a system wherein the government "listens to the people," "whose policies reflect public opinion" and whose authorities "serve the people" (*wei renmin fuwu*), in Mao's well-worn term that is still inscribed on all public buildings.[11]

This dominant viewpoint is reflected in the CCP's expressed intention since early in the 2000s to introduce a degree of "deliberative democracy" (*xieshang minzhu*), that is, a more or less formal process of consulting citizens. The idea is to take society's pulse regularly through opinion polls (often for internal use) and avoid promoting political leaders found to be too unpopular in their localities.[12]

Data regularly published by Asian Barometer Survey, a comparative research project on Asian countries set up by Taiwan's Academia Sinica, have also turned up similar findings: 63 percent of Chinese supported their political system as of 2016, while 72 percent declared their wish to live under the current regime; these numbers are lower than in Vietnam (93 and 88 percent, respectively) or Singapore (86 and 84 percent) but higher than in Taiwan (41 and 61 percent) or Hong Kong (40 and 54 percent).[13] While 66 percent of Chinese hold democracy to be the best form of government, just 42 percent believe it is preferable to any other system (compared, e.g., with 89 and 66 percent, respectively, in Japan).

The Chinese also voice optimism over the evolution in the country's level of democracy; evaluated by those polled at 6.7 on a scale of 1 to 10 against 5.4 "earlier" (no doubt before the reforms), it would in their view climb to 7.4 in the (indefinite) future. Paradoxically, Taiwanese views are not too different: 6.5, 6.1, and 8.2, respectively. In China as in the rest of East Asia, including democratic countries such as Japan, good governance and social justice are deemed to be two essential elements of democracy, much more than norms and procedures and even more than people's freedoms.

This level of importance attached to good governance is found in most surveys. In 2016, among aspects the Chinese appreciated the most was their government's ability to "resolve problems" (63 percent), just below the "pride" they felt in their system (69 percent). They were ready to support their political regime even when it faced problems (63 percent), and they were more concerned with the results the party-state was capable of showing them than with the procedures it followed, its transparency level, the way in which decisions were taken, or even checks and balances on political leaders' powers.[14]

One cannot avoid likening this conception of democracy to the traditional Confucian ideology, especially that of Mencius, who put the "people" at the heart of any politics, without however providing any representative system or limitations on leaders' powers. The formulation that "the people are the foundation of the country" (*min wei bang ben*) was quoted by Premier Wen Jiabao early in the 2000s in claiming legitimacy for the party's policies and its pursuit of the "interest of the community."[15] For Mencius, it was in cases of extreme abuse of power and injustice that the people had a right to revolt. As is well known, Mao was much inspired by this recommendation in ousting the KMT from power. And precisely in order to forestall any popular revolt or what are called "mass incidents," the party-state has been trying to prevent abuse and injustice; when they do occur, it acts to resolve them as quickly and at the lowest levels possible or to keep them secret. The party has done this not without some success despite a large (but undisclosed) number of such incidents occurring annually.[16] It should also be borne in mind that a great majority of these incidents are not of a political nature strictly speaking, and none to my knowledge since Tiananmen has questioned the nature of the regime. In general, they arise from job disputes or disagreements over the level of compensation for confiscated rural lands or urban dwellings, less frequently over environment problems, and even less often as nationalist mobilizations against a foreign country.

All studies on protest movements, workers' strikes, or peasant revolts confirm the great political caution shown by leaders as well as participants. Legitimate resistance against acts by the government or an enterprise seen as iniquitous is fine, and greater awareness among workers as well as peasants of their rights is also okay, but questioning the legitimacy of the one-party regime is not.[17]

According to Dickson's study, society's confidence in the central government and the party is at 7.5 to 8 on a scale from 0 to 10. More interestingly, despite some people's defiance of local governments, especially of administrative authorities they have had to deal with daily, this study shows that a majority (75 percent) of those surveyed were satisfied with official efforts in the areas of education and maintenance of order. Of course the polls are more guarded in respect to food security; just about half the people declared they were satisfied. However, these opinions confirm in a way the reactive nature as well as adaptation capacity of local authorities.[18]

Further, while Chinese people's confidence in local radio and television stations (50 percent) is lower than in national ones (70 percent) such as CCTV (90 percent), it is in both cases greater than their faith in foreign media. Even among those born after 1992, fewer than 40 percent have confidence in the latter (compared to 10 to 20 percent among those who are older).[19] This discrepancy between the society's levels of trust in central and local authorities has been confirmed by many studies, including Wenfang Tang's, who has concluded that dissatisfaction with local governments does not mean that more Chinese want more democracy, in the liberal sense of the term, or to embark on civil disobedience.[20]

Whoever lives in or has been to China quickly becomes aware of the diversity of viewpoints regarding the party-state's decisions or policies. One soon learns about the real generation gap that could in the future become worrying for the regime (see chapter 6). Young people are more sensitive to Internet censorship than are older groups. Dickson's survey showed that nearly 90 percent of young urban Chinese believed that state control of the Internet must not affect individual freedoms or the right to free expression. At the same time, the young have grown more cynical — or honest — about their reasons for joining the CCP; according to Dickson,

70 percent admitted that in fact career considerations rather than the idea of "serving the people" persuaded them to make that decision.[21]

More generally, the level of people's confidence in the party-state needs to be put in perspective; again according to Dickson, just 36 percent of urban Chinese believe government officials are truthful.[22] What is most striking is the degree of suspicion the people have among themselves beyond the limits of their families or the primary groups they belong to. Over the years there has been a lively debate in China about the nonexistence of "good Samaritans"—those who act in a genuinely disinterested manner—a phenomenon that both the authorities and large sections of society deplore. Risks attached to any altruistic action dampen the ardor of many willing to render help beyond their circle of acquaintance. Among the most cited examples is of a Good Samaritan being swindled by a fake victim through entrapment or having to pick up the hospital bills of an injured person one has helped.

The unprecedented desire for and possibility of exiting poverty and of enrichment, the absence of institutions able to limit the rights of the strongest, and mutual suspicions that nearly three decades of Maoism instilled—all these factors explain the high level of wariness and distrust in interpersonal relations. But far from harming the legitimacy of the regime, this situation has only boosted it, as has the confidence society places in authorities to maintain order, stability, and security.

A most interesting study has shown the extent to which Chinese society's ideological structuring—in terms of political preferences—helps in consolidating the current regime.[23] After confirming that Chinese society is indeed divided between "liberals" and "conservatives," the study demonstrates a high degree of correlation among their political, economic, and individual preferences. The "liberals" favor an expansion of civil liberties, of democracy, and of market mechanisms. They wish to see greater protection of individual rights vis-à-vis the state and greater economic opening globally, and they are quite pro-West and certainly "non-nationalists"; they are also more open regarding morals, such as with matters sexual. The "conservatives" for their part are attached to state ownership of the means of production, the social and economic protection that public authorities offer, and the CCP's leading role. They are generally protectionists in economic terms and are nationalists, and they respect more traditional and thus Confucian behaviors. The former tend to be richer; better educated; more urban; younger (between ages eighteen and thirty-five); and concentrated in coastal regions and big cities such as Beijing, Shanghai, and Guangzhou. The latter are in general more indigent; poorly educated; much less urbanized; older (thirty-five and older); and more numerous in interior provinces, such as Henan, Guizhou, and Guangxi.

More important, this divide does not correspond to a binary of opponents and supporters of the regime; while the "liberals" no doubt want a clearer political opening, they support the government as they see it as the promoter of economic reforms and liberalization. The "conservatives" on the other hand are hostile to any expansion of market mechanisms (and price rises) but see in the CCP and in its continued leading role a guarantee of political stability and increase in the country's might.

The Asian Barometer Survey on which this study partly relies also reveals unexpected differences between urban and rural youth. The former are not much more politically liberal than their elders, whereas the difference in age has much clearer consequences in the countryside: older people are more conservative, whereas those under age thirty-five want a reform of political structures (although its content is not defined). Analysts take pains to offer an explanation. Herewith are two of them: the first is that rural areas' middle-aged and old people are both disadvantaged and attached to traditions, and the second is that rural youth are often frustrated by the frequent rigging of village elections by local party bigwigs, such as in Wukan (Guangdong province) in 2011.

This is why China's new middle classes, probably inclined to be liberal, fail to constitute the force for political change that some observers and activists pin their hopes on.[24] Conversely, those "left behind" by growth have no protectors other than the party-state, even more so as it has become rich and disposes of greater means so as to be of help, even if for the moment social protection systems such as the guaranteed minimum income (*dibao*) or health insurance are still not just rudimentary but most unequal, favoring the richest cities and thus the coastal regions' middle classes.

Of course if the regime abandoned its proclaimed economic reforms or became too authoritarian or even totalitarian, "liberals" could reconsider their support. However, in the foreseeable future the fear of chaos will largely drive people's backing for the regime and its conception of democracy. In fact, Dickson's study shows that a majority of Chinese people believe that public demonstrations, multiplicity of political parties, or even the existence of groups espousing different points of view could pose a real danger to social stability.[25]

A MODERNIZED AND MORE EFFICIENT PROPAGANDA
AND CONTROL SYSTEM

Findings of such opinion surveys must be handled with caution for two main reasons. First, it is forbidden in China to criticize national leaders of the CCP, and thus it would be right to assume that those polled, or at least a part of them, have self-censored. Second, Chinese society is subject to a veritable daily drilling of anti-Western propaganda. This has been boosted under Xi but in fact has gone on uninterrupted since Tiananmen. Such propaganda consists of glorifying the regime while attributing much of the failures or weaknesses of pluralist democracies' economies or societies to their political system. For obvious reasons such attacks especially target Taiwan, whose parliamentarians' fisticuffs—today in fact much less frequent than in the 1990s, in the immediate aftermath of democratization—and mediocre economic results are broadcast with gusto on all Chinese television channels. But Chinese propaganda picks on all democracies and attributes to their basic nature developments such as Donald Trump's victory in the United States in 2016 or more generally the rise of populism and the distortions it has spawned among political regimes (Brexit and the emergence of xenophobic parties in Europe). Similarly, the Arab Spring's failure in 2011 was largely exploited by Beijing, which at the same time praised the success of authoritarian developing countries such as Ethiopia and Rwanda as well as al-Sisi's taking control of Egypt. Quite simply, the People's Republic is engaged in an undeclared ideological war, one that cannot but influence Chinese society's viewpoints.

However, these constraints should be seen in context. Several studies have shown that those polled are much less fearful than supposed.[26] Thus, the surveys discussed here reflect Chinese society's general sentiments. Conversely, official propaganda's impact on society does hit some limits: on the one hand, more Chinese people travel and are better informed than before, such as in 1989, about the advantages and inconveniences of liberal democracy; on the other, a rising proportion neither listen to nor read official media[27] but prefer to scan the most informative or critical blogs on political matters. The tightening of control over the Internet since Xi rose to power has hardly changed this state of affairs (see chapter 4). Nonetheless, Chinese people's views of the outside world and particularly liberal democracies are heavily influenced not only by what they can observe now—rising crime rates and insecurity, increasing poverty, uncontrollable illegal migration, and growing xenophobia and social frustration—but also by their own priorities and fears.

A SOCIETY DIVORCED FROM POLITICS

In reality, these polls show something else: even in sections of society exasperated by the CCP's authoritarianism, the struggle for democracy is not a priority. The Chinese somehow manage to derive satisfaction from the regime while going all out to extend their own autonomy and personal freedom. Thus, they get around Internet censorship by using VPNs (virtual private networks), which despite recent crackdowns help them reach a large number of sites banned in China. They associate with nongovernmental or religious organizations more or less tolerated by the regime, seeking to enlarge solidarity links they can draw on to better protect themselves from the party-state. But they avoid politics as such as a public space rather too official and most risky. As New Left intellectual Kang Xiaoguang remarked in 2002, China has become "a society without politics."[28] In other words, Chinese people ignore the party-state as much as possible rather than defying it, preferring to turn their backs instead of risking rattling the regime, feigning obedience while doing their best through all means possible to wriggle out from under its authority and its controls.

Some sociologists and political scientists relying on culturalist theses also see in this dominant attitude toward authority the continuation of traditional behavior, the complementary—but more dissenting without being threatening—side of Chinese society's general support for the current regime. Such is the case for Tianjian Shi (deceased in 2010), who thought that Chinese cultural norms have always had an influence on political behavior beyond differences of regime or structural changes occurring in society. Thus in his view, in authoritarian China as in democratic Taiwan, society tends more naturally than in the West to repose confidence in those wielding authority, whether inside families, schools, or enterprises or with regard to political leaders, and seems less inclined to question or confront authority. Taking this further, he argued that

Chinese traditional culture sees democracy more as a system able to ensure guardianship than as a set of procedures leading to a choice of
people's representatives and to control—and also limit—their powers; for
Shi, this view of the "good government" as the people's "protector" has
remained dominant to this day.[29] Other political scientists, such as the
Korean Doh Chull Shin, impute to this dominant opinion in Chinese
society (or other Asian ones) the manifestation of support for a system he
calls "paternalistic meritocracy."[30]

Such interpretations are debatable, especially regarding Taiwan and
South Korea, which have absorbed most of the principles of electoral and
procedural democracy. However, one can only marvel at the ease with
which so many in the PRC trust their government and identify with the
neotraditionalist and neo-Confucian discourse it puts out.[31]

Whether this impressive degree of trust in the government stems from
Mao's "mass line" ideology, as Wenfang Tang argues, is questionable.
His comparative surveys show a higher level of political trust in China
than in Taiwan, leading him to believe in the former's regime sustainability. I do agree with the idea that, strengthened by its growing nationalism
and its reactiveness to protests, China's "populist authoritarianism" has
much room to continue to prosper and survive. But was Mao responsive
to public protests? Actually, mass movements and mobilizations were
not only the antithesis of democracy, but rather strong weapons to prevent any criticism from reaching the ears of the leaders.[32]

My interpretation is that a return to tradition is the consequence more
of the rupture wrought by the events of 1949 than of the vicissitudes
during the rise of democratic ideas in the late Qing and republican eras.
The CCP has consistently tried to snuff out the quest for freedom and
democracy that Chinese elites had pursued before 1949 and some coura-
geously later than that, especially between the start of reforms and Tiananmen.[33] It has expressly kept Chinese society distanced from liberal
ideas and has only retained from past efforts at democratization and
modernization the need or rather obsession to strengthen the state vis-à-
vis society and foreign powers. Until Mao's death, it did so in the name of
communist revolution and since then has invoked economic development, reconnecting with the imperial past whose authoritarian character
it has deliberately instrumentalized and even expanded.

FACTORS FOR CHANGE

For all that, the political values dear to people in the PRC are not static in nature. Consumption, personal well-being, and security take precedence over democracy now. As I have written elsewhere, the Chinese became consumers before becoming citizens.[34] Moreover, society's continuing administrative compartmentalization, a rural society still encumbered in its movement by the *hukou* or resident permit system, a general lack of confidence among social and economic actors, and the weakness of institutions for seeking redress (courts, arbitrage, or mediation) all slow down the evolution of the dominant political culture and more generally of political mentalities.

However, people's political values are influenced by other factors, such as the rise in education levels; rapid urbanization; and increased contacts with foreign countries, or what I would call "liberal external China": Taiwan and Hong Kong, of course, but also overseas Chinese communities in Western countries (the United States, Canada, Australia, and countries in Europe).

Another glance at the study (2016) by Jennifer Pan and Yiqing Xu on Chinese people's political preferences shows the emergence of a majority potentially favorable to freedom and democracy, a majority that, albeit deeply nationalist and sovereignist—or Westphalian, one might say— adheres to a liberal vision of politics.[35] Also, the study showed that 66 percent of those polled disagreed with the idea of denying the vote to citizens not yet trained in democratic methods, a result that goes against the conviction often attributed to urban middle classes that the introduction of "one person, one vote" would mean giving power to representatives of a majority as yet lacking in education, rural inhabitants, and migrants (who together still comprise two-thirds of the population). Moreover, 73 percent of those polled reject the idea that a multiparty system is not adapted to China now, again a finding that directly contradicts official discourse. And 58 percent give precedence to the universality of human rights protection over sovereignty, once again going against principles dear to the government.

But Chinese people are more divided and reserved over "Western-style" freedom of speech, understood by them to be unrestricted, which is obviously an incorrect perception, given that in most democracies there are laws against, for instance, defamation and hate or racist speech, laws that are little known or unknown in China. In fact, 55 percent of those surveyed believe adoption of such levels of freedom would lead to "social disorders," while 44 percent think the opposite. Half are open to religious proselytization, while the other half oppose it. Of those polled, 51 percent believe force may be used to reunify with Taiwan if circumstances permit, and 65 percent think national unity and territorial integrity represent society's supreme interest. However, 74 percent criticize the argument, rehashed by the New Left and surreptitiously encouraged by authorities, that the United States and the West in general cannot accept China's rise to the rank of a major power.

In the economic arena, a majority seems to favor a mix of liberal and interventionist principles. People are more hostile to state enterprises' privileges (68 percent) and to protectionism (58 percent) and mostly favor privatization of land (53 percent), which the party rejects in principle, authorizing merely the commercialization of farmland use rights (*shiyongquan*). But 80 percent of those surveyed, concerned over steep increases in property prices, do not believe that state control of such prices would affect economic development. Aware of income inequalities between cities and the countryside, 63 percent think the state and consumers should support the prices of cereals. And 61 percent want people with high incomes to declare how these were acquired.

As for values, there are some contradictions: the Book of Changes (*Yijing* or I Ching), the source of many Chinese beliefs—and superstitions—is deemed more useful than Confucianism (59 percent compared to 34 percent); 70 percent of those polled say Chinese classics, mainly Confucian, should form part of the basis of education. At the same time, 67 percent would agree to recognize their children's relationships with someone of the same gender should they so choose.

Contemporary Chinese society is actually more tolerant than many outsiders may believe, a degree of tolerance long seen in Taiwan and well captured on screen in Ang Lee's wonderful film *The Wedding Banquet* (*Xi Yan*, 1993). In general, Chinese society is much less hostile than is assumed to liberal political values, which most people in Taiwan and Hong Kong are already well accustomed to.

Opinion surveys carried out in recent years show a relative decline in the level of confidence reposed in the party-state. Between 2010 and 2016 people's level of confidence in the government's ability to solve problems fell from 76 to 63 percent. Also, 69 percent (compared to 79 percent six years earlier) said they were proud of the political system, and 63 percent in 2016 (69 percent in 2010) were ready to support the regime even if it were facing problems.[36]

One should not jump to conclusions based on these few changes. Such levels of support are certainly impressive and confirm the importance a great majority of the people attach to results of government action rather than to the methods used in arriving at them. More generally, although broadly favoring democracy in general, Chinese society does not see the attainment of freedoms and establishment of institutions to protect them as a priority. In other words, people still have a firm belief in their leaders' capacity for reforms and political progress.

CONCLUSION

It is difficult to make sense of the political culture that stems from these sets of opinion polls. Clearly, political values are evolving, and it would be wrong to presume that in the future democratic ideas will not come to prevail. But for now, Chinese society's priority is not democracy or what some Anglo-Saxons call liberal democracy.

The weakness of democratic culture clearly acts as a brake on any democratization of the regime. Bluntly stated, despite all the opinions reported here, there is today in the PRC no strong demand for democracy. I discuss the liberal currents and partisans of democratization, such as Liu Xiaobo, in chapter 5. But I note here that these highly repressed forces remain a little-known minority in the PRC, whereas most of society identifies with the political system established in 1949. Society hopes at best that the regime will keep improving, becoming more efficient and better serving its interests, mainly by developing the economy and generally taking care of its well-being.

The Chinese are above all preoccupied with personal enrichment and consumption; although it was the main fuel for the country's economic take-off, Chinese society is not a catalyst for democratic transition. Of course a well-educated, urban, better-informed, leisured society has become more aware of its rights, more prompt to protest against abuses of power, and more demanding of freedoms and guarantees.

But Chinese society, including its middle classes, remains steeped in Confucian ideology, reverential toward authority, respectful of hierarchy, and lacking in familiarity with institutions and practices of truly democratic countries. Its own democratic values are superficial, still largely adulterated by the CCP's anti-West and now neo-Confucian propaganda and dominant elite discourse. In other words, the communist authorities have deliberately utilized traditional political culture, the better to maintain Leninist political culture's hegemony within the society, especially the elites. And one can only conclude that they have been successful.

NOTES

1. On Confucianism in China and Taiwan today, its autonomy vis-à-vis the authorities, and its multiple manifestations, see Sébastien Billioud and Joël Thoraval, *The Sage and the People: The Confucian Revival in China* (Oxford and New York: Oxford University Press, 2015). On the CCP's use of Confucianism, see Sébastien Billioud, "Confucianism, 'Cultural Tradition' and Official Discourses in China at the Start of the New Century," *China Perspectives*, no. 3 (2007): 50–65.

2. According to some studies, the middle classes included 420 million Chinese in 2012, representing only 31 percent of the population; see "How Well-Off Is China's Middle Class?," China Power, https://chinapower.csis.org/china-middle-class/. Regarding differences over the size of China's middle classes, according to a McKinsey study, 54 percent of urban households will form the upper middle class in 2022 (with an income of 106,000 to 229,000 yuan a year), compared to 14 percent in 2012, and more than 22 percent will form the lower middle class, compared to 54 percent in 2012; see "Mapping China's Middle Class," *McKinsey Quarterly* (June 2013), https://www.mckinsey.com/industries/retail/our-insights/mapping-chinas-middle-class. See also David S. G. Goodman, *Class in Contemporary China* (Cambridge, UK: Polity Press, 2014); and Minglu Chen and David S. G. Goodman, *Middle Class China: Identity and Behaviour* (Cheltenham, UK: Elgar, 2013). On the relationship between democracy and the middle classes, see Andrew Nathan, "The Puzzle of the Chinese Middle Class," *Journal of Democracy* 27, no. 2 (April 2016): 5–19.

3. See, for example, Minxin Pei, "The Beginning of the End," *The Washington Quarterly* 39, no. 3 (Autumn 2016): 131–142.

4. Among the first post-1989 studies are Andrew J. Nathan and Shi Tianjian, "Cultural Requisites for Democracy in China: Findings from a Survey," in *China in Transformation*, ed. Tu Wei-ming (Cambridge, MA: Harvard University Press, 1994), 95–123; Daniel V. Dowd, Allen Carlson, and Mingming Shen, "The Prospects for Democratization in China: Evidence from the 1995 Beijing Area Study," in *China and Democracy: Reconsidering the Prospect for a Democratic China*, ed. Suisheng Zhao (New York and London: Routledge, 2000), 189–206; Shiping Hua, ed., *Chinese Political Culture, 1989–2000* (Armonk, NY: M. E. Sharpe, 2001); and Suzanne Ogden, *Inklings of Democracy in China* (Cambridge, MA, and London: Harvard University Asia Center, 2002).

5. David Elkins and Richard E. Simeon, "A Cause in Search of Its Effect, or What Does Political Culture Explain," *Comparative Politics* 11, no. 2 (1979): 127–145; and Gabriel Almond, "The Study of Political Culture," in *A Discipline Divided: Schools and Sects in Political Science*, ed. Gabriel A. Almond (London: Sage Publications, 1990), 138–169. See also Wenfang Tang, *Populist Authoritarianism: Chinese Political Culture and*

Regime Sustainability (New York and Oxford: Oxford University Press, 2016), 2–5; Yang Zhong, *Political Culture and Participation in Urban China* (Singapore: Palgrave Macmillan, 2018), 3–4.

6. See Tang, *Populist Authoritarianism*, 15–19.

7. Bruce Dickson, *The Dictator's Dilemma: The Chinese Communist Party's Strategy for Survival* (Oxford: Oxford University Press, 2016), 232–237, on the relation between nationalism and support for the regime; and Asian Barometer Surveys, http://www.asianbarometer.org/survey.

8. Dowd, Carlson, and Shen, "The Prospects for Democratization in China"; Ogden, *Inklings of Democracy*, 123–124; and Yun-han Chu and Yu-tzung Chang, "Culture Shift and Regime Legitimacy: Comparing Mainland China, Taiwan, and Hong Kong," in *Chinese Political Culture, 1989–2000*, ed. Shiping Hua (Armonk, NY: M. E. Sharpe, 2001), 320–347.

9. "Building of Political Democracy in China," China Through a Lens, October 2005, http://www.china.org.cn/english/2005/Oct/145718.htm.

10. Tianjian Shi, "China: Democratic Values Supporting an Authoritarian System," in *How East Asians View Democracy*, ed. Yun-han Chu, Larry Diamond, Andrew J. Nathan, and Doh Chull Shin (New York: Columbia University Press, 2008), 209–237.

11. Dickson, *The Dictator's Dilemma*, 285–288. It should however be noted that Dickson's opinion surveys, conducted in 2010 and 2014, covered urban residents only; the countryside, which still accounts for 42 percent of the population, was excluded.

12. Jean-Pierre Cabestan, *Le système politique chinois: Un nouvel équilibre autoritaire* [The Chinese political system: A new authoritarian equilibrium] (Paris: Presses de Sciences-Po, 2014), 532–534.

13. Hsin-hsin Pan and Wen-chin Wu, "Quality of Governance and Political Legitimacy: Governance-based Legitimacy in East Asia," Global Barometer, Working Paper Series, no. 121, 2016, http://www.asianbarometer.org/publications//96047634fd37cd9b360485a62ea44a56.pdf; on Vietnam and China, see Regina Abrami, Edmund Malesky, and Yu Zheng, "Vietnam Through Chinese Eyes: Divergent Accountability in Single-Party Regimes," in *Why Communism Did Not Collapse: Understanding Authoritarian Regime Resilience in Asia and Europe*, ed. Martin K. Dimitrov (Cambridge, UK: Cambridge University Press, 2013), 237–275.

14. Yun-han Chu and Wen-chin Wu, "Sources of Regime Legitimacy in East Asian Societies," Global Barometer, Working Paper Series, no. 118, 2016, http://www.asianbarometer.org/publications//6d6966754cdbbde13ae3a5d24d79f52e.pdf.

15. See Wen's speech, "Turning Your Eyes to China" (presented at Harvard University, December 10, 2003, http://www.fmprc.gov.cn/ce/ceun/eng/xw/t56090.htm).

16. Since 2012 the Ministry of Public Security has stopped publishing "mass incidents" data. See chapter 6.

17. See studies published by the Hong Kong–based *China Labour Bulletin* at http://www.clb.org.hk. On peasant revolts, see Lucien Bianco, *Peasants without the Party: Grass-roots Movements in Twentieth-Century China* (Armonk, NY: M. E. Sharpe, 2001); Kevin J. O'Brien and Lianjiang Li, *Rightful Resistance in Rural China* (Cambridge, UK: Cambridge University Press, 2006); and Kevin O'Brien, "Rightful Resistance Revisited," *The Journal of Peasant Studies* 40, no. 6 (2013): 1051–1062.

18. Dickson, *The Dictator's Dilemma*, 187–199, 268–272.

19. Dickson, *The Dictator's Dilemma*, 65–67.

20. Tang, *Populist Authoritarianism*, 33–39; Zhong, *Political Culture*, 16–17.

21. Tang, *Populist Authoritarianism*, 60–73, 250–252.

22. Tang, *Populist Authoritarianism*, 122–123.

23. Jennifer Pan and Yiqing Xu, "China's Ideological Spectrum," *Journal of Politics* 79, no. 3 (July 2017): 792–803.

24. Nathan, "The Puzzle of the Chinese Middle Class."

25. Dickson, *The Dictator's Dilemma*, 243–245.

26. Xuchuan Lei and Jie Lu, "Revisiting Political Wariness in China's Public Opinion Surveys: Experimental Evidence on Responses to Politically Sensitive Questions," *Journal of Contemporary China* 26, no. 104 (March 2017): 213–232.

27. Those who consult media are more likely to be influenced by official propaganda; see Wenfang Tang, *Public Opinion and Political Change in China* (Stanford, CA: Stanford University Press, 2005).

28. Cited by Eva Pils, "Charter 08 and Violent Resistance: The Dark Side of the Chinese *Weiquan* Movement," in *Liu Xiaobo, Charter 08, and the Challenges of Political Reform in China*, ed. Jean-Philippe Béja, Fu Hualing, and Eva Pils (Hong Kong: Hong Kong University Press, 2012), 486.

29. Tianjian Shi, *The Cultural Logic of Politics in Mainland China and Taiwan* (Cambridge, UK: Cambridge University Press, 2014).

30. Doh Chull Shin, *Confucianism and Democratization in East Asia* (Cambridge, UK: Cambridge University Press, 2012), 106ff.

31. See the following interesting survey: Ashley Esarey, Daniela Stockmann, and Jie Zhang, "Support for Propaganda: Chinese Perceptions of Public Service Advertising," *Journal of Contemporary China* 26, no. 103 (January 2017): 101–117.

32. Tang, *Populist Authoritarianism*, 74–99, 152–166.

33. See Jean-Philippe Béja, *A la recherche d'une ombre chinoise: Le mouvement pour la démocratie en Chine (1919–2004)* [In search of a Chinese shadow: China's pro-democracy movement (1919–2004)] (Paris: Le Seuil, 2004); and Cheng Yingxiang (with Claude Cadart), *Dégel de l'intelligence en Chine, 1976–1989: Quatorze témoignages* [Intellectual thaw in China 1976–1989: Fourteen interviews] (Paris: Gallimard, 2004).

34. Cabestan, *Le système politique chinois*, 605.

35. Pan and Xu, "China's Ideological Spectrum," table A1. The data from this table are cited in the following paragraphs.

36. Chu and Wu, "Sources of Regime Legitimacy in East Asian Societies."

FOUR

Civil Society

Leashed by the Party-State

Does the civil society that has gradually taken shape in China since 1979 pose a threat to the regime? Not in the foreseeable future. As I discuss later, while pushing back to the extent possible against political restrictions, Chinese civil society remains embryonic, generally avoiding taking risks or venturing into the political domain, which today is particularly treacherous. Consequently, its members avoid politics, focusing their attention elsewhere, especially on social and charitable activities, education, culture, and religion, including via the Internet. The CCP is at pains to monitor this process. Nonetheless, to a large extent the party is able to stem overly direct political expressions, relying on major repressive as well as ideological, organizational, economic, and financial means to ensure the collaboration of large sections of society, with its monopoly hold over politics as well as its acts of coercion and control. Further, with the lid on politics, the party has continued to reform itself and improve the efficiency of post-Tiananmen mechanisms established to manage civil society and social conflicts.[1] This is best illustrated by the party's ability to attract new members, especially from among the elites and educated sections of society. Its nationalism has a good chance of continuing to help keep it in power. And problems posed by some ethnic minorities (Tibetans or Uyghurs) are not going to make it deviate from its path.

My hypothesis is that the party-state has on the one hand receded, leaving society more elbow room and autonomy, but on the other hand,

75

by using better adapted and more indirect methods, has tightened its hold and control over the nation.[2] Further, although for clarity of presentation I have set the regime and civil society in opposition, the thesis of a continuum, or an "interpenetration" between the two, remains valid, a process the party has a good chance to get the better of in the foreseeable future.[3]

A SUBSTANTIAL EXPANSION OF CHINESE CIVIL SOCIETY

Of course the very use of the concept "civil society" or "citizens' society" (*gongmin shehui*) can be contested, especially as it is taboo in China. The officially preferred expressions in China are "public society" (*gonggong shehui*) and "people's society" (*renmin shehui*), the CCP promoting what it sees as the more just and equitable nature of Chinese social organization. In reality, and for good reason despite their official admiration for the French Revolution, Chinese authorities have always been wary of the citizenship (*gongmin*) concept, behind which too often lurks a hidden democratic demand they have no intention of honoring.

Chinese civil society remains a work in progress and in permanent transformation.[4] Some social forces seek to transform it into a "public sphere," even a "political society" in Jürgen Habermas's sense of those terms.[5] However, the party-state has grown more vigilant in the face of this potential evolution and seems able for the foreseeable future to keep its hold over civil society Chinese style, especially over NGOs, which have proliferated since the early 1990s.

Since Tiananmen, one of the most important evolutions in Chinese society has been the bursting forth of the association phenomenon. But most of these associations have been established "from above"—that is, by the party-state itself or with its authorization and registered with the Ministry of Civil Affairs. These are official NGOs, or rather "social organizations" (*shehui zuzhi*), Chinese officialdom frowning on the term NGO. Many of them are actually what we often refer to as GONGOs or government-organized NGOs.

Numbering more than 760,000 in 2017 (up from under 5,000 in 1988), these organizations can be divided into three categories.[6] First are social groups (*shehui tuanti*, 355,000) authorized by an administration in their line of activity; these professional organizations are not really NGOs but more supple entities facilitating authorities' twisting of rules in respect of public audits and officials' recruitment. They include the CCP's traditional mass organizations like the Communist Youth League and the All-China Federation of Trade Unions (ACFTU). Obviously these are no source of potential challenge. Second are about 400,000 "civil noncommercial institutions" (*minban feiqiye danwei*); these are more autonomous and are engaged in diverse fields such as education, health, culture, children's welfare, senior citizens' care, and the environment. They are often an extension of the local state and have a wide reach. They include, for instance, chambers of commerce and industry; moreover, they are officially registered, having been abundantly prudent in not offending the authorities. Public security organs continue exercising power over them, ensuring they do not turn into political or activist organizations. In any case, this risk is insignificant, as most registered NGOs know the rules of the game perfectly, wisely skirting politics or taking to cultural and social fields.[7]

Third are the foundations (*jijinhui*, about 6,300 in 2017). Authorized since 2004, they organize the voluntary work and financing of charitable organizations and registered NGOs. Since 2011 foundations receiving private monies (*feigongmu jijinhui*), that is, financed by business circles, have outnumbered those getting public funding (4,629 and 1,678 respectively in 2017), which is not without potentially interesting political consequences to be considered. Of course they are all under the tight control of the party-state and rarely help the truly autonomous NGOs.[8]

There is also what I call a "nebula of unregistered NGOs," by definition impossible to quantify (two to three million by some estimates). They occupy a gray zone, their existence being particularly precarious; they could be informal, generally small, and organized in the form of a friends' or solidarity network, or more structured and larger, for protection's sake registered as an enterprise, a status easier to obtain in China than that of NGO. These nonofficial organizations are constituted around missions generally similar to those of official NGOs. Labor NGOs are a major exception; organized as quasi-law firms specializing in workers' rights, these NGOs take part in social movements (strikes and workers' demands) and often look like free trade unions in the making, hence the strict surveillance they attract and the repression that has become more fierce since Xi Jinping's advent, including in coastal provinces such as Guangdong, long free of such attention.

This last example highlights notable provincial variations in terms of NGO activities. For a long time Yunnan has been more tolerant than other provinces toward environmental protection NGOs. But on the whole surveillance of NGOs has been strengthened since 2012, and that of foreign NGOs even more so since a new law was enacted in 2016; they now have to register not with the Ministry of Civil Affairs but with the Ministry of Public Security.

Nonofficial NGOs may be formed for specific purposes, such as during major natural catastrophes like the 2008 Sichuan earthquake, or for a given issue, for example action against the installation of a polluting factory. But in such cases they are fragile and tend to be ephemeral in nature.[9]

More often, social or political activism—undeclared—develops more informally. It may be the result of a spontaneous mobilization facilitated by social networks. Or it could be spurred by a personality. Such was the case in the 2000s with the campaign in Henan by Dr. Gao Yaojie against the spread of AIDS through blood transfusions.

Be that as it may, it seems to me unrealistic to expect this multiplication of NGOs to lead to the formation of a force capable of compelling the regime to change. Instead, the party-state has been able to turn the situation to its advantage, allocating to a larger number of such organizations both financial support and tasks it cannot or does not want to undertake anymore. Like the KMT in Taiwan earlier, many Chinese NGOs now play a complementary role to the state's own in social and educational policy matters.

National and even official NGOs sometimes exercise a salutary oversight on local affairs in a region far from the center, exposing a social or environmental scandal, for instance. But the authorities accept such intervention and from time to time encourage it, as it forms part of the political system's adaptation and amelioration and also contributes to its consolidation.

Taking this further, since early in the 2010s the party has established its own local-level NGOs. Shanghai's CCP committee, for instance, has formed NGOs in charitable and elderly care domains. More interestingly, these structures have set up internal party committees whose task is to facilitate the mobilization of volunteers as well as government services.[10]

From this brief description, the dominant model that comes through is that of NGOs' "dependent autonomy" in relation to the party-state, part of a more general "consultative authoritarianism" model proposed by Teets and others.[11] For now, private foundations financing the NGOs have been unable to loosen these dependence ties.

Simply put, NGOs, which were previously decried by the party-state, are now out in the open. But to survive, they must collaborate with the authorities, who for their part will help them. The latter have until now shown they are able to maintain and control this state of affairs.

CAN THE INTERNET DEMOCRATIZE CHINA?

By itself the Internet cannot democratize China. It can contribute to spreading or speeding up an already unleashed democratization process; contribute to a pluralization of debates, especially on economic and social issues; and help mobilize people around a specific cause. But it would be naïve to believe that a new technical means of communication is capable of modifying mentalities by itself and of shifting the ideological fault-lines among the elites and in society unless a new "political offer" favoring democracy comes up, precisely what the party-state has thus far succeeded in preventing and will no doubt continue blocking into the foreseeable future.[12]

Clearly the explosive Internet growth in China has opened a pluralistic public space for discussion, previously nonexistent. The high rate of ownership of devices of various sorts (in 2018, more than 800 million people, over 200 million of them in rural China, had a smartphone) and of broadband access stokes such talks and more generally of Internet usage in a growing number of private and commercial activities (purchases, payments, banking, online games, etc.). Facilitated, among other sites, by Jack Ma's Alibaba, a private firm, such commercial usage is today more systematic in China than in Europe or even the United States.

However, the Internet in China remains under high political and moral surveillance. Right from the 1990s, the government set up what is widely known as "The Great Firewall" thanks to technology from Western companies such as Cisco Systems, or Chinese ones like Huawei. This wall closes China off from media such as Facebook, Google, and Twitter and blocks access to foreign sites and blogs deemed politically or morally dangerous. Messages of that type from abroad can also be censored. The Great Firewall represents the sovereignist approach to the Internet that China has long upheld and which it promotes in the international arena.[13] Combating pornography and vulgar sites is the authorities' often-used argument for imposing fierce censorship on anything they disapprove of. Moreover, the administration in charge of Internet oversight—strengthened under Xi, who personally took charge of a new CCP cybersecurity and informatization-leading small group (elevated to the status of commission in February 2018) in 2013—employs a large number of people whose task is to direct discussion on social networks and snuff out content deemed noxious.[14] These "Internet police," labeled by critics as Wumaodang (50-cent party) for the amount supposedly paid them for each politically correct post, initially numbered 40,000. But Internet policing has gone much further and now targets users accused of spreading "rumors," be they of a political, economic, or financial nature.[15] The number of "inspectors" in charge of "Internet clean-up" on behalf of administrations or private companies, estimated at two million in 2017, has now sharply increased.[16]

China is hardly alone in adopting such a security policy. It therefore counts on not inconsiderable international backing for continuing to "regulate" online traffic as it wishes. Barring a regime change, there is no reason for the party-state to relax its grip. Under Xi, it has been perceptibly boosted and has—and will mostly continue to have—the technical and financial means to do so. Nationalism also helps in this task (see below). Since 2016 there has been a burgeoning nationalist "troll army" or "Little Pinks" (*xiaofenhong*) voluntarily launching all-out attacks against anyone venturing to criticize the Party or Xi's policies.[17]

In this repressive climate, what room for maneuvering do Chinese netizens have? Much Internet traffic is not of a political nature. It may well be said that the explosion of online purchases and Internet-backed technical facilities has influenced Chinese people's propensity to focus on consumption, show business, sports, and online games and gambling. Such conduct only satisfies and reassures the authoritarian regime, which is only too happy to be of help with its unrestrained crackdown on all sorts of financial fraud, often fomented from abroad by Chinese (and Taiwanese) mafias, that Internet users fall victim to.

Moreover, the controls imposed by the authorities are not as effective as sometimes believed. Censorship is often erratic. Even under Xi, a large number of Internet users continue to have access to banned foreign sites by using highly sophisticated foreign VPNs (ninety million users) that can be bought online. These VPNs are often tolerated, especially because they are used by the elites and in particular by researchers looking for cutting-edge technologies or by Chinese and foreign enterprises (see chapter 6). There are provincial variations too, the VPNs having greater difficulty penetrating the Great Firewall in Beijing, the regime's nerve center, than in other cities.

In their own interest, the authorities are not as draconian as is generally believed. Online information and opinions are useful to them for better gauging changes in public opinion, nationally as well as locally. This is all the more useful as the new urban middle classes, or "angry youth" (*fenqing*), let off steam online, and thus the Internet serves as a safety valve for the authorities. The extent of freedom allowed for many blogs, such as that of the writer and rally driver Han Han, perfectly illustrates this reality.[18]

In recent years the authorities have tightened control on blogs opened on Weibo (a microblog site launched by the state-owned Sina Corporation in 2009, inspired mostly by Twitter) and other portals such as Tencent or Sohu. From 2013 onward, the portals were obliged to break with noted public intellectuals—the "Big Vs"[19]—who, like the artist Ai Weiwei and jurist He Weifang, tried to push too far the limits of what was permitted. Consequently, Weibo had just 220 million registered users in 2015, down from more than 500 million in 2012, just before people were made to register with their real names. (The number of users increased again to 462 million at the end of 2018.) In any event, it should be noted that China's ten most popular blogs on Weibo now are by film actors or television stars.

Although it only allows the exchange of rather short messages (five hundred characters) and accounts are regularly closed by the authorities, Weixin (or WeChat, the equivalent of WhatsApp; 1.1 billion users) remains mostly open. The same is the case for discussion forums on social networks such as *Baidu Baike* (Baidu encyclopedia, similar to *Wikipedia*), of course within known censorship limits. Internet users know the limits and are quite cautious when they discuss political issues, exercising a certain degree of self-censorship or communicating through "light-dark" messages, to use French China Internet expert Séverine Arsène's expression.

In China as elsewhere, new public spaces opened by the Internet and especially social networks are becoming increasingly fragmented and ephemeral. Netizens sharing the same ideas (e.g., New Left sites) or interests tend to gather among themselves, limiting pluralism in debates and supporting each other in their positions. Moreover, in China this space is truncated and thus distorted, with "liberal" sites and blogs, that is, those favoring real political reform, having been shut down one after the other. As Margaret Roberts has shown, censorship has become subtler, making access to critical information more difficult and distracting netizens with or diverting them to contrarian and progovernment messages.[20]

According to studies such as Dickson's, most Chinese Internet users, while declaring support for freedom of expression online in principle (see chapter 3), claim not to be affected by censorship (most users say they have never experienced blocked sites [72 percent], deleted messages [77 percent] or closed accounts [91 percent]). And if censorship does happen to affect their online activity, they often react with resignation (49 percent): "it doesn't matter!" (*wusuowei*).[21]

Finally, and this is most important for the regime's survival, the Internet has provided it with new tools, formidable in my view, to observe people, control them, and even predict their actions, such as virtual delinquents' future crimes. This is why the party-state lets debates take place online and tolerates a certain level of criticism. This new mode of expression helps the government manage risks and better prepare for preventive action. Moreover, security organs' accumulation of vast amounts of computerized data (big data), both individual and commercial, along with cross-checking of different files in all impunity, and on a permanent basis profiting from rapid development of artificial intelligence—one of the priorities of the current government—inevitably contributes to transforming the Chinese regime into a sort of Orwellian "Big Brother" worthy of *1984*. And it has an efficiency and freedom, since the Edward Snowden affair in 2013, far greater than that of the US National Security Agency.

In such circumstances, it is difficult to see how multiple frustrations caused by Internet censorship can engender an organized political movement for liberating this means of communication and more generally for freedom of expression. Isolated behind their devices and separated by their interests and opinions, Chinese netizens do not make for a political force capable of striking a new rapport with the authorities but are rather an aggregate of dispersed and more or less irritated consumers.

In short, the Internet has led the regime to accept some pluralism and to be more consultative, but this alone will not suffice to oblige it to democratize.

A MORE ATTENTIVE MANAGEMENT OF SOCIAL CONFLICTS

Every year in China there are tens of thousands of social conflicts of all sorts (180,000 in 2010, compared to 8,700 in 1993), not to mention larger numbers of "public disturbances" (600,000 in 2006). Such conflicts can arise from confiscation of farmland, workers being laid off, nonpayment of wages, environmental pollution, a badly handled criminal case, or some administrative injustice. Generally slotted in the media under the topic "mass incidents," can these conflicts lead to a change in the political regime?

The answer again is no. Since Tiananmen, the authoritarian but no longer totalitarian regime has learned to better manage social conflicts. Moreover, it has made social stability its top priority, the condition for pursuing national economic growth. The party-state's leading cadres know very well that their promotion depends at least partly—apart from the growth rate but taking precedence over environmental protection— on their ability to maintain order and prevent "mass incidents," and if they do occur, to nip them in the bud—that is, to resolve them as soon as and at the lowest administrative level possible, so as to prevent their spread through capillary action as it were from one village, enterprise, town, or district to another.

The number of such incidents rose steadily throughout the 1990s and the following decade, revealing not only much greater frustration among some segments of the population vis-à-vis governmental measures but also greater tolerance on the authorities' part in the face of demands they know to be well-founded: badly compensated land or house expropriations; the workers in failing public enterprises rendered jobless; wages unpaid or remaining too low despite a rising cost of living, especially in coastal regions; and installation of a polluting factory close to residential zones.

Since 2012 the Ministry of Public Security has stopped publishing figures on "mass incidents," although they continue to be estimated at around 200,000 a year, or more than 500 daily.[22] Most of these conflicts are not of a political nature; organizers of protest movements in cities (strikes and demonstrations), as in the countryside (marches to county or township government headquarters), take good care to ensure their action is not perceived as political by the authorities, and the size of the movements may vary enormously (from some fifty protestors to several thousand). Moreover, these disputes are mostly localized and rarely spread, except in major industrial cities such as Guangzhou or the Pearl River Delta, where migrant workers (*mingong*) in foreign private firms share the same demands or jointly contest the legitimacy of the official union, the local branch of the ACFTU, subordinated to the CCP.[23] The 2014 Honda factory strikes illustrated this potentially dangerous evolution in political terms. Nevertheless, these are exceptions. Generally, and this is quite important, social conflicts occur more because of a feeling of injustice (*yuan*, again) than in protest against situations of social inequality. Thus, contrary to what some Westerners (including Thomas Piketty in France) believe, although income inequalities are particularly flagrant and still deepening, they are better accepted in China than in Europe, or rather, they rarely lead to social mobilizations (see chapter 6).[24]

Such a configuration of social conflicts eases the authorities' task. The general strategy applied now combines repression and negotiation: repression and often arrests of ringleaders but pragmatic negotiation with the majority of complainants or a moderate party thereof. If the demands are directed at an enterprise, the local party-state acts as a mediator, but a partisan one, in most cases clearly defending the bosses against workers in the name of economic development. This tendency might seem paradoxical on the part of a party that still claims to represent the international communist movement, or what remains of it. But obviously the party-state's officials are mainly judged on the basis of their jurisdiction's growth rate; also they are often themselves entrepreneurs, engaged directly or indirectly through family members, and thus have a personal stake in not tilting the balance too much in workers' favor.

Mediation becomes more balanced and thus favorable to workers or employees on strike only when the firms are owned by foreign, Hong Kong, or Taiwan entities. It is in these enterprises that the 2008 Labor Contract Law, more protective of the salaried class, has been applied with rare zeal. As for Chinese firms, economic patriotism dictates that they frequently benefit from grace periods or levels of benevolence denied to foreign competitors.

The authorities are especially vigilant about "mass incidents" and have generally displayed both tolerance and firmness. When local authorities in charge of managing a crisis fail, the government at a higher level might intervene, not hesitating at times to take the protestors' side to restore order. Such was the case in Weng'an, a small town in Guizhou province where in 2008 rumors had spread like wildfire of a young girl's being raped and murdered by a local cadre. Faced with the police's refusal to investigate the case, several thousand protestors quickly rallied using SMS (short message service) and set fire to the municipal government office as well as several Public Security vehicles. Provincial authorities then intervened, restoring order by denouncing Weng'an officials and dismissing several of them from their posts.

What comes through from the handling of these social conflicts is the emergence, on the side of the party-state as well as public and private enterprises, of a capacity to negotiate not with duly recognized social partners but with the complainants or petitioners of the moment. As previously discussed, the CCP remains allergic to any sign of free unions emerging, closely watching labor NGOs that might display unionist intentions even at the most local level and dismantling them if need be. But the party amended the Trade Union Law in 2001 to allow independent delegates, in principle elected by personnel, to sit alongside official union representatives when labor disputes arise.[25] Although the law is far from being uniformly respected, such disputes are generally handled more flexibly so as to safeguard social stability. Moreover, a large number of major firms, such as Alibaba, prefer such methods if only to preserve their image. Similarly, local governments have increased compensation to farmers forced to vacate their lands for the needs of urbanization or industrialization (dams, factories, highways, etc.).

More generally, in the aftermath of the Asian financial crisis (1997–1998), the authorities have invested greatly in "preserving social stability" (*weiwen*). Since 2010 the budget for this has surpassed that of the PLA, covering not only repressive measures ("black jails," i.e., illegal detention centers for holding complainants before sending them back home, or arrested human rights lawyers), but also a notable integration aspect focusing on migrant workers (280 million), extending them social assistance, lodging, or education.[26]

Thus the party-state has learned to negotiate with society, having acquired the means for it. Such negotiations are much easier given that society is fragmented and structurally unorganized. Some observers have raised doubts about the authorities' ability to continue financing *weiwen* in the medium term, especially in the event of economic slowdown or social crisis. What can be said is that such a scenario is still far off. Today the Chinese administration is rich and has for a long time demonstrated its competence in raising revenues. And even if the means of modern communication make for much quicker and larger mobilizations, which might at times take the authorities off guard, the administration's, and particularly Public Security's, network within society is such that it remains nearly impossible for petitioners pursuing even a single cause to form an organization, let alone a political one.

Here again, authorities have established a "new authoritarian equilibrium" that has a good chance of enduring.

RELAUNCH OF JUDICIAL REFORMS AND EFFORTS AT AUTONOMIZING JUSTICE

Informal means of conflict resolution no longer suffice, and ever-growing segments in the world of business and the middle classes want the party-state to ensure greater legal safeguards.[27] Xi and his team are aware of this expectation. Thus, alongside the anticorruption drive, they launched judicial reforms in the autumn of 2014 (during the 4th Plenum of the 18th Central Committee) that has deepened since the 19th Party Congress. It consists mainly of better equipping courts and judges, already more professional compared to just ten years ago, against what is known as "judicial protectionism"—that is, local party authorities' interference in conflict resolution at lower jurisdictions. Currently, at each level judges and prosecutors as well as Public Security officials belong to party political and legal affairs commissions (*zhengfa weiyuanhui*). While this has gone unchallenged and continues to operate for any political matter (such as dissidents) or anything to do with state security, the reform has been aimed at better integrating the judicial institution vertically and guarding it against local authorities' interference. Thus cross-administrative-boundary jurisdictional entities have been established at the subprovincial level (in the counties or county-level municipalities). The Supreme Court has set up six circuit courts in charge of several provinces, and some provincial-level localities such as Shanghai have started to do the same at the lower level. Transregional courts in charge of adjudicating transregional cases have been created in Beijing and Shanghai. More courts specializing in intellectual property, financial affairs, or the Internet, as well as their own appeal courts, are also gradually being established. Moreover, courts' budgets are now distinct from local ones and centralized at the provincial level; judges are no longer paid by their constituency's government but by the judiciary.[28]

It is too early to take stock of this reform. Clearly its aim is not to attenuate the regime's repressive character. The abolition in 2013 of reeducation through labor camps (*laojiao*) has not ended arbitrary detentions, either. The arrests in July 2015 of some two hundred lawyers suspected of taking up political cases abundantly show the limits of this change. But the intention is clear: to introduce more legal safeguards, first for economic actors and then for private persons in dispute with legal entities, individuals, or even the administration, and finally for workers in conflict with their employers. Creating a legal environment favorable for economic development, intellectual property protection, and innovation and preserving social stability are the main motivations behind this reform.[29] Meanwhile, the isolation of dissidents and activists, their relatively small number, and most Chinese people's ignorance of their fate help the regime to appear reformist while being repressive and to consolidate its legitimacy, whereas in the West the regime is seen as weakening it.

RELIGIOUS RENEWAL AND POLITICAL CHANGE

Another notable phenomenon in China today is religious revival.[30] While this phenomenon reflects the moral void created by the country's feverish course for enrichment and especially its political and economic elites' unbridled accumulation of wealth, it raises several issues for political scientists. Is this religious revival not a part of society's autonomization, as discussed previously? If it is, will religious organizations or at least the more independent among them not become spearheads of social and even political demands, as happened in South Korea and Taiwan decades ago? Does Christianity's unprecedented expansion in China and the conversion to it of a noticeable number of activists not favor the struggle for democracy?

At the outset, it should be noted that while religious practice is allowed in China, except for CCP members, legally constituted religious organizations (Buddhist, Daoist, Muslim, Protestant, and Catholic) are all strictly controlled by the regime, via the erstwhile State Administration for Religious Affairs and since March 2018 directly by the CCP's United Front Work Department.

At present, unlike in the Mao era, the party-state is not opposed to religions. It even holds that they play a positive role, for several reasons: they propagate moral values, which were deeply and repeatedly jeopardized through the political extremism of the Cultural Revolution and the triumphant egoism of the reform and opening era; somewhat like NGOs, especially through their charitable work, legal religious organizations help the state's social policies; and invoking past practices, they mobilize the society around spiritual ideals, steering it away from politics and any questioning of the regime, or that at least is the CCP's hope. Thus, sticking to Marx's well-known assertion, religion is still seen by the party as "the opium of the masses," but a useful one, at least in reasonable doses.

On the whole, religious organizations and practices that have revived and been growing in China since 1979 and even more so from 1989 hardly constitute a threat to the party-state. Most religious practices, even outside of authorized organizations, as they did in China earlier, ignore the regime and focus on pastoral activities and the rebuilding of primary groups for solidarity and faith.

However, religious revival does pose several risks for the party-state, which it is fully aware of. This is why, above all, it privileges "Chinese" or "national" religions such as Daoism (1 percent of the population) and Buddhism (16 percent), although the latter is of Indian origin, or even popular religions (22 percent) over so-called Western ones: Christianity (ninety-three million adherents, or 7 percent of the population, in 2017 compared to seventy million in 2010 and six million in 1982) and Islam (twenty-three million).[31] This dichotomy has been accentuated under Xi, who has shown greater tolerance for the "Chinese" religions.

Jiang Zemin ruthlessly cracked down on the Falungong in 1999, and his successors have kept at it, but this unrecognized Buddhist group, which accords importance to the practice of *qigong*, a Chinese system of physical exercise and breathing control, had defied the regime by indulging in "politics"—that is, showing that it had in place a highly structured national organization and demanding that authorities legalize it. Daoist and Buddhist temples and monasteries flourish throughout China as religious places as well as tourist destinations and are income generators for local organizations and governments overseeing them. For now, except for Falungong, ipso facto deemed an "evil cult" (*xiejiao*) but that nevertheless counts tens of millions of adherents, no other Daoist or Buddhist organization has tried to become political or take to dissidence. And while in principle party members are required to be atheists, the authorities tend to overlook their practice of Daoism or Buddhism but not that of Islam or Christianity.

Islam poses a special problem that I return to when I consider the issue of Xinjiang. Suffice it to say here that the principal Muslim minority in China are not the Uyghurs (eleven million) of China's western region but the Hui (twelve million), mostly concentrated in Ningxia but also present in numerous cities and provinces. Difficult to distinguish from the Han and well-integrated in the system, the Hui are not a centrifugal force or a real political threat to Beijing, in spite of the growing frustration that some of them manifest against Xi's strict control of their religious activities. Moreover, while there has been a return to religiosity among many Chinese Muslims, Islam does not extend beyond the ethnic groups that have traditionally practiced it.

More daunting problems for the authorities stem from the unprecedented rise of Christianity in China.[32] Here again, all the risks are not of the same magnitude or nature. Catholicism presents well-known difficulties, PRC-Vatican diplomatic relations not having been restored since their rupture in 1951. Tortuous negotiations are under way that should eventually lead the two sides to reach an agreement on the nomination of bishops (in future probably appointed by the Holy See based on a Beijing-prepared list) and thus facilitate reconciliation between the Patriotic Church loyal to the party-state and the underground Church only obedient to Rome. But for the present, Chinese Catholics (nine to twelve million, including about six million affiliated with the official Church) do not constitute a notable force among political reformers or dissidents, unlike in Hong Kong, where for specific reasons (the best schools are Catholic) they are overrepresented among both the official elites and the prodemocracy camp.

It is the various Protestant congregations that constitute the main source of political risk for the authorities. The rapid and unprecedented rise in the number of Christians (more than 10 percent annually), with some statistics indicating that they outnumber CCP members (one hundred million against ninety million), obviously worries the authorities. However, this situation needs to be seen in perspective. The risks do not stem from the tightly controlled official Church (the Three-Self Patriotic Movement, with twenty million adherents) or from the ranks of charismatic cults (such as the Evangelists or Pentecostals), millenarians, or esoterics; some of these groups, such as Quannengshen (Church of Almighty God), are dangerous because they sometimes use violence in rallying new converts.[33] The government comes down hard on such misdemeanors when it notices them, much to the satisfaction of the majority of the public, and it is difficult to envisage a political movement similar to the Taiping Rebellion (1850–1864) arising from these sects.[34] Finally, such risks are not posed either by the so-called House Churches (two-thirds of all Chinese Christians, according to some estimates[35]), private "family" churches (*jiaqing jiaohui*), or "urban" ones (*chengshi jiaohui*), which for the most part are engaged in spiritual or social activities.

In fact, the highly decentralized nature of non-Catholic Christianity in China as well as elsewhere both strengthens and weakens the risk of politicization. Two parallel phenomena have gradually arisen: some underground congregations, sometimes linked to sister organizations abroad (especially the United States, Canada, Australia, Hong Kong, and Taiwan), have become politicized; and a growing number of political activists and dissidents have declared themselves Christians and rely on their religious faith for the courage they might exhibit, which they often need. While many Christians are to be found in the Yangzi delta (Anhui, Jiangsu, Zhejiang, and Shanghai), a politically important region, they are also traditionally concentrated in the less-developed Henan, Hebei, and Fujian provinces. Elsewhere they are sparse. Above all, underground or "political" Christianity seems relatively weak and fragmented.

For the foreseeable future, the party-state has the means to contain the rise of "political Christianity," on the one hand by gradually integrating House Churches in official Christianity and tolerating only those churches that eschew politics,[36] and on the other by cracking down on Protestant groups that are politicized or have forged links with foreign organizations. Such links prove to be double-edged: they bring in funding and other forms of support but attract attention and surveillance from the Public Security and State Security (counterespionage) authorities, risking being labeled by the CCP as "hostile Western forces." This is especially the case with Chinese religious groups connected to American evangelists, known for their conservatism, and in particular Bob Fu's

China Aid Association, a structure openly dedicated to helping China's House Churches.

Chinese Protestant churches maintaining links with their coreligionists in Hong Kong or Taiwan are also in the security organs' sights, and more so since Xi's rise to power. However, some groups with deep roots in China (Methodists, Presbyterians, and Anglicans) or that adhere to local Christianity (such as Lingliangtang or the "Bread of Life" church, highly influential in Hong Kong and among overseas Chinese), are more difficult to suppress. They have penetrated the new elites (entrepreneurs, private company cadres, and students) and have an opening to the liberal world, which by nature can potentially boost their role in any democratization of mainland China. Some new House Churches that emerged in China in the 1990s, such as the Beijing Ark House Church, which the dissident Yu Jie belonged to before his exile to the United States in 2012, have a declared political agenda: propagate democratic ideas.[37] Others, such as Shouwang (literally "keeping watch"), have more modest but also political plans: persuade the authorities to recognize underground churches.[38] Although they are much more clandestine owing to the far greater hounding they face from security officials than they did in Taiwan or South Korea before those countries' own democratization, such politicized churches already play a role in the structuring of Chinese dissidence. In the long run, therefore, they could form part of social forces facilitating the regime's political evolution.

More generally, Christianity, especially its evangelical branch, is on the ascendant in China. Some studies predict that by 2030, Christians might number 225 million (16 percent of the population).[39] Among religious organizations active in China, it is the Christian ones that are perceived as the greatest threats the CCP faces,[40] all the more so as a growing number of party members say they could combine their active participation in an organization that is atheist in principle with their Christian faith. The CCP leadership's efforts to contain this trend appear increasingly to be in vain, in spite of the campaign that it launched in 2018 to ask party members to choose: renounce their religious faith or leave the party.

However, unlike countries that were part of the "third wave" of democratization, the Chinese regime keeps tight control over religious organizations, including underground ones, to ensure they remain obedient or fragmented. The authorities know full well that such entities' autonomization and consolidation could weaken and even wreck the regime. More important, Christianity is likely to remain a minority religion in China, perceived as Western and thus illegitimate in many nationalist eyes. Although popular among elites, it would be wrong to exaggerate its long-term influence and its ability to weigh in on the country's political future.

A CCP THAT REMAINS HIGHLY ATTRACTIVE

The CCP competes with India's BJP (Bharatiya Janata Party) for the world's largest political party status in number of members. Dethroned in 2015 (87.8 against 88 million), the CCP seems to have regained its top spot since then (89.56 million members in late 2017). Regardless of whether it is the largest party (some data indicate that the BJP has 110 million members), its size presents a major challenge for anyone seeking to join. Party membership is not only a necessary condition but an insufficient one for a public sector career in the broad sense: administration, public enterprise, or institution and of course, party organs. It is the best strategy that new elites can adopt to obtain recognition, legitimacy, benefits, and protection from political authorities. Some entrepreneurs, scholars, intellectuals, and liberal professionals may well opt to join one of the eight "democratic parties" permitted and operating under the CCP's leadership. Such a move could help their integration into the regime's formal institutions (people's congresses, people's consultative conferences), in which a proportion of noncommunists are given membership (30 and 70 percent, respectively) (see chapter 1). But with a total membership of under a million members, these formations remain marginal.[41]

The party is an elite organization and intends to remain so. Moreover, it is becoming increasingly elitist. The percentage of the population with CCP membership has notably risen since Tiananmen, from 4.4 percent in 1993 to 6.5 percent in 2016. But the admission process has remained lengthy and is replete with numerous tests that have increased in number and toughness since Xi's ascendancy; he has sought to raise the professional, ideological, and moral quality of new members. Consequently, the increase in membership has slowed—up 1.3 percent in 2014, 1.1 percent in 2015, 0.8 percent in 2016, and 0.1 percent in 2017—and its percentage of China's population has begun to decrease (6.4 percent in 2017).[42]

In a way the CCP is somewhat like an ethnic minority: the vast majority of the population does not identify with it; they are not interested in politics in the sense understood in the People's Republic—affairs of the state, or rather the party-state; and they believe that their daily lives as well as future plans do not depend on their relation with the party, that is, the administrative authorities. They thus think, perhaps rightly, that they have no reason to seek membership. At any rate, given the entry criteria in operation and the priority given to integrating new or future elites (entrepreneurs, managers, engineers, scholars, and students) and a higher number of women (27 percent of members in 2017 compared to 14 percent in 1988), a large section of society seems unconcerned by such prospects.

Yet it is difficult, even impossible, to ignore the CCP, given its hegemony over the state and society. Almost all officials, PLA officers, and public sector cadres are party members. While the rate of adhesion is much lower in other sectors of activity, it has become more important for the middle classes (managers, engineers, and technicians) than for workers and farmers (who in 2017 made up 36 percent of party members, compared to 44 percent in 2005), in line with societal changes.[43] Today, 48 percent of CCP members are university graduates, compared to 29 percent in 2005.[44]

Beginning in 2006, some sources showed that one-third (4.3 million or 34 percent) of the 12.7 million private entrepreneurs was party members. This proportion has no doubt risen, but due to poor data, it is impossible to be sure, especially as private enterprises have more than doubled in number (27 million in late 2017). Moreover, in recent years the party has enrolled only a small number of representatives of what it calls "new social classes," that is, entrepreneurs. In 2016 some fourteen thousand from this category joined (compared to ten thousand in 2005). In fact, most small entrepreneurs have no particular reason to invest in politics. They are too busy with professional plans and the future of their businesses to seek party membership. However, should their companies grow in size and appear to succeed, the party would begin to take an interest, interfering in various ways in their businesses and inviting them to join. Such interest could be predatory (demand for advantages in cash or kind). But it could also, and more generally, stem from a desire to both support and control: support for any local generator of economic wealth of whatever sort and control of the most significant among them so as to prevent the formation of a bourgeoisie independent of the party and potentially the bearer of a political project (see chapter 5).

Since the start of the twenty-first century, the strategy of attraction and acculturation of new elites launched by Jiang has been fully operational, and its clear aim is to establish links of both allegiance to and dependence on the party. Conversely, private entrepreneurs who have major businesses find that they need to multiply their relations with the state, with party membership becoming an asset and often a quasi-necessity, facilitating via bribes their transactions with the administration or lowering their costs. Some among them prefer not joining, the better to safeguard their autonomy. They may join the local people's congress or the people's consultative conference, where they can wield some influence—albeit limited—on local political matters and above all acquire better protection against the regime's arbitrariness. In any case, the CCP has managed to maintain close links of dependence with private entrepreneurs, limiting their elbow room and any interest in challenging the current political system's basis (see chapter 5).

In the new socioeconomic context, what does it mean to adhere and belong to the party? The move to join on the part of most new members is pragmatic if not cynical, although a sort of idealism among a minority of members cannot be ruled out. Belonging to the CCP brings a number of advantages in terms of access to information, participation in intraparty political discussion and, more important, a network of useful and protective relations. But membership also entails several nonnegligible constraints: payment of fees ranging from 0.5 to 3 percent of monthly income (notably higher for entrepreneurs and other high-value members), regular participation in long and boring meetings mainly meant to assimilate and eventually propagate central directives, and restrictions on freedom of movement and foreign travel. To these constraints, which under Xi operate more than in previous eras, must be added the feelings of powerlessness and no doubt also frustration among ordinary members about decision-making processes and appointments, which remain highly centralized despite the campaign for "intraparty democracy" that Hu Jintao launched in 2007, and which quickly proved short-lived and is now long forgotten.[45]

Hence the number of "dormant members" is large and has tended to grow. Major population movements and urbanization of society have added to this tendency. For instance, many students distance themselves from the party without, however, handing in their cards once their studies are complete, especially if they work in the private sector or pursue higher studies abroad. Moreover, the party is struggling to rejuvenate itself (24.9 percent of members were under age thirty-five in 2017, compared to 27 percent in 1988), and 19.6 percent of members are retirees. Thus the typical CCP member is a male aged between forty and fifty, a university or technical school graduate occupying a cadre's post generally in the public sector.

More generally, the profile of the basic communist has greatly evolved, making way for more diverse social and political identities, at the risk of fracturing the CCP into several rival ideological tendencies. Having become a "ruling party" of a "catchall" and "nationalist" bent, somewhat like the KMT of yore, the CCP includes those pining for the Mao era (many among the party apparatchiks, retirees, and intellectuals) and liberals (no doubt mostly representing the private sector, academics, and those living in coastal regions), but primarily an immense mass of conformists who will jump according to circumstances, given the balance of power and indications from the top.

In sociological terms, some political scientists have divided the party into five distinct strata:[46]

1. Major leading cadres (650,000): the ones who make the rules.
2. The business elite, both state enterprises' managers and owners of private companies: as noted previously, with access to economic resources and enjoying close relations with the authorities, this elite is influential.
3. The intellectual elite and those from the education sector: including opinion leaders, this stratum could prove influential on the condition that its advice is accepted by the first two strata.
4. Passive members: mid-level cadres, engineers, technicians, and employees, who have the right to vote (especially to choose among candidates proposed by the organization) and to speak but little influence (25 percent of members).
5. Lower classes: farmers, workers, retirees (especially former employees of state enterprises), and students (66 percent of members), who enjoy more or less the same rights as the previous stratum.[47]

Thus, the party is controlled by a tiny group of people, fewer than 10 percent of its members (eight million). This situation is full of tension and uncertainty. But for now, the CCP's attractiveness generally outweighs the inconveniences of remaining a powerless member: in 2017, nearly 20 million people applied to join, but a mere 1.98 million were admitted, or just one out of ten.[48] And those disappointed with the party prefer to distance themselves quietly rather than seek to reform it from within because any attempt to influence matters seems in vain, at least for the rank and file.

Therefore, one may conclude that the great mass of members constitute a factor for regime stability and longevity. It is not from this mass that political change will emerge. They are too dependent, powerless, and pragmatic for that. Changes can only come from party elites, whom I discuss in chapter 5.

"SOCIAL CREDIT" AND MANAGEMENT OF SOCIETY

As the party-state modernizes, grows rich, and acquires sophisticated technical means, it gains the ability to better control society; this is the "social governance" (*shehui zhili*) or "social management" (*shehui guanli*) system. This approach has a strong security dimension that was strengthened under Xi; his decision in late 2013 to establish a new National Security Commission that he presides over is part of this integral vision of society and thus of social stability maintenance.

Since 2014 the party-state has gradually acquired a new instrument for greater control of citizens and companies: the "social credit system" (*shehui xinyong tixi*). Copied from Western credit institutions, its aim is to assess and note the reliability of people and entities not only regarding their repayment ability but on a number of extremely vast and varied criteria: respect for law; repayment of loans; and political, social, and moral conduct. Thus individuals marked as asocial for not visiting their parents or behaving badly on public transport or worse, being labeled as dissidents or dangerous for social stability in view of, for instance, their participation in an underground church or in a workers' rights NGO, could receive a negative evaluation and attract a certain number of sanctions or constraints: ban on travel in public transport, especially high-speed trains or aircraft; no access to social housing or public jobs; prohibition from leaving the territory; and so forth.

This task is facilitated through the accumulation by the party-state, and especially by its security services, of a vast amount of data on any

organized group or individual (big data), the generalization of facial recognition devices, and advances in artificial intelligence, a priority for
Chinese innovation.[49]

Conceived of in the early 2000s for controlling businesses and compelling them to show greater respect for their legal, economic, and social
obligations (adhering to rules and their own entrepreneurial engage-
ments, tax returns, environmental protection, energy saving, etc.), the
social credit system has gradually been set up on the basis of local trials
and since 2014 has been extended to control citizens, at least in some
regions where it is currently being tested.

It is the second aspect of the system that is of particular interest, as it
obviously places society under far greater surveillance, thus helping further consolidate regime stability. Interestingly, the main aim of the social
credit system has been to restore the trust citizens might have in economic actors or in fellow citizens, which only attests to the high level of
mutual distrust that has engulfed Chinese society since the start of reforms and to some extent since 1949. Mainly covering enterprises, Chinese or foreign, the project has also aimed at reducing the cost of transactions and cutting economic risks by obliging the government to gather a
great deal of legal, financial, and commercial information on the firms. As
of 2018, 75 percent of such information has been made public, with the
rest having restricted, mainly government, access.[50]

This new system links mechanisms for holding individuals responsible with social control methods. On the one hand, society is induced to
take part in the system, as such participation would allow access to diverse services and advantages; on the other, involvement in the system
opens society to potential sanctions, that is, holds it responsible.[51]

Although it could help clean up the internal economic environment,
improve economic actors' behavior, reduce corruption, and regulate the
market, this new project manifestly contains an Orwellian dimension that
Internet growth can only enhance (see above). The introduction of social
credit increases the party-state's right to oversee business activities, its
interference in market mechanisms, and its control over the private sector, including foreign companies. It confirms the CCP's intention to remain on top of the system and prevent the emergence of economic forces
out of its tight leash. The social credit system establishes above all a level
of surveillance and micromanagement of citizens that is particularly anti-

freedom, ignoring among other things respect for privacy and the right to be forgotten.

For the present, the social credit system is in force only partially and is far from being centralized; a large amount of data is being held and managed by local authorities. It has already attracted numerous criticisms in society and among economic circles on account of its attack on freedoms, the inconsistency of the data gathered, and the potentially arbitrary nature of the grading system. Moreover, for technical reasons the target of general adoption by 2020 might not be met.[52]

Nevertheless, the social credit system seeks to reassure credit enterprises, consumers, parents, and the government, highlighting the need for security and predictability that Chinese society is obsessed with, much more than with individual freedoms or privacy. This also confirms the low level of interpersonal confidence within Chinese society, the priorities of a majority of its members, and the dominant political culture.

In any case, the introduction of the social credit system adds to the many factors behind the regime's ability to maintain in the foreseeable future the means not only to control society but also to prevent in time any social manifestation that could weaken or a fortiori destabilize the political regime.

NATIONALISM

Quite clearly nationalism has become the main factor rallying society around the party. In Chinese this is referred to as the "cohesive force" (*ningjuli*) of nationalism (*minzuzhuyi*). Chinese nationalism—ideology, instrument, and emotion all rolled into one—is a paradoxical reality that I have described elsewhere.[53] In their personal conduct, the Chinese are not that nationalistic, much less for instance than the Japanese or Koreans. To be sure, Chinese nationalism has a Han racial basis ("race" being the original sense of *minzu*), making it difficult for all non-Han citizens to internalize it, all the more so as the Han have an annoying tendency to act superior to ethnic minorities. Nevertheless, the Chinese buy foreign products; put their money where it fetches the best returns, unconcerned with national boundaries; send their children to the best US universities if they can afford it; and are curious to discover the world, even if such curiosity is rather superficial among most of them. These behaviors are perceptible not only among the middle classes; they are shared by a great majority of elites, including those of the political or intellectual New Left, known for their uncompromising "patriotism," whose activities are rarely in step with their ideas.

But no one can deny the strength of Chinese nationalism, which is increasing. Since Tiananmen, nationalism has largely replaced communist ideology, despite ritual references to "socialism with Chinese characteristics" punctuating official discourse. More important, the CCP intends to remain both the only leader and guarantor of Chinese nationalism.

On the one hand, as the sole source of political authority, the party reserves for itself the task of defining nationalism's contours and content; it is for the CCP to choose the battles society must fight and specify the means to be used. While it has shown skill in instrumentalizing popular emotions, it has thus far known when to impose limits it deems necessary on these flashes of what I have called "nationalist moments." Simply put, the authorities have thus far succeeded in calling a halt to outbreaks of popular fervor. That was the case during anti-US protests in 1999 following the accidental NATO aerial bombing of the Chinese embassy in Belgrade, regarding the anti-Japanese movement of 2005 that was provoked by the strengthening of the US-Japanese coalition over Taiwan, in response to the anti-French rally of 2008 after the Olympic torch fiasco in Paris, and when Chinese students sought to mobilize against Japanese occupation of the Senkaku islands (Diaoyu in Chinese) in 2012. As soon as protesters begin acting in response to the CCP's sluggishness or its lack of concern for society's feelings, security forces move in to persuade organizers to cease their campaign.

On the other hand, it is crucial for the CCP to maintain its monopoly over nationalism. Not only must it sustain the perception that is constantly at the forefront of this battle; it must also keep delegitimizing any other nationalist project, whether its historical enemy the KMT (despite the latter's partial rehabilitation for reasons that have more to do with Taiwan rather than the republican era) or prodemocracy personalities and groups such as Liu Xiaobo or members of the constitutionalist movement, who all know too well that no political reform can afford to overlook nationalism.

For now, the CCP has forged far ahead of its detractors on this front. All Chinese leaders have contributed to it, Jiang and especially Xi, of course, with greater success than Hu Jintao. In fact, since 2013 the "Chinese dream" of power, greatness, and prosperity, as well as the two "centenaries"—of the party in 2021 and of the People's Republic in 2049—seem capable of continuing to rally the majority of Chinese society around the CCP and its chief, whose "thought" has been enshrined in the Party Constitution since October 2017. Rising tensions in the East China Sea with Japan, in the South China Sea with some Southeast Asian countries, especially Vietnam, or with India over the Himalayan border, and more generally the heightening of Sino-US rivalry for global leadership, help unify society around the party-state. This raises the question of whether the assertion of power at play since 2008 and the symbolic moment of the Beijing Olympics in fact have served the party's internal plan: consolidating Chinese society's support for its leading role.

There certainly are opinion groups or public intellectuals such as the New Left and media outlets such as *Global Times* (*Huanqiu Shibao*) that take a more nationalistic stance than the government, especially on international matters, and often sound "hawkish," exerting real pressure on Chinese diplomacy. Moreover, top party leaders, especially the "princelings" and more generally the nomenklatura, do not exactly have an impenetrable armor; the corruption that came to light after the Bo Xilai affair has opened many Chinese people's eyes to the hypocrisy of their nationalist claims.

However, the potency and consistency of nationalist propaganda diffused by the authorities and some segments of society are in my view capable of containing such risks. The party's propaganda services continue to rely on films and accounts of the Sino-Japanese War that highlight the courage and determination of communist guerrillas and delegitimize, albeit less vigorously than previously, the role of Chiang Kai-shek's Nationalist army. But this message has worn thin, prompting the propaganda organs to try to revamp themselves, but with little success on the whole. For instance, the 2017 film made for the PLA's ninetieth anniversary, *The Founding of the Army* (*Jianjun Daye*), had patchy success, artificially boosted by tickets given free to public institutions and the highly limited number of foreign films distributed in China.

But the regime can often rely on projects undertaken by individual initiatives with private funding to spread a nationalist message close or identical to its own. Such was the case with the 2017 film *Wolf Warrior 2* (*Zhan Lang Er*), directed by actor and martial artist Wu Jing. Beating all foreign films at the box office right from the first week, this full-length film, with undeniably good technical quality, clearly touched a sensitive chord in the Chinese collective consciousness, evoking a much more positive response than previous nationalistic films had managed.

The film depicts the adventures of a sort of Rambo who lands up in Africa and manages somewhat by chance to save a Chinese community threatened by American mercenaries and arms sellers and in the process to ease the task of the Chinese Navy dispatched there. It thus skillfully deals with the current main obsessions of the regime as well as of society: the security of Chinese expatriates, the PLA's projection abroad, China's positive and major role in Africa, and Sino-US rivalry and the rise of national ambitions. The message is clear: the CCP works for the people, has the power and the means to protect them, and can even lead China to surpass the United States and replace it as guarantor of world peace. As *Wolf Warrior 2* shows, "whoever attacks China will be killed however far away the target lies!"

Obviously the film had the authorities' backing and assistance, technically (with elements of the PLA participating) as well as in terms of its script, largely approved by the party's propaganda services.[54] But the way in which it was made and the success it has enjoyed show the extent to which the state's nationalism has been internalized by Chinese society and how the constant reaffirmation of national strength and pride has become the best asset for the regime's survival. Received with much greater reservations abroad, the film also testifies to the increasingly irreconcilable and thus dangerous nature of Chinese nationalism, an evolution that could weaken further the advocates of better relations with the West, in particular the United States. Such an evolution also contributes, as discussed in the next section, to vitiating relations between the Han and ethnic minorities, at least with some of them within China itself.

More generally, as long as the CCP keeps pursuing its nationalist dream of power and greatness, it will be difficult for any opposition force to even weaken much less dethrone it.

MINORITY ETHNICITIES' MARGINALIZATION AND POWERLESSNESS

What challenges does the regime face from ethnic minorities, at least from some among them? Could Tibetan, Uyghur, or Mongol proindependence groups really provoke the undoing of the PRC's current borders?

The answer is no, given the extreme asymmetry of the forces present. And even if a change of regime in Beijing could improve the autonomy status of non-Han ethnicities as they wish, the general state of affairs will remain. A breakup of the Chinese empire is in my view unlikely, even in the longer term.

In the nationalist context discussed in the previous section, what can ethnic minorities hope for, or rather fear? They will face much greater pressure to assimilate, that is, to be proficient in Chinese, at the risk of gradually losing their own culture, and to identify with the Chinese nation (*Zhonghua minzu*), defined mainly in racial terms; much greater restrictions on the already superficial autonomy granted by the PRC's constitutional order; and of course no hope of independence, which is not only a taboo concept but an objective deemed "criminal" under Chinese law.

Here I briefly note the vastly contrasting situation of ethnic minorities in China. Comprising just 8.5 percent of the population (114 million in 2010) and divided into fifty-five officially recognized ethnicities, the groups are highly unequal in size. While the Yi of Sichuan and Yunnan number 9 million, the Koreans of Manchuria are fewer than 2 million and the Kirghiz of Xinjiang hardly 200,000. Most of these groups are relatively well integrated and ask for little more than the safeguarding of their way of life and religious practices. This is the case with the Zhuang in Guangxi (17 million) and the Hui of Ningxia and Gansu and other provinces (11 million). Constituting in general a minority of the population in their own regions, these groups are represented in their formal institutions (people's congresses) and take part in administrative matters but rarely head party organs, which are mostly controlled by Hans. Where they are concentrated in large numbers, these groups have a constitutionally guaranteed autonomy status (*zizhi*) at the provincial level—China has five "autonomous regions"—as well as at lower ones. Although in principle political, in reality this status grants them merely relative freedom in economic, social, cultural, or religious matters. Han officials posted in minority areas do not usually learn the major minority languages, as no policy dictates it.

During the establishment of the short-lived Jiangxi Soviet Republic in 1931, the CCP had offered to grant independence to ethnic minorities that wanted it. But from 1949 onward this idea was abandoned, replaced by the autonomy status, most often devoid of meaning, the party apparatus guaranteeing the centralization of the bureaucratic edifice.

Whereas since 1979 there has been a real cultural revival among most ethnic minorities that economic development and tourism have fostered but also tended to mangle, the political problems concerning the minorities are concentrated in three specific "autonomous regions"—Inner Mongolia, Tibet, and Xinjiang—and three relatively large groups: Mongols (6 million), Tibetans (6.3 million), and Uyghurs (11.3 million).

What is common to the three regions is both their late and fitful integration into the Chinese empire and the aspirations for independence of their peoples. In a way they also share the practical impossibility of their dream of independence: the human, economic, political, and military balance of power is too unequal. Beyond these common points, the nature of their problems and the seriousness of tensions on the ground are quite different.

In Inner Mongolia (24.7 million inhabitants in 2010), Mongols represent a mere 17 percent of the population. Mongolia's partition into two entities dates back to 1911 and their respective relationship with the Manchu court; Outer Mongolia was much more loosely connected to it. A proindependence movement did appear in Inner Mongolia during the democratization of the Mongolian People's Republic in 1990, demanding reunification of the whole nation. But it was quickly sidelined owing to differences between the two Mongol communities, internal difficulties in the Republic of Mongolia, and China's rapid economic growth. Today, some Mongols in China, backed by a few US-based organizations, express identity-linked demands, mainly cultural and linguistic. But paradoxically, they are concentrated in Inner Mongolia's quite Sinicized urban centers and not in the more traditionally Mongol steppes. Despite growing relations with their northern cousins and greater cultural awareness, the Mongols in China have globally adjusted to Beijing's tutelage and cohabitation with the Han.

Tibet, however, is more complicated. The Tibetans do not feel Chinese and say they belong to a nation dominated by Tantric Buddhism, one that had long been independent. A government in exile has been based in Dharamsala, in northern India, since 1959, when the fourteenth Dalai Lama escaped from Lhasa, following an uprising against PRC rule.

Placed under Chinese suzerainty by the Mongols (Yuan) under Kublai Khan in the thirteenth century, Tibet was again separated from China under the Ming (1368–1644). The Manchus, thanks to their political alliance with the Mongols, reintegrated Tibet into the empire and began exercising the right to a say in the choice of the Dalai Lama, the spiritual and temporal chief of the main Tibetan Buddhist sect. But until 1911, and even 1949, the control of Tibet by the Chinese central government was loose and symbolic.

What weakens some Tibetans' demand for independence is the hesitation shown by Tibetan chiefs of the republican era to establish an independent state, as Outer Mongolia did. But unlike Ulaanbaatar, previously Moscow's protégé, Lhasa could count on no foreign power, not even Britain, to advance its cause. Moreover, the British had in 1914 recognized Chinese "suzerainty" over Tibet.

Since 1951 Tibet has been under PLA control and PRC administration. While the Tibetans' condition has gradually improved since 1979 in economic and religious terms, the CCP's refusal to share political power and consequently to negotiate true autonomy with the Dalai Lama is the main cause of the current impasse. Since 1988 the Dalai Lama and Dharamsala have abandoned the demand for independence, calling merely for greater autonomy, similar to that accorded to Hong Kong since 1997 through the "one-country, two-systems" formula. It cannot be ruled out that a democratic Chinese government would accept such an arrangement, although the Tibetans' wish for extending it to historic Tibet—that is, to Kham (high plateaus in Sichuan) and Amdo (Qinghai)—might never be granted. So long as the CCP is in power, there is little chance of the situation changing and tensions easing. Although still mostly populated by Tibetans (90 percent of 3.2 million inhabitants), the region has changed greatly, its urban centers now being dominated demographically and economically by Han colonizers. Tourism development has mainly benefited the settlers, while Public Security officials inspect in a particularly tortuous manner all monasteries and religious activities. This has contributed to endangering Tibetan culture and language, deepening the divide between the communities.

Beijing is waiting for the Dalai Lama's death to take charge of the choice of his successor and thus buttress its hold over Tibetan monks. It could be a Pyrrhic victory, as Tibetans might pick their own fifteenth Dalai Lama or eliminate the post. The balance of power between the Chinese and Tibetans can only deteriorate in the future, and barring a regime change, put off any prospects for real political and religious autonomy. Were such a change to occur, any Chinese central government would reject all talk of independence and continue managing Tibet's foreign affairs and militarily controlling the still partly disputed vast border with South Asia, especially India. And it will mostly likely have the means to do so.

Xinjiang (population 24 million) is arguably the region that presents the gravest security problem for Beijing, due to the Uyghurs' persistent demand for independence as well as, since the 1990s, the rise of Islamic fundamentalism, this despite genuine and rapid economic growth. But here again the forces present are unfavorable to the Central Asian Muslim communities, especially the Uyghur majority. In fact, although the Han account for, at least officially, just 36 percent of the population, compared to 48 percent Uyghurs and 64 percent for the total Muslim ethnicities (Kirghiz, Kazakh, Hui, etc.), they dominate the politico-administrative institutions, the economy—partly via the *bingtuan*, the still extant military farms established in the 1950s (with 2.5 million employees)—and geographically the region's more developed north (Urumqi, Turfan, Hami, Karamay, and Ili). More important, despite the recrudescence of violent attacks by the most radical fringes of Uyghur political movements, Chinese security organs (the PLA, Armed Police, and State Security) have all the means to restore order whenever it is disturbed; to pursue, detain, and reeducate, if need be, identified "terrorists"; and to control borders with neighboring countries (Kazakhstan, Kirghizstan, Tajikistan, and Pakistan in particular), in other words to keep Xinjiang in China's fold. And this can be done without help from the Shanghai Cooperation Organization set up in 2001, which includes, apart from the above-mentioned states, China, Russia, Uzbekistan, and India.

Evidently the length and legitimacy of Xinjiang's incorporation in the Chinese empire divides Chinese and Uyghurs: the former say it goes back to the Han (first century CE), while the latter believe non-Chinese dynasties (Yuan and Manchu) were behind the annexation. Regardless, this frontier region between empires remained disputed until 1949, and the PRC became the first regime to completely and closely administer Xinjiang, facilitating from the 1950s Han implantation (Han were less than 5 percent of the population in 1949).

Since the early 2000s, tensions between Uyghurs and the Han have intensified; the 2009 anti-Chinese riots in Urumqi and subsequent repression led to the installation of a sort of rampant apartheid between communities. Augmentation of diverse restrictions imposed on Muslims and the practice of their religion—not to mention the detention of around one million of them for reeducation since 2018—is resented by them.[55] Mainly represented by the World Uyghur Congress (WUC), the diaspora has become more active, taking advantage of improving relations with Central Asia and Turkey as well as the presence of "compatriots" in Kazakhstan and Kirghizstan.

But for the great majority of Chinese, Xinjiang's independence is inconceivable. Although the WUC seems to have moderated its demands, asking only for significant political autonomy, it is far from commanding unanimity among those opposed to Chinese rule. The numbers of armed attacks by Uyghurs seem to indicate a fragmentation of the movement, and this can only strengthen the position of security organs and of Han authorities in general. Again, barring major political change in Beijing, it is difficult to see the situation in Xinjiang improving. Even if a democratic regime were to take shape in China, the type of political formula that can resolve the region's problems and usher in harmonious cohabitation among communities would be difficult to achieve. Unlike the French in Algeria, the Han settlers will have the means to resist any forced departure; the central government will most likely continue to seek to manage the region's external affairs and security (border control and public order); and if religious extremism does not ebb, the government will be tempted to maintain tight surveillance of imams, Muslim religious venues in general, and their relations with foreign entities.

These ethnic problems inherited from the imperial past are not regarded with the same importance abroad and within China. Abroad they are often exaggerated, while in China they are generally perceived as secondary, even marginal. But it should be borne in mind that, representing a third of the PRC territory, Tibet and Xinjiang have a strategic importance for any central government. Two contradictory tendencies are at work: on the one hand Tibetans' and Uyghurs' demands for autonomy and even independence are most likely to persist; on the other, arguing that these communities have already received much in terms of cultural autonomy and economic development, a majority of Han Chinese will continue to oppose their demands and to believe, wrongly, that these regions' modernization and the minorities' enrichment will gradually kill such aspirations. Even though these two communities and the ethnic minorities more generally struggle to identify with the Chinese nation of the CCP's conception, they will have to take into account in their future strategies the irredentist power of nationalism that the party has propagated in Han society.

Quite simply, the risk of Tibet or Xinjiang becoming independent is minimal, and even less for Inner Mongolia. And any increase in such a risk can only be an obstacle to democratization of the Chinese regime, rather than the opposite.

CONCLUSION

The CCP is no longer seeking to prevent the emergence of a civil society; that would be in vain and counterproductive. But it has generally managed to neutralize and in a way tame it.

The party-state is far from being on top of things, and new manifestations of civil society activities abound: multiplication of autonomous and unregistered NGOs; opening up of new online public space and the impossibility of achieving total Internet surveillance; the growing might of religions, especially Christianity, tending toward politicization; and the proliferation of social conflict and tensions between society and local authorities. More generally, despite Xi's firm hand, Chinese society enjoys a much higher degree of autonomy and freedom than at the beginning of the reforms. The country's unprecedented economic development and enrichment have played a key role in this evolution.

However, the regime has adapted to the new environment and has things in hand, certainly more so than, say, five years ago. It has persuaded most NGOs to collaborate with it; the great majority of religious practices do not threaten it, and in fact quite the contrary; it has been modernizing the judiciary's workings and improving legal safeguards; it has become more adept at managing social conflict; large numbers still seek CCP membership each year; the nationalism it has been plugging constantly is helping to ensure society's backing for it much more than in earlier eras; and the worries caused by the Tibetans and Uyghurs are no more than flea bites.

China's civil society is vibrant, but it will remain embryonic and rudderless into the foreseeable future. In these circumstances, more than any expansion of movements favoring democracy, only a division among elites can get things going.

NOTES

1. Yang Lijun and Shan Wei, eds., *Governing Society in Contemporary China* (Singapore: World Scientific, 2017).

2. Notably, this point has been developed by Stein Ringen in *The Perfect Dictatorship: China in the 21st Century* (Hong Kong: HKU Press, 2016), 137.

3. Elizabeth J. Perry, "Trends in the Study of Chinese Politics: State-Society Relations," *The China Quarterly*, no. 139 (September 1994): 704–713.

4. Jean-Pierre Cabestan, *Le système politique chinois: Un nouvel équilibre autoritaire* [The Chinese political system: A new authoritarian equilibrium] (Paris, Presses de Sciences-Po, 2014), 485ff.

5. Jürgen Habermas, *The Structural Transformation of the Public Sphere: An Inquiry into a Category of Bourgeois Society*, trans. Thomas Burger (Cambridge, MA: The MIT Press, 1989); Steven Seidman, ed., *Jürgen Habermas on Society and Politics: A Reader* (Boston: Beacon Press, 1989).

6. *2017nian Shehui Fuwu Fazhan Tongji Baogao* [Social Services development statistical report 2017], http://www.mca.gov.cn/article/sj/tjgb/2017/201708021607.pdf, 13–14.

7. Jessica C. Teets, *Civil Society under Authoritarianism: The China Model* (New York: Cambridge University Press, 2014).

8. Shawn Shieh, "Same Bed, Different Dreams? The Divergent Pathways of Foundations and Grassroot NGOs in China," *Voluntas* 28, no. 4 (August 2017): 1785–1811.

9. On the CCP's management of the Wenchuan earthquake and the short-lived relaxation of control over media and semiofficial NGOs, see Christian P. Sorace, *Shaken Authority: China's Communist Party and the 2008 Sichuan Earthquake* (Ithaca, NY: Cornell University Press, 2017).

10. Patricia M. Thornton, "The Advance of the Party: Transformation or Takeover of Urban Grassroots Society," *The China Quarterly*, no. 213 (March 2013): 1–18.

11. Teets, *Civil Society Under Authoritarianism*; and Yiyi Lu, *Non-Governmental Organisations in China: The Rise of Dependent Autonomy* (London and New York: Routledge, 2009).

12. See Séverine Arsène, *Internet et politique en Chine* [Internet and politics in China] (Paris: Karthala, 2011); see also Jacques Delisle, Avery Goldstein, and Guobin Yang, eds., *The Internet, Social Media, and a Changing China* (Philadelphia: University of Pennsylvania Press, 2016); and Gianluigi Negro, *The Internet in China: From Infrastructure to a Nascent Civil Society* (Cham, Switzerland: Palgrave Macmillan, 2017).

13. Séverine Arsène, "Internet Governance in Chinese Academic Literature: Rebalancing a Hegemonic World Order?," *China Perspectives*, no. 2 (2016): 25–36.

14. Gary King, Jennifer Pan, and Margaret Roberts, "How the Chinese Government Fabricates Social Media Posts for Strategic Distraction, Not Engaged Argument," *American Political Science Review* 111, no. 3 (2017): 484–501.

15. Wu Mei, "China's Crackdown on 'Internet Rumors' and 'Illegal' Internet Publicity Activities," in *Governing Society in Contemporary China*, ed. Yang Lijun and Shan Wei (Singapore: World Scientific, 2017), 41–56.

16. No figures have been officially published. Ian Williams, "China's Internet Crackdown Is Another Step Towards 'Digital Totalitarian State,'" NBC News, September 6, 2017, https://www.nbcnews.com/news/china/china-s-internet-crackdown-another-step-toward-digital-totalitarian-state-n798001.

17. Brice Pedroletti, "La Chine vaillamment défendue par son armée de trolls" [China vigorously defended by troll army), *Le Monde*, June 4, 2017.

18. Han Han, *Blogs de Chine* [China blogs] (Paris: Bleu de Chine—Gallimard, 2012).

19. Phil Muncaster, "China's 'Big Vs' disown selves online to avoid new gossip laws," *The Register*, September 18, 2013, https://www.theregister.co.uk/2013/09/18/verified_accounts_weibo_unverify_rumour_crackdown/.

20. Margaret E. Roberts, *Censored: Distraction and Diversion Inside China's Great Firewall* (Princeton, NJ: Princeton University Press, 2018).

21. Bruce J. Dickson, *The Dictator's Dilemma: The Chinese Communist Party's Strategy for Survival* (Oxford: Oxford University Press, 2016), 71–73.

22. Dali L. Yang, "China's Troubled Quest for Order: Leadership, Organization and the Contradictions of the Stability Maintenance Regime," *Journal of Contemporary China* 26, no. 103 (January 2017): 48.

23. Chloé Froissart, "Negotiating Authoritarianism and Its Limits: Worker-led Collective Bargaining in Guangdong Province," *China Information* 32, no. 1 (March 2018): 23–45; and Chloé Froissart, "L'évolution de la dynamique des grèves en Chine et leur impact sur la démocratisation au sein des entreprises" [Changes in strike dynamics in China and their impact on democratisation inside firms], in *Travail, luttes sociales et régulation du capitalisme dans la Chine contemporaine* [Work, social struggles and regulation of capitalism in China today], ed. Clément Sehier and Richard Sobel (Lille, France: Presses universitaires du septentrion, 2015), 103–121.

24. Martin King Whyte, *Myth of the Social Volcano: Perceptions of Inequality and Distributive Injustice in Contemporary China* (Stanford, CA: Stanford University Press, 2010). See also Le Blog de Thomas Piketty, "De l'inégalité en Chine" [Inquality in China], February 14, 2017, http://piketty.blog.lemonde.fr/2017/02/14/de-linegalite-en-chine/; Piketty estimated that in 2015, the richest 10 percent in China held 67 percent of private wealth, compared to 41 percent in 1995.

25. Han Dongfang with Michaël Sztanke, *Mon combat pour les ouvriers chinois* [My struggle for Chinese workers] (Paris: Michel Lafon, 2014). Han is director of *China Labour Bulletin*, a Hong Kong–based NGO that reports on labor troubles in China and advises parties implicated in them (http://www.clb.org.hk).

26. On migrants, see Chloé Froissart, *La Chine et ses migrants: La conquête d'une citoyenneté* [China and its migrants: the conquest of a citizenship] (Rennes, France: Presses universitaires de Rennes, 2013); see also a review of the book by Eric Florence in *China Perspectives*, no. 4 (2014): 66–67.

27. Andrew Nathan, "The Puzzle of the Chinese Middle Class," *Journal of Democracy* 27, no. 2 (April 2016): 5–19.

28. See "White Paper on Judicial Reform of Chinese Courts," *China Daily*, February 27, 2017. See also Susan Finder's blog at http://supremepeoplescourtmonitor.com for regular reports on the various steps and features of the current judicial reform. On the current operation of Chinese courts, see Kwai Hang Ng and He Xin, *Embedded Courts: Judicial Decision-making in China* (Cambridge, UK: Cambridge University Press, 2017).

29. Yang, "China's Troubled Quest for Order," 50–52; Jacques DeLisle, "Law in the China Model 2.0: Legality, Developmentalism and Leninism Under Xi Jinping," *Journal of Contemporary China* 26, no. 103 (January 2017): 68–84.

30. Vincent Goossaert and David Palmer, *The Religious Question in Modern China* (Chicago: University of Chicago Press, 2010); Benoît Vermander, "Religious Revival and Exit from Religion in Contemporary China," *China Perspectives*, no. 4 (2009): 4–15;

and Ian Johnson, *The Souls of China: The Return of Religion After Mao* (New York: Pantheon, 2017).

31. Katharina Wenzel-Teuber, "Statistics on Religions and Churches in the People's Republic of China, Update for the Year 2016," *Religions & Christianity in Today's China* 7, no. 2 (2017): 26–53. For a good account of the situation of religions, see "International Religious Freedom Report for 2016, China," https://www.state.gov/documents/organization/268968.pdf; and Viola Zhou, "China's Underground Churches Head for Cover as Crackdown Closes In," *SCMP*, September 10, 2017, https://www.scmp.com/news/china/policies-politics/article/2110433/chinas-underground-churches-head-cover-crackdown-closes.

32. Eleanor Albert, "Christianity in China," Council on Foreign Relations, May 7, 2015, https://www.cfr.org/backgrounder/christianity-china.

33. On this sect, see Nuala Gathercole Lam, "Police Arrest Disciples of Chinese Female Jesus," Sixth Tone, July 26, 2017, http://www.sixthtone.com/news/1000581/police-arrest-disciples-of-chinese-female-jesus. On Pentecostals, see Edmond Tang, "'Yellers' and Healers—'Pentecostalism' and the Study of Grassroots Christianity in China," Churches Together in Britain and Ireland, September 2002, https://web.archive.org/web/20060905143444/http://www.ctbi.org.uk/index.php?op=modload&name=knowledge&file=kbasepage&LinkID=148.

34. See Jonathan D. Spence, *God's Chinese Son: The Taiping Heavenly Kingdom of Hong Xiuquan* (New York and London: Northon & Co., 1996).

35. About 30 million Christians are affiliated with official churches. The rest of the 93 to 115 million Christians belong to a large number of unregistered churches; and Viola Zhou, "China's Underground Churches Head for Cover as Crackdown Closes In," *SCMP*, September 10, 2017, https://www.scmp.com/news/china/policies-politics/article/2110433/chinas-underground-churches-head-cover-crackdown-closes.

36. Carsten T. Vala, *The Politics of Protestant Churches and the Party-State in China: God Above Party?* (London and New York: Routledge, 2017).

37. Gerda Wielander, "Bridging the Gap? An Investigation of Beijing Intellectual House Church Activities and Their Implications for China's Democratization," *Journal of Contemporary China* 18, no. 62 (2009): 849–864.

38. Carsten T. Vala, "Protestant Christianity and Civil Society in Authoritarian China," *China Perspectives*, no. 3 (2012): 43–52. Shouwang was formed in 1993 by an ethnic Korean Chinese. See Vala, *The Politics of Protestant Churches*, ch. 8.

39. Fenggang Yang, "The Other Chinese Miracle: Great Awakening Shifts Growth of Global Christianity to the East," *GlobalPlus*, December 1, 2015, Archives, http://globalplus.thearda.com/globalplus-religion-in-china/.

40. Fenggang Yang, *Religion in China. Survival & Revival under Communist Rule* (Oxford: Oxford University Press, 2012), 22.

41. On "democratic parties," see Cabestan, *Le système politique chinois*, 354–367.

42. "2017nian Zhongguo gongchandang dandnei tongji gongbao" [Internal statistical report of China's Communist Party 2017], *Xinhua*, June 30, 2018, http://www.gov.cn/shuju/2018-06/30/content_5302456.htm.

43. Jie Chen, *A Middle Class Without Democracy: Economic Growth and the Prospect for Democratization in China* (Oxford: Oxford University Press, 2013).

44. *Xinhua*, June 30, 2018; and Lea Shih, "Centralized Leadership—Heterogeneous Party Base," *Merics China Monitor*, Mercator Institute for China Studies, August 16, 2017.

45. In his report to the 19th Party Congress (October 2017), Xi Jinping revived this objective but insisted far more on strengthening discipline than on intraparty democracy.

46. Zhu Yuwei and Xiang Zeng, "Dangyuan jiecenghua dui dangnei minzhu chansheng de yingxiang" [Influence of stratification of members on intra-party democracy], *Lilun yanjiu* [Theoretical studies], no. 5 (2017): 2021, cited in Shih, "Centralized Leadership," 6, 10.

47. Today, technicians, specialized personnel, and managers make up 25.7 percent of party members, while workers and farmers, retirees, students, and other employees make up 65.9 percent of members. *Xinhua*, June 30, 2018; and Shih, "Centralized Leadership," 6, 10.

48. *Xinhua*, June 30, 2018.

49. Rob Schmitz, "Facial Recognition in China Is Big Business as Local Governments Boost Surveillance," NPR, April 3, 2018, https://www.npr.org/sections/parall els/2018/04/03/598012923/facial-recognition-in-china-is-big-business-as-local-governm ents-boost-surveilla.

50. Mirjam Meissner, "China's Social Credit System," *Merics China Monitor*, Mercator Institute for Chinese Studies, May 24, 2017.

51. Samantha Hoffman, "Managing the State: Social Credit, Surveillance and the CCP's Plan for China," *China Brief* 17, no. 11 (August 17, 2017), https://jamestown.org/ program/managing-the-state-social-credit-surveillance-and-the-ccps-plan-for-china/.

52. Martin Chorzempa, Paul Triolo, and Samm Sacks, "China's Social Credit System: A Mark of Progress or a Threat to Privacy?," *Policy Brief* 18-14, June 2018, Peterson Institute for International Economics, 4–11, https://piie.com/system/files/ documents/pb18-14.pdf.

53. Jean-Pierre Cabestan, "The Many Facets of Chinese Nationalism," *China Perspectives*, no. 59 (May–June 2005): 26–40.

54. Gao Wencheng, "Commentary: To Enjoy the Chinese Film Wolf Warrior II, Shed Your Biases," *Xinhua*, August 16, 2017, http://www.xinhuanet.com/english/2017-08/16/ c_136530175.htm; and Stephen K. Hirst, "'Wolf Warrior 2,' China's Answer to 'Rambo,' Is a Map of the Nation's Future," *Salon*, August 19, 2017, http://www.salon.com/ 2017/08/18/wolf-warrior-2/.

55. Adrian Zenz, "Thoroughly Reforming Them Towards a Healthy Heart Attitude: China's Political Re-Education Campaign in Xinjiang," SocArXiv Papers, September 7, 2018, https://osf.io/preprints/socarxiv/4j6rq/.

FIVE

The Role of Elites

Shaping Political Evolution

The party-state's enduring capacity to fetter civil society makes practically impossible any regime change through societal pressure alone, at least for now. As I discuss later, while some segments of civil society, with their mobilization, can manage to divide the elites, the former are too closely watched, fragmented, and even atomized to kick off a political movement for democratization.

This situation inevitably compels us to turn our gaze on the elites. I have discussed how within the CCP it is they who can hope to exert any influence at all on the political system. But Chinese elites have become increasingly diverse. In this discussion I have included what I call "counter-elites," that is, political activists and dissidents who face risks and dangers in agitating for their country's democratization. Elites and counter-elites are not watertight compartments; as I show here, there are multiple links and contacts among them, albeit discreet if not secret, and powerless in the foreseeable future to upset the state of affairs.

China's political, economic, and intellectual elites today are mostly regime supporters or at least show no sign of organization and even less of mobilization capable of forcing the party-state to evolve toward greater transparency, political opening, and in fine, democracy. Political activists favoring a total democratization of the regime are weak, isolated, and divided and are hounded vigorously and effectively by the authorities.

Economic, political, and international circumstances could well modify this situation in the future and facilitate the emergence of deeper fault-lines among the CCP political elite (see chapter 6). But one should not hope for a democratic impetus from these elites, and even less from economic and intellectual elites mostly dependent on and fed by the regime, as well as acculturated to the party's modus operandi. Both within the party and outside it, liberal currents are weak and marginalized by the New Left, nationalists, neoconservatives, and anti-Western voices. And the former's persistent failure to gain representation in the party's highest echelons blocks any evolution.

PARTY POLITICAL ELITES

The party political elites are probably those we know the least about. Officially they stick to the political line set by the party leadership and are not authorized to air a different opinion, at least in public. Any outside observer would be struck to note how party officials—the approachable ones—carefully stick to the ideas of the current top leaders and regurgitate the priorities set by them; in this sense, such elites are mere political functionaries.

Such apparent unanimity is not anodyne. It is strategic and even vital for the party; after Tiananmen, Deng and his successors drew lessons from the CCP's internal divisions being exposed to international media. Party leaders subsequently reinforced internal instructions warning cadres against any deviation from the line. And even more under Xi Jinping than in earlier periods, a show of unity is the rule and the risks attached to any transgression are high.

Clearly such a demonstration of unanimity is more myth than reality. The fragmentation of power noticed under Hu Jintao has led to public expression of different and rival political plans within the Politburo itself. The contention in the years 2007–2012 between Bo Xilai, then head of the sprawling Chongqing metropolis, and Wang Yang of the affluent Guangdong province best illustrates this. Backed by New Left intellectuals (see below), Bo not only intended to combat corruption and restore to glory the Maoist songs of the Cultural Revolution; he also wanted to introduce a more socialist program of economic development and social protection, and to combat inequalities. These plans had at that time won the backing of many national leaders, including Xi, then PRC vice president and Hu's successor-designate. Conversely, Wang, acclaimed by liberals for having used democratic methods (village committee reelection) to sort out in 2011 (albeit provisionally) the crisis in Wukan, a village unjustly dispossessed of its land, and equally opposed to corruption, prioritized the transformation of Guangdong as an industrial zone featuring high technology and innovation, with help from private and foreign capital. Bo's fall and Xi's rise to power put an end to this rivalry as well as both men's ambitions. But the rival plans of Bo and Wang have continued to divide the leadership and no doubt pit partisans of Xi, closer to Bo, against allies of Premier Li Keqiang, who favor Wang. Wang's promotion to the Politburo Standing Committee in October 2017 and in March 2018 as head of the CPPCC has hardly affected the balance of power, which is increasingly favorable to Xi.

Do the party's main leaders disagree on issues as vital as the political system's future? In the PRC's type of system, democrats in power must necessarily remain concealed until the end, that is, as long as the balance of power is tilted against those favoring an exit from the one-party system. Moreover, the principle of collective leadership fosters prudence rather than a show of initiative: any iconoclastic proposal or isolation within the leadership could lead to removal from power. Conversely, concentration of power in the hands of the party number one—Xi today—places on his shoulders the responsibility for any political reform project, even the least bold.

In 2012 some observers speculated on Xi's proreform inclinations. Their view was that Xi had to first consolidate his power before undertaking "liberal" economic and political reforms he wished to impose. Such speculation, based mainly on reservations expressed by his father, Xi Zhongxun, over the Tiananmen crackdown, has been contradicted by most of the decisions Xi has taken since assuming the top post, including the repression in 2013 of the constitutionalist movement (the arrests of Xu Zhiyong, Pu Zhiqiang, etc.) and in 2015 of more than two hundred rights defense lawyers, as well as increased surveillance of the Internet and foreign NGOs. In the economic sphere, for Xi and his advisers a clearer recourse to market mechanisms has not in the least meant the public sector's marginalization; rather, it has been consolidated and finds itself more assured, thanks to the new behemoths and monopolies established, of continuing to dominate the sectors deemed strategic for the economy.

As already noted, Xi and no doubt a majority of the leadership intend to continue modernizing and improving the one-party system so as to consolidate it and ensure its long-term stability. Those favoring an exit from this system have little chance of being co-opted onto the organization's highest rungs.

This hardly means the leaders agree on everything. Xi's proclaimed priorities and policies have kindled veiled criticisms inside the apparatus. His anticorruption drive sparked a brouhaha leading to stasis and resistance in the face of economic reforms decided soon thereafter. Similarly, in 2016 the fast-deepening public debt divided the leadership, with Xi and his advisers, such as Liu He, wanting to first solve this problem, whereas Premier Li seemed to favor staying with ongoing economic activity and high growth through relaunch plans. Since late 2018, ironically, Xi and Li appear to have swapped positions, the president being now mainly worried about the economic slowdown and social stability. Further, the status Xi acquired in 2016 as "core" of the party leadership; the enshrining of his ideas officially as "thought" during the 19th Party Congress; and his decision, approved in March 2018, to revise the state constitution so that he can stay in power for ten more years—that is beyond 2022–2023 if not for life—have met with far from unanimous acclaim. And the party's uproar against Xi has intensified since the summer of 2018, also fed by the growing trade war with the United States.

But identifying such divergences remains arduous and subject to multiple uncertainties. Moreover, they have no bearing on the country's general political orientation; currently it can be said there is consensus among the nomenklatura to pursue modernization and consolidation of the one-party system based on the methods and within the limits prescribed from above. It can also be said that a majority probably favors investing Xi with greater powers than his predecessors had, the better to confront gathering storms. Among the motivations of the nomenklatura, it is obvious that they have too much to lose politically, economically, and socially if there is any challenge to the current state of affairs.

This does not mean that CCP leaders are not influenced by economic or intellectual elites or even counter-elites. The economic elites' influence has persuaded them to accept several major policy and legal changes, such as the private sector's inexorable expansion, now representing 60 percent of GNP, and greater protection of intellectual property. The economic elites have also corrupted the party leaders. But they have not in any way sought to persuade them to open up the political arena (see below). Nor have the intellectual elites done so, because despite pluralism of ideas catching on, the regime has made sure that such elites are dominated by the New Left and the nationalists, sidelining liberals and democrats (see below). One might even go further and suggest that divisions in the country's policy direction and even in the party-state apparatus reflect this imposed and distorted balance of power observed among opinion groups. As for counter-elites, in the current context of repression, it is impossible to measure their influence on the most reformist of Chinese leaders.

ECONOMIC ELITES

It is hardly easier to gauge economic elites' opinions regarding the political system's future. These elites are still made up of two distinct segments: on the one hand state sector administrators and managers, and on the other private entrepreneurs. While we would be right to be interested in the former's political tendencies, the latter, given the bourgeoisie's historic role in the Marxist sense—owners of the means of production—in the rise of democracy in the West, must receive all our attention here. State sector officials, being appointed by the CCP and mostly belonging to it, are more akin to the political elites discussed previously than to private entrepreneurs. One might say they remain divided on the public policy issues discussed previously or by competing interests rather than by a hypothetical exit from the current political system. In any case, as cadres, they are forbidden to express their political ideas in public and few test this rule because of the risks to their careers. I therefore concentrate here on private entrepreneurs.

First of all it should be noted that the distinction just made is not as neat as is often believed: the ownership structures of a number of private businesses, and not insignificant ones, are far from clear. For example, Lenovo, which bought IBM in 2005, is registered in Hong Kong and is thus largely private, but the Chinese Academy of Sciences, equivalent to France's CNRS (National Centre for Scientific Research), which helped set it up in 1984, still holds 36 percent of its shares. Huawei, the well-known private telecommunications firm based in Shenzhen, was founded by Ren Zhengfei, a former PLA officer who enjoys especially close relations with the party-state, leading to deep suspicions about the

nature and aims of the company long before his daughter, Meng Wan-
zhou, was arrested in December 2018 in Canada at the request of the
United States, which has sought her extradition for violation of Iran sanctions. More generally, a number of private entrepreneurs who "jumped
into the sea" (*xiahai*) in the 1990s or later are former party cadres who
have retained multiple links to it.[1]

Equally important, the private sector's status remains relatively precarious in China. The idea of "privatization" is still largely taboo. The
authorities prefer to speak of the "nonpublic" sector (*feigongyouzhi*). More
so under Xi than his predecessors, the party leadership accords priority
to state enterprises and promotes cooperation between public and private
sectors, especially in R&D and innovation. The big bosses of China's new
capitalism remain vulnerable, on "ejection seats" as it were, with the
party keeping the option of dropping them for the slightest economic or
political folly. Examples of sudden falls abound. The detention in 2017 of
Wu Xiaohui (worth $4.5 billion), head of Anbang insurance group, de-
spite his being Deng's grandson-in-law, is just one of the most recent.

In such conditions, it is no surprise that most "private" entrepreneurs
are legitimists; all studies on the issue tend to show—not without a certain consistency since early in the 2000s—loyalty to the regime and a
feeble inclination for democracy.[2] Those among them who risk being
seen as reformers or criticizing the political system constitute a tiny minority. And generally they remain guarded in their reproaches, focusing
for instance on public policy issues such as antipollution measures or
migrant workers' protection. Those calling for political reform or even
associating with activists seeking evolution in the system are quite rare.

Among the most politicized of businessmen is Wang Gongquan, an
investor who did not hesitate to financially back the New Citizens Movement (*xin gongmin yundong*), an informal political group founded in 2010
promoting citizen awareness and more generally constitutionalism until
its repression and the jailing of its leaders, including Xu Zhiyong, in 2013
(see below). For urging their release, Wang was himself detained for a
few months that year, and his blog (1.5 million followers on Sina Weibo)
was shut down. Since his release in January 2014, Wang has been much
more careful, but with others such as Pan Shiyi (16 million followers),
founder of Soho China property group, he continues to seek greater
transparency on the government's part, especially regarding environ-

mental protection, and for businesses to contribute more to social progress.

In March 2016 Ren Zhiqiang, a property tycoon (thirty-eight million followers), was in the news for openly defying Xi's injunctions that the media should strictly follow the party line. Ren declared that rather than serving the party, media must "serve the people." He got off with a minor sanction: a year's probation from the CCP, of which he is a member. Said to be a protégé of Wang Qishan, then in charge of party discipline, he escaped expulsion. However, his microblog was suspended. The fracas ended there.[3]

Equally interesting is the third example, Liu Chuanzhi, founder of Lenovo (and Legend Holdings), who regularly targets private entrepreneurs' lack of courage and social responsibility—in short, their timidity and self-centeredness. However, in an opinion piece published in *Caijing* magazine in October 2012, he opposed the election of "political leaders" through universal suffrage at least "in the near future," preferring their selection by "elites of the society." Nevertheless, worried about corruption, he said China must give priority to establishing a "rule of law" (*fazhi*), that is, better legal safeguards. Representative of business circles (although the precise extent of its popularity cannot be gauged), this viewpoint is shared by an intellectual current, as discussed later. It could also be the opinion of large segments of the Hong Kong establishment, especially those overrepresented thanks to the "functional constituencies" (thirty of seventy seats) in the Special Administrative Region's Legislative Council. A semidemocracy that gives top billing to elites: isn't this what privileged Chinese dream of?

Since then, no doubt influenced by the Xi-imposed "new normal," Liu has become more circumspect, advising businessmen to avoid airing their views when political conditions are not favorable and at any rate never to cross the "red line."[4] This has earned him some criticism from his "liberal" entrepreneur friends and led him to nuance his pronouncements; later, adjusting his stance but not taking risks, he admitted that it was difficult for economic elites to avoid being interested in politics.[5]

As a final example, some private economy figures have advanced iconoclastic ideas. In a November 2016 interview with the business news site Yicai, Liu Qiangdong, chairman and CEO of e-commerce giant JD.com, who ranks thirtieth on the *Forbes* China Rich List (worth $6.7 billion), said that with the technological advances of recent years, communism or "a society with neither poor nor rich people and with all companies nationalized" could indeed be achieved in the near future.[6] Though not entirely following suit, Jack Ma, head of Alibaba and China's richest man (worth $39 billion) voiced his backing in May 2017 for the adoption of a planned economy with the gradual conquest of big data, remarking, "We may thus be able to find the invisible hand of the market."[7]

While these statements had the manifest intention of flattering the regime and perhaps also protecting the speakers, they were corrected by party experts, who asked the representatives of economic elites to be more careful in using the term "communism." This was perhaps owing to a rash of sarcasm that such comments by rich capitalists provoked online rather than due to the sacred nature of the concept in the party's official statutes.[8]

Thus, private entrepreneurs do not always avoid politics and despite Xi avoid it less than before. As for intellectual elites or counter-elites, fame, connections, or age protect them or at least render them less vulnerable and more audacious, such as in the cases of Lenovo's Liu and the tycoon Ren Zhiqiang. In general these entrepreneurs are careful, at least in public, given their dependence on the regime and the risks any political engagement entails. Thus, among the first 303 signatories of Charter 08, drafted in 2008 by Liu Xiaobo (see below), there were just 17 businessmen.[9]

More crucially, a majority of entrepreneurs are seeking out a path in the current political system, especially in formal institutions. They are also largely behind growing inequalities, lack of mobility, and greater elitism in society, often belonging themselves to the privileged class since the Mao era and sometimes even before 1949.[10]

Their influence on the party-state has incontestably increased. At the local and even national levels, major private entrepreneurs have acquired an unspoken political role. It could take institutional form through their participation in people's congresses or people's consultative conferences, whose relative powerlessness has already been discussed, but it is mostly done through chambers of commerce and industry. Although officially under the party-state's tutelage, these chambers have become business lobbies that the regime has to reckon with; studies on the ground bear this out. New capitalists' regular donations to foundations and other charitable organizations contribute to boosting their influence and fame and thus their function as role models in society.

Political influence can also be informal. The very economic weight of major entrepreneurs imposes on the politico-administrative authorities new constraints, forcing them to form alliances with these new actors. Ma Huateng, also known as Pony Ma, CEO of Tencent (second on the *Forbes* China Rich List and worth $38.5 billion); Jack Ma of Alibaba; and Ren Zhengfei of Huawei (eighty-third on *Forbes* China Rich List and worth $2 billion) are by no means strong enough to defy Xi and in any case would definitely avoid attempting anything of that sort. Their strategy consists more of being able to steer in a favorable direction public policies that concern their own businesses and obtaining as many guarantees and protections as possible from the party-state.[11] Such roles and political influence are not without limits. Restrictions imposed by the government in 2017 on major private actors wanting to invest abroad and spread their companies' risks—such as Wanda, Fosun, and HNA (Hainan Airlines)— show that the private sector's mounting strength has worried the authorities. These groups' bosses—Wang Jianlin, until 2016 China's richest man (then worth $30 billion; number 4, with $23.4 billion in 2019); Guo Guangchang (number 26, $7.5 billion); and Chen Feng (number 205, $1.7 billion), all three of whom are CCP members—have at times and in varying degrees been at odds with the authorities. Jack Ma's sudden announcement of his retirement as Alibaba CEO in September 2018 has also underscored the CCP's persistent influence on China's new tycoons, the Chinese government making public at the same time Ma's early decision to join the party in the 1980s.[12]

Labeled "gray rhinos" (*hui xiniu*) in view of the generous state-owned bank loans they have obtained thanks to their high-level connections, some companies have tended to act and invest with a freedom logically flowing from the Chinese economy's globalization, but also possibly going against the party-state's interests. This is one of the major contradictions of the Chinese political system: some of its economic decisions are motivated more by clientelism than by financial considerations or profitability.

This contradiction was glaringly revealed through the case of billionaire Guo Wengui, founder of Beijing Zenith Holdings, who in 2013 sought refuge in the United States. From there he launched regular attacks against leaders who had betrayed him, such as Wang Qishan, then in charge of discipline inspection in the party, and Chen Feng, the head of HNA, whose cover-ups Guo denounced. No democrat himself, Guo had enjoyed protection from a number of now-fallen leaders, including Ma Jian, former vice minister of public security. Guo declared backing for Xi and attacked systemic corruption, prominently including that of Wang, who retired in October 2017 before being elevated in March 2018 to the vice presidency of the People's Republic. It was no doubt a defense strategy, and many aspects of the affair lack credibility and remain unclear. Similar is the case of the January 2017 abduction from Hong Kong and illegal repatriation to the mainland by Chinese Public Security officials of billionaire investor Xiao Jianhua. His role as manager of the fortunes of many in the nomenklatura, including Xi's elder sister (Qi Qiaoqiao) and brother-in-law (Deng Jiagui), as well as his links to Wanda, were said to have led to his arrest.[13] Guo's revelations and Xiao's disappearance highlight the complexity and closeness of relations between the party-state and private entrepreneurs.

These turns of events also shed light on the autonomization of major groups and their ability, at least for a while, to get around state-imposed restrictions. What will this incestuous as well as complicated relationship between the party and private entrepreneurs lead to? For now the CCP has managed to keep the latter on a leash, at least up to a point. This could well change, especially in the event of economic recession or social crisis, because more than ever before the regime needs the private sector to ensure growth and create jobs. But the new elites' dependence on the party indisputably blocks change.

Barrington Moore coined the famous phrase: "No bourgeoisie, no democracy."[14] Will China disprove this statement by one of the American fathers of historical institutionalism? For now, the answer is yes. As Kellee Tsai has shown, a majority of private entrepreneurs believe the political system generally "works for them."[15] But perhaps it will be "no" in the long term, as China's twentieth-century history and today's private entrepreneurs' desire for independence, as well as their crucial economic role, could eventually prove Moore right.[16] That being so, and as discussed presently, the bourgeoisie's autonomization remains a necessary but insufficient condition in any democratization process, especially in China.

INTELLECTUAL ELITES

What role can intellectual elites play in any evolution of the political system in China? On the one hand, there has been an intellectual renewal since the start of reforms. Despite Tiananmen, debates among academics and more generally "public intellectuals" (*gonggong zhishifenzi*) on China's future politics have been rich, pluralistic, and lively. These debates have featured different schools of thought that gradually emerged after 1989, notably the so-called (at times pejoratively) New Left (*xinzuopai*), cultural and Confucian nationalists, neoconservatives, and liberals, to name just the main groups.[17] The fragmentation noted in the 1990s was followed by a form of Left-Right polarization, especially between the New Left and liberals, which must be understood in the opposite sense of Left and Right in the West, with Chinese intellectuals deemed to be conservative and favoring retention of an authoritarian political system representing the Left and reformers and democrats in the political arena constituting the Right.

On the other hand, censorship, repression, the near-totality of intellectuals' financial dependence on the party-state, and the latter's own ideological needs fundamentally distort the balance of power among these schools of thought, giving much greater weight to all the nonliberals and especially the conservative, nationalistic, and often neo-Confucian Left that favors "meritocracy" or "Chinese democracy" than to supporters of a Western-style, electoral, and pluralistic democracy. Visible since the early 1990s and constantly manipulated by the CCP, this imbalance has accentuated since Xi's rise to power. Of course some liberals close to counter-elites, whom I discuss later, continue to speak out. But they need to be extra careful and have often been reduced to silence.

This balance of power and the nature and at times incoherence of propositions advanced by those whom Emilie Frenkiel calls "organic intellectuals" has other causes, often for the older ones more generational and linked to the traumatic experience of the Cultural Revolution and at times deeper and more structural, stemming from the fundamental rupture the establishment of the PRC in 1949 constituted (see chapter 2). Thus, all idea of revolution is mostly banned, and only reform may improve the political system or show a way out. It is striking to note, as discussed later, the extent to which Chinese intellectuals using the pretext of a return to Confucianism or traditional political culture remain "for-

matted" by CCP ideology and its interpretation of otherwise liberal concepts such as democracy, freedom, and subjective rights.[18]

Stated simply, while most Chinese intellectuals—though not all—
seem to favor their political system's evolution toward democracy, as
does much of Chinese society (see chapter 3), there is profound misunderstanding about the concept's meaning. Some intellectuals, such as
Yu Keping, the best known reformist thinker in the CCP, adhere to the
party's definition of "socialist democracy," merely seeking under liberal
pretexts (such as suggesting an extension of local elections) to perfect and
legitimize its functioning.[19] Others, such as People's University professor
Yang Guangbin, argue that China is already largely democratic, given the
party-state's gradual adoption of consultation mechanisms and the attention accorded to various interest groups in society. Yet others, such as
Tsinghua University's Cui Zhiyuan, former adviser to Bo Xilai in Chongqing, believe China can democratize even while retaining the one-party
system. He argues that the CCP represents the government of the majority both because its internal functioning is democratized and because it
remains the best guarantor against diverse interest groups; "economic
democracy"—that is, combating inequalities—is more important than
electoral democracy; and China, with its institutional innovations, has
established a new political "model." Another Bo ex-confidant, Wang
Shaoguang, who has for long taught at the Chinese University of Hong
Kong, shares these ideas, opposing what he calls "substantial democracy"—deemed to be more participative and more equal to electoral democracy—whose weaknesses and distortions he vehemently denounces.
Rather than elections, for Wang and others such as Hu Angang, the priority is the state's strengthening and modernization, a well-known obsession of late Qing reformers (see chapter 2). A similar preoccupation
prominently underpins the work of New Left thinker Wang Hui, who
believes that China can modernize Marxism as well as socialism in adapting it to globalization while at the same time keeping its one-party system. To do so, Wang proposes "repoliticizing" a CCP that is too much
affected by "statism" or reintroducing in it internal theoretical debates
and political struggles with the help of Mao's "mass line" as a way to
increase political participation.[20]

Much more than among these New Left figures, the promotion of the
"Chinese model" finds favor with Confucian nationalists such as Tsinghua professor Kang Xiaoguang, who claims its authorship. Elitism and

meritocracy are for him the foundations of this model, which should abandon Marxism and rebase its ideology on traditional Chinese political culture.

Some Chinese intellectuals, and not only liberals, have an understanding of democracy close to the Western one, holding it to be incompatible with the retention of a one-party system and with the repression of anyone opposing it. However, that does not mean they want such a democracy introduced in China. Many of them are fiercely opposed to that idea. That is the case with cultural nationalists such as Kang Xiaoguang and Jiang Qing, founder of the Yangming Academy in Guizhou. The same is true of Peking University's Pan Wei, who ardently believes in the possibility of establishing a rule of law without democracy, somewhat like Singapore, although that city-state has in fact adopted a certain measure of electoral pluralism (see chapter 6). Similarly, Gan Yang, a former liberal, now advocates the establishment of a "Confucian socialist republic." And some, such as Kang Xiaoguang and Jiang Qing, go further: while promoting "Confucian constitutionalism," they also wish to institutionalize Confucianism and restore its status as the guiding ideology of the country and a state religion.[21]

Another group, mainly gathered around "neoauthoritarian" and "neoconservative" scholars such as Shanghai Normal University's Xiao Gongqin, thinks that given the population's "insufficient quality" (*suzhi di*), China is not ripe for democracy. This idea is widespread among political elites and in urban society, particularly its middle classes. These intellectuals believe an authoritarian transition is necessary and must be based on Chinese political and ideological tradition in order to maintain national cohesion. This viewpoint is part of Chinese political thought of the twentieth century, at the start of which reformers of the empire such as Liang Qichao belatedly and for the same reasons became partisans of "enlightened despotism" (*kaiming zhuanzhi*) (see chapter 2). But Xiao Gongqin does not oppose democracy itself, saying it can be adopted when the middle classes dominate in society.[22] For this reason, he tends to favor a Taiwan-style evolution in China.

Xiao is not alone in advocating this gradualist and peaceful path to democratization. Some jurists, such as Shanghai Jiao Tong University's Ji Weidong, hold that the advent of rule of law and greater respect for established procedures should precede it: a rather original idea in the PRC, where traditionally legal procedures are neglected.[23]

This penchant for gradualism is also shared by most liberals and democratic counter-elites. It originated in an understandable rejection of revolution immortalized by Li Zehou and Liu Zaifu in their 1995 book *Gaobie geming* (Farewell to revolution), a view shared by bloggers such as Han Han. This attitude also stems from a visceral criticism of radicalism, one of the best-known representatives of this view being Confucian thinker and democrat Yu Ying-shih, long settled in the United States.[24]

Liberal intellectuals are as disunited as members of other schools of thought; some are reformers solely in economic matters and thus prioritize the rise of the private sector and market mechanisms. But most, concerned about social and political consequences of ongoing economic growth, favor an extension of freedoms, greater bureaucratic transparency, a real development of pluralistic elections, and a gradual evolution toward a constitutional democracy ending the CCP's monopolistic power, even if this last and ultimate objective often remains unexpressed.[25]

Zhu Xueqin, who has long taught at Shanghai University, is representative of this liberal current, as also are figures such as Xu Youyu, Qin Hui, Li Qiang, Yao Yang, He Weifang, and Liu Junning, despite some differences among them. Xu, a former Red Guard and later victim of the Cultural Revolution, who retired from the Chinese Academy of Social Sciences (CASS), opposes copying American or European political systems without adaptation. Tsinghua professor Qin is the main promoter in China of social democracy, hoping without success thus far to reconcile liberals and the New Left. Peking University's Li is more nuanced; he acknowledges the CCP's achievements in building and modernizing the state but thinks the issue of constitutionalism and democratization remains untouched and sooner or later will need to be addressed. Somewhat like Yu Ying-shih, Peking University economist Yao Yang holds Chinese tradition to be compatible with liberal democracy. The same institution's law professor He Weifang wants to prioritize judicial reform and autonomization of courts.[26] Finally, former CASS scholar Liu, often seen as a proponent of liberalism, has sought to establish the Chinese roots of liberalism. Like Xu, He, and many other liberals, he too signed Charter 08, drafted by Liu Xiaobo, calling for China's gradual democratization. To this list may be added some economists worried about rigidities of the political system and structural obstacles to economic reforms and thus to the pursuit of sustainable growth—simply put, over the prospect of a middle-income trap (see chapter 6). However, most economists avoid venturing into the political reform terrain.[27]

Thus the liberals' links with the counter-elites are many, and one hesitates to put liberals who have identified with the constitutionalist movement in the camp of "organic intellectuals," seeing how they are muzzled and threatened by the authorities. This hesitation also concerns former communists close to Hu Yaobang and Zhao Ziyang, the two major reformers of the 1980s, lately turned liberals (in the Chinese sense of the term) of the social democratic tendency, such as Li Rui (who died in February 2019 at age 101) or Du Daozheng, and until July 2016 gathered around the magazine *Yanhuang Chunqiu*.[28] After the publication was suspended and put under the control of "intellectuals" close to the regime, the liberal current was clearly reduced to silence and marginalized. This silence is likely to never be complete. In July 2018, Xu Zhangrun, professor of constitutional law at Tsinghua University, wrote an open criticism of Xi Jinping's dictatorial inclinations, including his decision to perpetuate his reign, which, although censured in China, has been widely circulated among the elites. While more than a hundred Chinese academics openly supported him, Xu has been banned from teaching and put under investigation.[29]

Consequently, chances are that most "organic intellectuals" in the full sense of the term can only continue to back the regime and help it along the authoritarian path, rather than play a catalyzing role in its democratization. It may be added that most Chinese experts on international relations, while not directly taking part in these debates, base their analyses and their optimistic projections on China's rise to the top rung of major powers on the maintenance of a strong and authoritarian party-state. These experts are thus for the most part opposed to any democratization or even liberalization of the political system; they cannot even contemplate such a prospect.[30]

This argument may be taken further, advancing the idea that the New Left and cultural nationalists, who are close to the regime and dominate official media, have become dangerous through their influence. Not only are their theories the result of intellectual patchwork that only some, like Peking University philosopher Liu Dong, recognize as being haphazard, but they knowingly present a "distorted" definition of democracy.[31] In fact, how is one to believe, for instance, that inner-party democratization—a process about which there is no tangible proof and which hasn't at all prevented the CCP from remaining a secret society—can constitute the first step toward the country's democratization? Or that rule of law can emerge with the courts remaining under the CCP's control? Or that the party has decided to give priority to reducing social inequalities, when they glaringly continue to deepen? Promoting a social Darwinism introduced by Yan Fu in the nineteenth century and an unswerving elitism, defending a major part of Maoist heritage, and unreservedly criticizing Taiwan's democracy, these conservative intellectuals are in reality sycophants of the regime and harbingers of an ideological fight against values the West champions.

This balance of power could change, of course, but that ultimately depends on the evolution of the political system and thus among political elites. The good news is that among liberal intellectuals and even neoconservatives, as well as some economists, there exist multiple affinities with counter-elites that a change in political circumstances could buttress. Voluntarily suppressed now, these often iconoclastic discussions of the 1980s constitute a precedent in this regard.[32] The bad news is that most intellectual elites believe China's economic success and the pursuit of its rise to power depend on retaining the current regime. They continue to depend pathologically on the party-state and the discourse it propagates in the society. They also help render this discourse credible and ensure its dominance in society. And the CCP leadership will for long continue to do all it can to vilify the Taiwan experience and promote a Singapore-inspired model without, however, opening up the political arena (see chapter 6).

COUNTER-ELITES

I define counter-elites as activists and public intellectuals who are frequently gagged and repressed by the party-state because of their political criticism of the current regime and their legal or illegal, but legitimate, actions or stances aimed at steering it toward democracy. If this definition of counter-elites is accepted, it includes human rights lawyers who are fighting against administrative and judicial arbitrariness; political activists seeking, most often unsuccessfully, to contest local people's congresses' elections at the grassroot levels (townships and counties); those behind the constitutionalist movement, now mostly behind bars or under constant surveillance; and all those who have openly sought to create a political movement, even an opposition party, and have risked arrest or immediate dismantling of their organizations. Needless to say, all such initiatives are closely watched by the Public Security authorities and, if there is an external ramification, those of State Security. They have therefore little hope of success.

Three important questions arise: (1) What is the size and influence of these counter-elites, both within the society in general and among elites in particular? (2) If their movement were to spread, would Public Security authorities be able to continue keeping tabs on them? (3) How can the counter-elites play a role in a future evolution of the political system?

Today the counter-elites and their movements are weak, divided, and marginal. First of all, given China's size, counter-elites seem minuscule. Constituted following the Sun Zhigang incident in 2003—in which a student was found dead in a repatriation center for illegal migrants—the "rights protection movement" (*weiquan yundong*) probably counts no more than 1,000 lawyers out of a total of 300,000 in the country. At that time the incident sparked strong reactions among jurists and forced the government to abolish the rule regarding migrants' repatriation.[33] But activist lawyers quickly realized the limits imposed by the regime. And the repression their movement was subjected to in July 2015—some 200 of them being arrested—seems to have halted their expansion, although most human rights defenders were subsequently released.[34]

Charter 08, drafted by Liu Xiaobo and others and advocating a constitutional and democratic system, was initially signed by just 303 public figures and eventually garnered around 10,000 signatures, including from a number of dissidents living abroad.[35] The New Citizens Movement (*Zhongguo xin gongmin yundong*), founded in 2010 to promote the constitutionalist struggle and led by Xu Zhiyong, Teng Biao, and Pu Zhiqiang, has perhaps five thousand members and at most ten thousand, since the repression and the arrest of its leaders, including Xu and Pu, in 2013.[36]

Divergences in aims and strategies have contributed to fragmenting this network that favors China's democratization. Full-time activist lawyers are few in number and do not belong to a "movement" as such, while those who occasionally take on a delicate case prefer to keep their distance from the full-time activist lawyers. Waves of repression against these de facto or genuine political movements have also divided and weakened them, persuading some to be more careful and others, such as Teng Biao, to go into exile, first in Hong Kong and then the United States.

These recent crackdowns have also led some activists to challenge the gradualism advocated by most Chinese reformers. Illustrating this new fragmentation is these more radical activists' criticism of what they called Liu Xiaobo's "moderatism" and even "capitulationism"; at the end of his trial Liu famously said, "I have no enemies."[37]

Marginalization of counter-elites is evident. It is striking to note that the great majority of Chinese people are ignorant of the very existence of people like Liu Xiaobo, who died of cancer in 2017 while serving an eleven-year jail sentence, or of the rights protection movement. This lack of knowledge about and indifference toward the fates of the leaders of these movements are shared and amplified by most mainstream intellectuals, highlighting the lack of political and moral consciousness in Chinese society today.

Nevertheless, despite the asymmetry of their struggle against the regime, Chinese political activists are today more numerous, and the influence of their ideas is growing, including inside the party. Charter 08 had greater reverberations among elite officials than is generally believed. The large number of influential figures who signed it, not only from among academics and intellectuals but also writers, artists, and businesspeople—8,484 including a few living abroad—worried the authorities.[38] Added to that was the awarding of the 2009 Nobel Peace Prize to Liu, given the international as well as internal repercussions of the decision. And despite Liu's immediate arrest and sentencing to a stiff jail term for "inciting subversion of state power," signatories such as the economist Mao Yushi, lawyer Mo Shaoping, and former local deputy Yao Lifa did not desert the cause or give up the struggle. On the contrary, a number of them have rallied behind the constitutionalist movement, which continues to progress despite the jailing of its leaders.

Obviously, for the foreseeable future the authorities will keep wielding the means for watching over and even microcontrolling the potential troublemakers and will contain their public expression. But the multiplication of repressive measures by Xi exposes a paranoia that, from a security point of view, is probably justified. Real or illusory, the specter of "color revolution" (*yanse geming*) has reappeared in China.[39]

In other words, the spread of democratic ideas and the interest among substantial sections of Chinese society in Taiwan's democratic transition and experience and, particularly in the country's south, in Hong Kong's resistance against Beijing's authoritarian objectives since the 2014 Umbrella Movement, worry the CCP.[40] It has therefore sought to limit Taiwan-bound tourism and keeps a close watch on young Chinese studying in Hong Kong or Taiwan. In general, the multiplication of relations among counter-elites inside and outside the country, especially those living in the United States, has led to an increase in such surveillance, but this raises the issues of financial and practical limits, as well as their effectiveness.

Charter 08's publication resulted from a relative relaxation of control over civil society. In the 2000s, the Gongmeng group (Open Constitution Initiative) was founded following the Sun Zhigang incident, at the initiative of Charter 08 signatories Xu Zhiyong and Teng Biao, then was dismantled in 2009. By several accounts, the repression that followed Charter 08's publication, and even more that let loose after Xi's rise to power, surprised the democrats, who had wrongly thought the time had come to air their demands. As early as 2008, the party-state became convinced it had to be more vigilant. The Arab Spring of 2011 only added to its nervousness.

Clearly China is still far from the tipping point where the cost of repression becomes prohibitive, that is, higher than that of political opening and reform. In fact the party-state has already invested a great deal of money in surveillance of society, above all of counter-elites, and it has the financial and technical means, notably thanks to big data, to sink even more resources into surveillance, so dependent is the long-term survival of the regime on such methods.

However, the authorities face a dilemma: they want to keep silencing all political opposition, but changes in society, the country's opening, and external pressures are compelling them to moderate their repressive measures. For instance, among the Charter 08 signatories, Liu Xiaobo was the only one to have been dragged before the courts. Five years later Xu Zhiyong was given just a four-year prison term. Lawyer Pu Zhiqiang, arrested in 2014, got a relatively minor sentence—three years suspended—before being released, though of course he was barred from practicing law. Most other activists and dissidents are subject to costly surveillance measures, requiring numerous security personnel, that are less and less dissuasive. More seriously, these developments deepen the distance between state and society, weakening the impact of its political discourse and of its aggressive stances while on the other hand gradually pushing the society—especially its urban and educated parts, given their lifestyles and daily experiences—toward the liberal and democratic ideas developed by the counter-elites.

By being lenient toward those who make honorable amends and treating recalcitrants harshly (*tanbai congkuan, kangju congyan*), the authorities seem to believe they have found the best solution for containing political activism. Thus on December 26, 2017, while lawyer Xie Yang, who had modified his initial deposition under torture and confessed ("incitation to subversion of state power"), was freed, blogger Wu Gan was sentenced to eight years' imprisonment for refusing to admit his crime ("subversion of state power"). Nevertheless, it is unlikely that the movement for better protection of human rights and political freedoms will end anytime soon.

At present it is impossible to measure this current's influence in society or among political and intellectual elites. I close this section on counter-elites by advancing the hypothesis that the vast majority of Chinese society remains both indifferent to politics and under the constant influence of CCP discourse, and that official elites are being mobilized against liberal ideas in a struggle more bitter than is often supposed.

Liu Xiaobo's death was an occasion for some democrats, such as Wang Dan, one of the student activists during Tiananmen and now based in Washington, DC, to compare him to politicians who, during the Qing dynasty, tried to reform the empire: while Liu followed Kang Youwei's path, Wang said, he shed his blood like Tan Sitong, a reformer who was decapitated in 1898 following the failure of the Hundred Days' Reform.[41] Although Liu was not executed, the comparison is quite apt; who in the time of Kang and Tan would have believed they would become heroes in China's political modernization? While Liu could never enjoy the Czech statesman Václav Havel's turn of fortune, he could well occupy an equal place in Chinese history.

CONCLUSION

Which segment of Chinese elites can get things moving? Certainly not the party's political elites or a majority of intellectual elites, at least in the short term. There is a potential for politicization among private entrepreneurs, but they continue to appear defenseless, vulnerable, and most reluctant to take risks to advance any cause other than their own economic interests, in the current Xi-imposed "new normal." As for counter-elites, they need to await better days just to raise their heads. Consequently, the almost patently "class" alliance, a brazen one, among the party-state nomenklatura, new capitalists, and large segments of the intellectual elite has good prospects of remaining invincible in the decade or two ahead.

At the same time, another coalition of liberal elites, counter-elites, and some elements among economic elites is also emerging. Charter 08 was its first, albeit stuttering, expression. The party-state will certainly do all it can to nip in the bud, contain, or divide any coalition favoring political change, should one be formed.

What can change things is discussed in the next chapter. This chapter sought to show the elites' essential role in any future exit from the current political system. It should be borne in mind that such a change or political rupture can generally be the work of a limited number of actors. Democratization processes in South Korea and Taiwan demonstrate that. Civil society and the society as a whole will join in only if initiatives taken by counter-elites and other initially minority movements succeed in influencing and mobilizing substantial segments of the more conservative elites and then manage to exert pressure on the authorities, fracturing them and eventually forcing the regime to change.

NOTES

1. Huang Yasheng, *Capitalism with Chinese Characteristics: Entrepreneurship and the State* (New York: Cambridge University Press, 2008). See also Carl Walter and Fraser Howie, *Red Capitalism: The Fragile Financial Foundation of China's Extraordinary Rise* (Singapore: Wiley, 2012).

2. Bruce J. Dickson, *Red Capitalists in China: The Party, Private Entrepreneurs, and Prospects for Political Change* (Cambridge, UK: Cambridge University Press, 2003); Marie-Claire Bergère, *Capitalismes et capitalistes en Chine: Des origines à nos jours* [Capitalisms and capitalists in China: Origins to the present day] (Paris: Perrin, 2007); Kellee Tsai, *Capitalism without Democracy: The Private Sector in Contemporary China* (Ithaca, NY: Cornell University Press, 2007); Bruce J. Dickson, *Wealth into Power: The Communist Party's Embrace of China's Private Sector* (New York: Cambridge University Press, 2008); and Jie Chen and Bruce J. Dickson, *Allies of the State: China's Private Entrepreneurs and Democratic Change* (Cambridge, MA: Harvard University Press, 2010).

3. "China Puts a Tycoon, Ren Zhiqiang, on Probation for Criticizing Policies," *New York Times*, May 2, 2016, https://www.nytimes.com/2016/05/03/world/asia/china-ren-zhiqiang.html?mcubz=3.

4. Simon Denyer, "China's Reluctant Entrepreneurs," *Guardian*, September 3, 2013, https://www.theguardian.com/world/2013/sep/03/china-reluctant-entrepreneurs.

5. Amy Li, "Lenovo's Founder Liu Chuanzhi 'Talks Politics' Again," *SCMP*, January 1, 2014, https://www.scmp.com/news/china-insider/article/1394668/lenovos-founder-liu-chuanzhi-talks-politics-again.

6. *Forbes*, February 26, 2019, https://www.forbes.com/profile/richard-liu-1/#8dfbc 36182d9; all other Chinese private entrepreneurs' ranking and wealth estimates are from the same *Forbes* webpage. "Technology Can Help Realize Communism: JD.com CEO," *Global Times*, August 20, 2017, http://www.globaltimes.cn/content/1062242. shtml.

7. "Can Big Data Help to Resurrect the Planned Economy?," *Global Times*, June 14, 2017, http://www.globaltimes.cn/content/1051715.shtml.

8. Shan Jie, "Tycoons Spark Discussion on Realization of Communism," *Global Times*, August 21, 2017, http://www.globaltimes.cn/content/1062482.shtml.

9. Zhang Zuhua and Li Xiaorong, eds., *Lingba xianzhang* [Charter 08] (Hong Kong: Kaifang chubanshe, 2009), 16–25.

10. David S. G. Goodman, "The Changing Face of China's Local Elite: Elite Advantage and Path Dependence in Business Communities," *Chinese Political Science Review* 3, no. 2 (2018): 115–128.

11. On how large-tech groups such as Alibaba are "co-opted into national policies," see Duncan Clark, *Alibaba: The House That Jack Ma Built* (New York: HarperCollins, 2016); see also Louise Lucas, "The Chinese Communist Party Entangles Big Tech," *Financial Times*, July 20, 2018, 7.

12. "How Jack Ma Changed the Chinese View of Entrepreneurs," *Knowledge@wharton*, September 25, 2018, http://knowledge.wharton.upenn.edu/article/how-will-alibaba-fare-without-jack-ma/.

13. Michael Forsythe, "A Missing Tycoon's Links to China's Troubled Dalian Wanda," *New York Times*, August 10, 2017, https://www.nytimes.com/2017/08/10/business/dealbook/china-wanda-xiao-jianhua.html. The Panama Papers had also revealed that in 2016 Deng Jiagui had offshore bank accounts in Panama; see Michael Forsythe, "Panama Papers Tie More of China's Elite to Secret Accounts," *New York Times*, April 6, 2016, https://www.nytimes.com/2016/04/07/world/asia/china-panama-papers.html.

14. Barrington Moore, *Social Origins of Dictatorship and Democracy: Lord and Peasant in the Making of the Modern World* (Boston: Beacon Press, 1966).

15. Tsai, *Capitalism without Democracy*; see also Kellee Tsai, "Cause or Consequence? Private Sector Development and Communist Resilience in China," in *Why Communism Did Not Collapse: Understanding Regime Resilience in Asia and Europe*, ed. Martin Dimitrov (Cambridge, UK: Cambridge University Press, 2013), 205–236.

16. Bergère, *Capitalismes et capitalistes en Chine*.

17. Timothy Cheek, David Ownby, and Joshua Fogel, "Mapping the Intellectual Public Sphere in China Today," *China Information* 32, no. 1 (March 2018): 107–120; and the five reports included in this issue as well as *China Information* 32, no. 2 (June 2018). See also Emilie Frenkiel, *Conditional Democracy: The Contemporary Debate on Political Reform in Chinese Universities* (Colchester, UK: ECPR Press Monographs, 2015); and Daniel C. Lynch, *China's Futures: PRC Elites Debate Economics, Politics, and Foreign Policy* (Stanford, CA: Stanford University Press, 2015).

18. See on this the acerbic criticism by Yu Ying-shih, "The Chinese Communists Are Not Confucianists," *China Change*, July 1, 2015, https://chinachange.org/2015/07/01/the-chinese-communists-are-not-confucianists/.

19. In his book *Minzhu shi hao dongxi* (Beijing: Shehui kexue wenxian chubanshe, 2006), Yu remains attached to the CCP's leading role. See *Democracy Is a Good Thing:*

Essays on Politics, Society, and Culture in Contemporary China (Washington, DC: Brookings Institution Press, 2009).

20. Shi Anshu, François Lachapelle, and Matthew Galway, "The Recasting of Chinese Socialism: The Chinese New Left since 2000," *China Information* 32, no. 1 (March 2018): 139–159, esp. 150–151.

21. Jun Deng and Craig A. Smith, "The Rise of New Confucianism and the Return of Spirituality to Politics in Mainland China," *China Information* 32, no. 2 (June 2018): 294–314.

22. An idea that converges with American sociologist Seymour Martin Lipset's requisite of a "diamond-shaped" social structure in which the middle class is the most populous, for the demand for democracy to emerge and consolidate. See Andrew Nathan, "The Puzzle of the Chinese Middle Class," *Journal of Democracy* 27, no. 2 (April 2016): 9, 17.

23. Ji Weidong, *Building the Rule of Law in China: Ideas, Praxis and Institutional Design* (London and New York: Routledge, 2017).

24. Yu Ying-shih, "The Radicalization of China in the Twentieth Century," *Daedalus* 122, no. 2 (1993): 125–150; and Yu, "The Chinese Communists Are Not Confucianists."

25. Tang Xiaobing and Mark McConaghy, "Liberalism in Contemporary China: Questions, Strategies and Directions," *China Information* 32, no. 1 (March 2018): 121–138; and Lu Hua and Matthew Galway, "Freedom and Its Limitations: The Contemporary Mainland Chinese Debate over Liberalism," *China Information* 32, no. 2 (June 2018): 315–335.

26. He Weifang, *In the Name of Justice: Striving for the Rule of Law in China* (Washington, DC: Brookings Institution Press, 2012).

27. Lynch, *China's Futures*, 20–67.

28. Li Rui, *Li Rui xin zhengjian: Heshi xianzheng dakaizhang* [Li Rui's new political position: When will a constitutional government be established?] (Hong Kong: Tiandi tushu, 2009).

29. "Xu Zhangrun: Women dangxia de kongju yu qidai" (Xu Zhangrun: Our Fears and Expectations), *The Initium*, July 24, 2018, https://theinitium.com/article/20180724-opinion-xuzhangrun-fear-hope/. Translated into English by Geremie Barmé under the title "Imminent Fears, Immediate Hopes—A Beijing Jeremiad," *China Heritage*, August 1, 2018, http://chinaheritage.net/journal/imminent-fears-immediate-hopes-a-beijing-jeremiad/.

30. Lynch, *China's Futures*, 15–184, 247–249.

31. Frenkiel, "Conclusion," in *Conditional Democracy*.

32. Jean-Philippe Béja, *A la recherche d'une ombre chinoise: Le mouvement pour la démocratie en Chine (1919–2004)* [In search of a Chinese shadow: China's pro-democracy movement (1919–2004)] (Paris: Le Seuil, 2004); Cheng Yingxiang (with Claude Cadart), *Dégel de l'intelligence en Chine, 1976–1989: Quatorze témoignages* [Intellectual thaw in China 1976–1989: Fourteen interviews] (Paris: Gallimard, 2004); Merle Goldman and Edward Gu, eds., *Chinese Intellectual Between State and Market* (London and New York: Routledge, 2004); and Wu Guoguang and Helen Lansdowne, eds., *Zhao Ziyang and China's Political Future* (London and New York: Routledge, 2008).

33. On the Sun Zhigang case, see Keith J. Hand, "Citizens Engage the Constitution: The Sun Zhigang Incident and Constitutional Review Proposals in the People's Republic of China," in *Building Constitutionalism in China*, ed. Stéphanie Balme and Michael W. Dowdle (New York: Palgrave Macmillan, 2009), 221–242.

34. Eva Pils, *China's Human Rights Lawyers: Advocacy and Resistance* (London and New York: Routledge, 2014); and Rachel E. Stern, "Activist Lawyers in Post-Tiananmen China," *Law & Social Inquiry* 42, no. 1 (Winter 2017): 234–251.

35. Zhang and Li, *Lingba xianzhang*, 16–25, 233–319. The English translation of Charter 08 is found in Jean-Philippe Béja, Fu Hualing, and Eva Pils, eds., *Liu Xiaobo, Charter 08 and the Challenges of Political Reform in China* (Hong Kong: Hong Kong University Press, 2012), 289–298 .

36. Xu Zhiyong, *To Build a Free China: A Citizen's Journey* (Boulder, CO: Lynne Rienner, 2016). Sentenced to four years' imprisonment, Xu was freed in July 2017. After nineteen months in detention, Pu was given a three-year suspended sentence and freed in December 2015.

37. Robert Mackey, "Jailed Chinese Dissident's 'Final Statement,'" *New York Times*, October 8, 2010, https://thelede.blogs.nytimes.com/2010/10/08/jailed-chinese-dissiden ts-final-statement/.

38. Zhang and Li, *Lingba xianzhang*, 233–319.

39. Willy Wo-Lap Lam, "China Brief Early Warning: Xi Jinping Warns Against the 'Black Swans' and 'Gray Rhinos' of a Possible Color Revolution," *China Brief*, February 20, 2019, https://jamestown.org/program/china-brief-early-warning-xi-jinping-warns-against-the-black-swans-and-gray-rhinos-of-a-possible-color-revolution/.

40. At the same time, many mainland Chinese people, perhaps a majority, strongly resent the rise of localism and proindependence ideas in Hong Kong, as well as the Taiwanese proindependence movement, which fuels their opposition to "Western democracy" and their support for the one-party system.

41. Wang Dan, "Liu Xiaobo: Walking the Path of Kang Youwei, Spilling His Blood Like Tan Sitong," *China Change*, July 20, 2017, http://chinachange.org/2017/07/20/liu-xiaobo-walking-the-path-of-kang-youwei-spilling-his-blood-like-tan-sitong/.

SIX

China's Future

Toward an Authoritarian and Imperial Political System

This is the book's most speculative part. In previous chapters I outlined some tendencies and hypotheses. Obstacles to any political change, be it a smooth evolution or a rupture, are easily discernible: the party-state's strength and ongoing modernization, the Soviet-style and thus efficient nature of its repressive system, the undeniable and even prodigious economic success it can boast of, society's depoliticization, its nationalism and the superficiality of its democratic culture, civil society's fragility, and the general conservatism of economic and intellectual elites and their dependence on CCP political elites.

What factors therefore might facilitate a change in the political system and perhaps even a break with the regime established in 1949? Observers most often cite four: an economic slowdown or crisis, a social crisis, a political crisis, or an international crisis.

Clearly these are not necessarily disjointed factors: an economic crisis might spark a social one; a social crisis can turn political and lead to an outbreak of division and conflict in the party's topmost levels; similarly, an international crisis stoking a political one or vice versa cannot be ruled out; or a deep social crisis may lead the regime to undertake an external adventure. However, for clarity's sake and demonstration purposes, I consider the four scenarios one by one.

My hypothesis is that in the foreseeable future the current authoritarian political system will be able to overcome potential crises and continue adapting successfully. In the longer term, signs of its atrophy will become clearer and compel it to transform itself. Will it therefore democratize? More likely, the PRC will change into a regime that is superficially communist but still largely authoritarian, elitist, paternalistic, extremely nationalistic, and increasingly imperial, with its economic and diplomatic clout persuading it to promote its own development model worldwide.

SLOWDOWN OR ECONOMIC CRISIS

Many China experts rightly think that unprecedented economic expansion has contributed to the political system's stability, boosting its legitimacy as well as life expectancy.[1] But some among them conclude, rather hastily I believe, that a slowing or an economic or financial crisis could weaken the CCP's domination and lead to political change. Others hold that without major political changes, the party-state would no longer be able to ensure economic development, its structures being too rigid, anti-freedom, and unsuited to the globalized environment in which it finds itself and therefore detrimental to innovation.[2] As discussed below, these scenarios are far from conclusive. The economic and financial problems China faces, as well as tensions between the modern economy and the one-party regime, must be seen in perspective. In the event of economic difficulties or social crisis, the party-state commands more political and security resources to keep itself afloat than is generally believed.

China's Economic Problems in Perspective

China's economy is immense, complex, and diversified. Second largest in the world since 2010, it contains, as has been suggested, multiple structures. There are state enterprises, both central and local; collective ones, mostly local and modest in size; and the private sector, wherein some major national and provincial groups coexist with myriad small firms. In the "gray" sector, firms that issue shares are private in principle but in fact state controlled. Finally, agriculture features mostly fragmented family holdings that are hardly profitable, despite a gradual but too lethargic concentration of holdings (or at least of land use rights) and therefore of their operations' modernization in some regions.

Despite an undeniable but salutary slowing of its official growth rate, China's economy continues to develop at a pace most countries envy (6.8

percent in 2017 and 6.6 percent in 2018, compared to 10.6 percent in 2010). That average figure hides major regional disparities. Some interior provinces or former industrial bases (in the northeast) are stagnating, while coastal China continues to post creditable growth rates. While the state sector is being consolidated and is generally declining profits, it remains barely remunerative with regard to fixed assets and is partly in a deficit, whereas creation and growth of jobs depends more on private companies and expansion of the services sector.

Chinese authorities are aware of the need to urgently deal with several serious economic challenges. These include transition from an economy built on investments and exports to one fueled by domestic consumption, innovation, and development of services; worrying levels of debt among local governments and especially enterprises (170 percent debt to GDP ratio, which constitutes the major part of a total internal debt amounting to 250 percent of the GDP at the end of 2017); and an overproduction crisis plaguing a number of sectors, in particular heavy industry (steel, aluminum, etc.), shipbuilding, solar panels, and cement. More generally there is the risk of getting caught in the middle-income trap, that is, becoming an economy whose production costs, particularly of labor, have risen too high for it to remain competitive but whose acquisition of modern technologies and professional skills is insufficient to join the ranks of developed economies.[3]

All these are real risks that Chinese economists are acutely aware of.[4] The transition to a new growth model is slow and incomplete, the economy being regularly propped up by public investment from 2008 onward. Economic actors' debts are revealed through the existence of a parallel and unregulated financial system (shadow banking) that no one knows the real size of (half of all loans, according to some estimates), and no one controls its activities.[5] Domestic debt is expected to reach 300 percent of GDP by 2022 if no corrective measures are taken.[6] Several major sectors, including construction, have trouble reining in production and have let bubbles build, some of which have burst, setting off property price collapses in some regions and medium and small cities (known in China as third- and fourth-tier ones). And the trade war with the United States, "declared" in the spring of 2018, has begun to bite, affecting economic actors' trust in the Chinese economy's future, depreciating the value of its currency (the yuan or the *renminbi*), and contributing to the economic slowdown. Bear in mind also that the middle-income trap has been avoided by only a few economies, for example Japan, South Korea, and Taiwan.

Nevertheless, the one sphere Chinese authorities are well aware of the need to pay attention to is economy. At the risk of oversimplifying, I believe that more than most other governments, the Chinese party-state has the necessary tools to overcome most of these difficulties. Although savings remain high (46.4 percent of GDP in 2017 compared to 52 percent in 2008), private consumption is rising, from 35.6 percent of GDP in 2010 to 39.1 percent in 2017.[7] This ratio is low, but all indicators project a rapid increase in retail consumption in the coming years; it is expected to contribute 51 percent of GDP in the 2020–2030 decade, compared to 41 percent in the previous decade, while investment's share in GDP will fall from 42 to 34 percent.[8] Services are also growing apace, stimulated by changes in household consumption structures; they represented 51.6 percent of GDP in 2017, compared to 46 percent in 2013 and 43 percent in 2010.[9] Some labor-intensive industries (textiles, leather, and consumer electronics) have already left China, moving to Southeast Asia, South Asia, and even Africa.

Further, backed by a mountain of private savings, the state has the necessary financial reserves to tackle the indebtedness of local governments and most state enterprises, forcing the most vulnerable of them to opt for bankruptcy or merger.[10] It also has the means to persuade large private groups to invest in public firms it intends to promote. For instance, in mid-2017 Alibaba, Baidu, and Tencent Holdings bought stakes in telecommunications company Unicom, attracted by advantageous synergy prospects.[11] Despite restrictions introduced in 2017, shadow banking remains a necessary complement to a banking system still almost exclusively public.[12] After the mess of the stock market panic of August 2015 and the sudden depreciation of about 4 percent of the *renminbi* against the US dollar, the government introduced stabilization measures. Moreover, on many occasions it has demonstrated its monetary and financial wisdom. It continues to closely manage the yuan, internationalizing it without making it convertible, and to check capital flows, since 2016 limiting investments abroad by Chinese firms, especially private groups. Thus, after falling from $4 trillion in June 2014 to under $3 trillion in January 2017, notably due to sales aimed at slowing capital outflows, China's foreign exchange reserves stabilized at $3.1 trillion in November 2017.

Moreover, using methods reminiscent of Colbertism or Gaullism, the Chinese government is steadily piloting economic modernization.[13] Launched in May 2015, the strategic plan "Made in China 2025" encapsulates China's ambition to become not only the world's leading industrial power but also the leader of many key sectors of tomorrow's globalized economy. The plan has in particular set targets to increase the domestic content of core industrial components and basic materials to 40 percent in 2020 and 70 percent in 2025.[14] As a result, the government is investing massively, by itself and through incentives, in research and development (more than 2 percent of GDP); innovation; and cutting-edge sectors such as electric vehicles, robotics, artificial intelligence, space, aeronautics, biotechnologies, and nanotechnologies. It is encouraging public-private partnerships using subsidies in all major industrial areas, including the military, aware of private firms' key role in innovation. And it is encouraging national trailblazers as well as private companies with major financial resources to acquire foreign high-technology units, in order to ensure China's rapid command of such technologies.

Briefly stated, China is arming itself with the necessary means to succeed in its economic transition and overcome the middle-income trap, and it is better placed than many countries to succeed in this endeavor.

Does the Party Impede Economic Progress?

In this scenario, it is difficult to contend that the CCP, even under Xi, is posing an obstacle to economic progress. That argument, based on American liberal ideology, errs through amnesia. The "Four Dragons" of the 1960s and 1970s (South Korea, Hong Kong, Singapore, and Taiwan) modernized before democratizing (and not all of them have democratized), and that modernization owed a great deal to the state's crucial economic role throughout the process and to selective protectionism adopted at that time.

This argument also errs by underestimating the CCP's capacity to adapt. As I have tried to show in previous chapters, the party-state has dedicated itself entirely and quite literally to economic development. This means it has modulated the political system's functioning to ensure it places no hurdles in the way of the country's modernization, cadre formation (engineers, technicians, economists, managers, administrators, jurists, etc.), scientific research, innovation, investment, consumption, or exports. As noted previously, Internet censorship, albeit antifreedom, has not prevented acquisition and spread of modern technologies. More generally the party-state may continue to offer necessary privileges (higher salaries, easier access to property) to all actors, especially elites, who contribute to modernization. In recent years it not only has shown a real ability to welcome back talented Chinese people who had left before or after Tiananmen—the famous "sea turtles' (*haigui*)—but also has persuaded a rising number of foreign engineers and scientists to move to and work for China.

Clearly Chinese economic and scientific elites are far from unanimous in accepting the party's rules and often complain about Internet censorship.[15] Some leave, taking their companies or a part of their interests abroad, migrating to freer countries or better-paying research centers. But the great majority of them have no choice but to keep developing their businesses in China and have worked out a modus vivendi with the regime, although negotiating under Xi's rule has become trickier. Several industrial advances already achieved testify to the success of the CCP's strategy: bullet trains, space launches, nuclear plants, renewable energy, the digital economy,[16] and so forth, as well as the rise of many private companies, from Huawei to Alibaba. The internationalization of Chinese firms both public and private—although since 2015 it has led to some capital flight, which the regime is trying to check—stems from an economic logic and strategy of expansion and spreading of risks. This has helped these firms capture greater market shares from their foreign competitors.

"Cassandras" will no doubt say China has thus far been merely copying developed countries and that it must now innovate. This objection can be countered in many ways: going by the number of invention patent applications filed annually (1.34 million in 2016 and 1.38 million in 2017), innovations (albeit often incremental) are already numerous, with China ranking third behind the United States and Japan.[17] More than any other emerging country, China has the talent and financial resources needed to innovate and is in a good position to compete with more advanced economies and in several sectors. This is so even if it is far from certain to gain a leading position in all the sectors targeted by its Made in China 2025 industrial policy.[18] The size of its domestic market and the economies of scale that it facilitates also help China in realizing its ambition.

Barring a speedy but improbable politicization of economic and scientific elites, with organizing such a process being even less probable, this strategy is likely to continue bearing the fruit the CCP hopes for.

What of an Economic Crisis?

Nonetheless, the outbreak of an economic crisis and its leading to a social one cannot be ruled out. China's economy is so diversified that such a crisis could grip a region particularly hit by recession or slowing of activity. A crisis spreading across the country cannot be ruled out either. Among the scenarios that are advanced, somewhat as Japan's economy did in the early 1990s, China's economy could undergo a bout of stagnation and, under the weight of contracted debt and in a scenario identical to that in Latin America in the 1980s, could get caught in the middle-income trap already mentioned. Some economists believe China already shows signs of both types of evolutions: Japan's stagnation as well as Latin America's debt crisis and middle-income trap.[19] In either case, the economic difficulties encountered (unemployment, a sharp decline in incomes and social services) could well provoke a social crisis and lead to acute forms of society-regime confrontation.

But is the regime totally devoid of ability to tackle these difficulties? As I discuss below, economic development is not the only basis for the CCP's legitimacy; it has more resources to fall back on when needed. But first I consider other factors that could lead to the outbreak of a social crisis and eventually a political one.

Conversely, would the regime's evolution toward less political control, what David Shambaugh for instance calls soft authoritarianism or a semidemocracy, really help it overcome looming economic and social challenges? This is far from certain, particularly for Chinese decision makers. In fact, the aggravation of economic risks that China faces explains to a large extent the regime's increasing paranoia since 2008 and more so since Xi's rise to power in 2012 as well as the concentration of powers in his hands and the perpetuation of his reign.

SOCIAL CRISIS AND RISKS OF ITS POLITICIZATION

China's society is already pregnant with numerous social tensions that would not necessarily need an economic crisis to explode. Among the better known are deepening income inequalities; a steep rise in cost of living in urban and coastal regions fueled by property price bubbles; growing frustration among young university graduates in search of decent and well-paying jobs; the rudimentary nature of social coverage systems; the presence in cities of about 280 million migrant workers, whose status remains precarious; the gradual marginalization of the countryside, where glaring poverty has been building; and finally a generation gap between those who witnessed the end of the Mao era plus the beginning of reforms and those born post-1980 and post-1990, the *jiulingnianhou*. On top of these issues is the supplementary burden for the regime and society of dealing with serious problems posed by irreversible environmental damage; a rapidly aging population; and the need to improve the quality of education, especially at higher and professional levels.

Again, are the tensions so serious as to provoke a social crisis and set off a political one? Even if they do turn serious, are they capable of weakening the regime, even forcing it to engage in a liberalization if not a democratization process? Would a softer authoritarianism or a semidemocratic system be better able to manage tensions and resolve the challenges the CCP confronts? In the following sections I consider one by one what I believe are the main sources of tensions and social problems.

Main Sources of Social Tensions

The first source of tension is the direct product of China's unprecedented modernization and transformation processes: rising expectations of the society.[20] If the authorities do not hold to their commitments or make decisions deemed unjust or iniquitous (*bu gongping*) by a part of society, the most affected segments tend to more quickly and directly react than in earlier times.[21] Loosening of the regime's hold on society and the more targeted nature of repression against dissidents have contributed to this. Hence there has been an increase in "mass incidents," as noted previously, but also greater attention to them on the regime's part.

Another major change that can multiply conflict sources is the fast-growing inequality. China has become one of the most unequal countries, with a Gini coefficient nearing 0.50 (compared to 0.30 in the 1980s) closing in on Brazil's (0.53), if not yet South Africa's (0.63). At the top is a stratum of millionaires and the leisure class (1 percent) sitting on a third of the country's wealth (compared to 42 percent in the United States), with the bottom 25 percent of the population having just 1 percent of the wealth. China today boasts 3.14 million (dollar) millionaires and 596 billionaires, more than even the United States.[22] Although this number is falling, the country still has 43 million poor people earning less than a dollar a day (or 2,300 yuan a year).[23] But have these inequalities, rightly speaking, caused the urban protest movements and peasant revolts of recent years? Isn't the cause rather political leaders' corruption and illegal rent seeking? As many sociologists, including Martin Whyte, have noted, Chinese society, somewhat like US and Latin American societies, is more accepting of inequality than are European ones (see chapter 4). Again, it is decisions by the regime or authorities in general (such as of a company) that are deemed arbitrary, as well as officials' corruption, that provoke a reaction from society.[24] This is why the party-state is paying greater attention to all protests against injustices[25] and why Xi launched the anticorruption campaign (see below).

This does not mean that in case of an economic crisis, some segments of society would not be tempted to target some attributes or symbols of social inequality (e.g., billionaires' cars or houses) or even corrupt leaders themselves who flaunt their wealth too openly—against Xi's instructions. But in China's current context it is difficult to see this type of action emerging and further, receiving support from large strata of urban society, including the middle classes (around one-third of the population today). Rather, as in other societies that have undergone rapid modernization, especially in Asia, China's middle classes are more likely to remain regime allies or what some political scientists call "a stabilizing force."[26] However, as noted previously, this is not to say the middle classes would not mobilize to defend their own interests or push back against the government on specific issues, such as installation of a polluting factory or a railway line too close to a residential area. Such struggles will likely continue to use peaceful and more often legal methods, above all avoiding getting politicized. I return to this below.

More worrying in my view is the third factor in potential tensions: rapid urbanization since the 1990s and the way it has come about. In 1978 just 18 percent of Chinese people lived in cities. Today 58 percent (or 820 million of 1.42 billion) do, and this number will rise to 70 percent by 2030 (1 billion of 1.45 billion). Further, the urban population is divided into two types. In the first category are so to speak legitimate residents who have full-fledged urban resident permits (*hukou*), giving them access to all social services that the municipal government, according to its financial capacity—there being huge inequalities among cities—can place at their disposal (schools, hospitals, minimum wages, and pensions). In the other category are migrant workers, second-class citizens, who are denied most social services and have to send their children to private and thus fee-paying schools, for instance. Of course the richest municipalities are taking steps to integrate them gradually, knowing that most of them will never return to the villages they left in order to improve their daily lives and ensure a better future for their children. But regular residents often oppose such reforms, fearing the loss of some of their social benefits.[27]

On top of these potential tensions is the fact that the concentration of a majority of the population in urban zones undeniably facilitates mobilization of malcontents, speeds the spread of demands, and thus heightens the risk of confrontation with the regime.[28] More generally, as in Europe and elsewhere, urbanization constitutes a profound social upheaval, the source of much progress and hope but also of multiple frustrations and disappointments. One cannot rule out a paupers' revolt by migrants or those denied the fruits of economic growth. But do they have a chance, as He Qinglian believes, of influencing political change?[29] Paradoxically, as He has herself acknowledged, urban society's fragmentation contributes to regime stability and to the middle classes' egoism on the one hand and to the isolation of migrants on the other, making any anti-regime mobilization and politicization particularly difficult.

The Chinese countryside's evolution as a source of social tensions is often overlooked. The vastly disparate situations frustrate analyses, as do peasant society's traditional divisions and rural flight. Perennially low incomes from land, its fragmentation (holdings of 0.6 hectare on average), and the consequent high costs of production have led many rural folks to seek work in cities or choose other activities (trade, services, crafts, small industry, or tourism) despite state subsidies and support for mechanization. In 2015 Chinese farmers' average annual income was officially $1,175, much lower than urban incomes (at that time more than $10,000) and overall per capita GNP ($8,000). Fewer than 44 percent of rural Chinese residents are farmers. Solutions to their persisting poverty lie in land consolidation, mechanization, crop diversity, and emergence of a class of rich farmers. But the CCP hesitates to back this last development, although on the ground it has no choice but to tolerate it; many holdings are sublet to those staying on in villages, and several farms have stopped growing cereals, which are generally less profitable and thus concentrated in large holdings such as in the northeast. Some crops, such as soybeans, are now mostly imported.

Transformations in peasant—more generally rural—society have led to scattering and individualizing of demands instead of unifying them. Most often stemming from unjust compensation for lands expropriated for the needs of urbanization, tensions continue to prevail and are dealt with by the party-state's local structures and occasionally by Public Security authorities or Armed Police. Meanwhile, rural society remains largely legitimist and much less prone than urban areas to question CCP supremacy.[30] Moreover, rural problems and the injustices committed there often stem from governance deficit and local elites' criminalization.[31] For these reasons, I do not see Chinese rural society today as a major source of a social crisis and even less a political one. The origins of such crises and their possible politicization will be urban.

Finally, the issue of the generation gap must be addressed. Changes in mind-set, focus of interest, and behavior have been too rapid, adding to communication problems between generations and between youth and authorities. Population aging aggravates these problems. The one-child policy, which was enforced rigorously until 2015 during a period of runaway economic growth, led to the emergence of generations of spoiled children, overprotected and micromanaged by parents and grandparents and thus lacking autonomy. Born in more comfortable surroundings; obsessed with consumption; and quickly enslaved by gadgets, online games, and social networks, these "little emperors" (*xiao huangdi*) are accused of being narcissistic, egocentric, and incapable of maturing, of becoming responsible and independent. As psychoanalyst Wu Zhihong said in a best seller that was quickly banned, they have turned China into a "nation of giant infants" (*juyingguo*).[32]

Today these young Chinese, including graduates of universities or specialized institutions, confront adult life just when good jobs are already taken, property prices in most big cities have become prohibitive, and money making is more difficult. Generally depoliticized and belonging to the middle classes, their only interests are personal and professional. Some among them are less invested in their work than their elders and have absorbed a culture that in Chinese is called *sang*, characterized by "a reduced work ethic, a lack of self-motivation and an apathetic demeanor."[33]

Such lack of interest in politics among "little emperors" and those in the grip of *sang* culture can only please an authoritarian regime. But doesn't such distancing from politics and from the party they have never thought of joining pose dangers? Can young Chinese become a source of social tensions, even revolt against a regime too removed from their concerns and incapable of communicating with them? Can they organize themselves, become politicized?

Chinese young people's egocentrism and the resultant atomization hardly push them to get organized even if they often face identical social problems. Of course, no change can be ruled out. It is striking to note, for instance, that young Hong Kongers, known for consumerism and political apathy, got politicized earlier in the 2010s, becoming the main actors in the 2014 Umbrella Movement that demanded real democratization in the process of electing the territory's chief executive and its legislature. It is no less striking to note how, despite failing in that effort, young Hong Kong democrats used and diffused Gene Sharp's strategies and methods for nonviolent action and civil disobedience.[34] However, differences between the two political environments (Hong Kong and China) must be underlined: one is relatively liberal, the other authoritarian. In Hong Kong, before its handover to Chinese sovereignty in 1997, Beijing had initially promised full democratization of institutions, but it went back on its word and, perhaps more important, gave the strong impression to Hong Kongers of having done so.[35] In China for now, the youth neither demand nor expect political reforms, but mainly well-paid jobs and affordable housing, demands the government is at pains to meet and to which it intends to give priority and let urban youth know it is doing so. To date, no peaceful civil disobedience movement has taken shape in China, although such a mobilization could well happen sooner or later.

Moreover, young Chinese are much more nationalistic than Hong Kongers. Mostly children of the rich (*fu'erdai*) or of affluent government officials (*guan'erdai*), those among them who study abroad (over 600,000 in 2017), far from imbibing democratic values they could be expected to admire, have an increasing tendency to defend their country and government, sometimes outrageously, attacking the West and particularly the United States. Further, their numbers and rising financial contribution to universities in the West (European, North American, and Australian) have led their hosts to practice a form of self-censorship, which only reassures the young Chinese. It would be wrong to generalize, but group pressure and the party's vigilant eye, via its embassies in host countries, have led to boosting conservatism among some of the youth and consequently greater fragmentation.[36]

Despite this development, the generation gap associated with the regime's political rigidity continues to distance youth from the party. Both the CCP and its dedicated mass organization, the CYL (eighty-one million members in 2018, compared to ninety million in 2012), have been adopting novel methods to keep attracting youngsters between ages fourteen and twenty-eight.[37] This is part of the Xi-imposed reforms in Hu Jintao's former fiefdom. With this aim, the League's budget was slashed and its former primary mission—training future CCP cadres—was modified to focus on ideological and moral education. For instance, the League now has a presence on Bilibili, or B-Station, a video-sharing site for Chinese fans of anime, manga, and online games mainly of Japanese origin. It also offers services and advice by those well-versed in communicating with and influencing young people. But its actions are easily seen through, eliciting numerous sarcastic user comments. The League does not directly criticize Japanese manga featured on the site, but just the "harmful" ideology of some of them. It also offers courses on various themes, including "How to Resist Western Colonization of the Mind" and "Why China Wins."[38] Such a strategy's effectiveness is questionable.[39]

Briefly put, so long as young Chinese remain apolitical and self-centered, there is nothing for the party to worry about. But beware the day they change, become politicized, and start holding their rulers accountable for their lack of political say or more simply the problems they face. Having grown up mostly in an urban, more modern, and relatively comfortable environment, they could well turn into centers of protest or even challenge the regime. Among the battles that could arise is for freer access to Internet and foreign sites. But urban Chinese society is not there yet, and it might be future generations of young people (born after 2000 or 2010) who find in politics a way of expressing themselves, influencing, and existing.

For now, the problems that will continue to engage both urban society and government are air and water pollution, adaptation of the economy, and social services to the rapidly aging population (there will be 240 million people over age sixty in 2020 and 360 million in 2030, compared to 180 million in 2018), and a relative workforce reduction (on the order of 250 million by 2050), as well as the need to make changes in training to meet labor market needs.[40] There are many arenas on which the regime's political reforms have little impact other than stoking more demands and social pressure on the government, which the party-state is fully aware of but which have persuaded it more than ever to persevere with the strict authoritarian line adopted under Xi.

In sum, two main social forces have the potential to weigh on the regime, to become politicized and provoke a political crisis: urban society at large and urban youth. Their higher levels of education and globalization and greater demands on the government constitute potential political change factors. But the activation of these forces depends on the way the regime and its elites will manage them and choose to suppress them, canalize them, or use them according to their own political interests.

POLITICAL CRISIS

What can set off a political crisis in China? What kind of political crisis can challenge the party-state's domination or compel it to move toward a less rigid authoritarianism, even a semidemocracy?

First of all, the regime has much greater political and security resources than many observers realize to snuff out any possible politicization of economic and social demands arising from society. Should the usually mobilized resources ever prove insufficient, maintenance of the political leadership's unity would become the topmost priority. In such circumstances, which forces would be capable of sundering this unity? And what could be the outcome of a division or open conflict at the party's summit?

A distinction should be made between political crises resulting from personal conflicts, power struggles such as the 2012 Bo Xilai affair, and those provoked by fundamental divergences over, for instance, major structural reforms or even more seriously the regime's political orientation. Only the latter interest us here, as they can be destabilizing, even though the former do reveal systemic tensions and weaknesses that could potentially shake the party's hegemony.

The CCP's Political and Security Resources

An argument sometimes advanced is that in the event of recession and economic or social crisis, the CCP's domination could be questioned, even threatened. This reasoning is generally based on the idea that the sole consideration for the regime's political legitimacy is unprecedented economic growth. But that is not the case. Of course the party-state needs some minimum growth, of 3 to 5 percent (not 7 percent as has been long believed), to usher in the promised "moderate prosperity" by 2021 and, more prosaically, to implement various social programs it has adopted: health insurance, unemployment insurance, pensions, construction of low-cost housing (*liangzufang*), minimum wages, and combating poverty. Politically it has invested much in realizing these social protection schemes, gathered since the 2000s under the "people's livelihood" slogan (*minsheng*). Having appropriated the third of Sun Yat-sen's (and KMT's) Three Principles of the People (see chapter 2)—as well as the first, "nationalism," but certainly not the second, "democracy"—CCP propaganda harps on it ad nauseam.[41]

Apart from improving the average standard of living, the CCP relies on other crucial sources of legitimacy: stability and nationalism; in other words, its ability, on the one hand, to maintain society's stability and security, and on the other, to incarnate the country's national interests as well as to claim a monopoly on Chinese nationalism.

These two pillars of CCP legitimacy date back to 1949 and the party's victory in the civil war against the KMT. The first pillar, disrupted by Mao, was restored to primacy by Deng, who presented it to his successors as the condition for China's economic modernization. It was by invoking the need for stability that Deng ordered the bloody suppression of the 1989 democratic movement. Since then, whenever there is social unrest or a few activists demand greater freedoms, it is in stability's name that the party's armed might descends on troublemakers. This stability maintenance argument has a good chance of not only continuing to be used by the regime and helping prevent any real political mobilization but also of finding a favorable response among the people, especially the middle classes.[42]

We have seen how much priority Chinese society, particularly its middle classes, attaches to personal safety and the security of their possessions, blaming migrant workers (especially Uyghurs and other Muslims) whenever they feel unsafe. There is undoubtedly a tendency the French would label "Lepenist"—in reference to Jean-Marie Le Pen, the former leader of France's extreme right-wing party—in this hierarchy of civic values dear to China's new middle classes. It should be noted that this inclination accords with the party's security policy and its ability to suppress any deviant or dissident behavior.[43]

Of course in the event of an economic crisis it would be difficult to predict the attitude that those segments of society directly affected would adopt. However, what is certain is that the party-state will give priority to stability maintenance. As it has shown many times, it will use all means at its disposal to attain this aim. It will offer solidarity measures while sticking to maintenance of order and if need be suppression; it will endeavor to put out by doing whatever it can any fires as it were that break out that could cause it embarrassment. Another scenario is that any possible fall in the Shanghai or Shenzhen stock exchange will certainly bankrupt and frustrate many middle-class or rich Chinese. But will they have any options but to accept, as they did in 2015, the reassurances of and corrective measures taken by the government? Aren't protests by small shareholders, dear to Berthold Brecht, the easiest to contain?

We have also seen how the CCP has sought to embody Chinese nationalism in a quasi-monopolistic way, with help from fellow-travelers who have agreed to be part of its United Front. China's increasing might, its continuing and on the whole successful quest for international respect, and the unprecedented modernization of its armed forces—all these developments have undeniably stoked this nationalism. But can a recession or social crisis weaken it, or more seriously, alienate Chinese nationalists from the CCP?

I don't think this could happen. The party-state controls all official media and is thus able, in case of economic or social problems, to ensure the majority of society rallies round. As in the past, it will use adversity to persuade people to support the government and shift responsibility for the ills confronting the country to a minority of unscrupulous economic actors or more simply foreigners and Western capitalism, particularly the United States. And this will be done without ceding ground to warmongers (see below).

In other words, the CCP is not lacking in political and security resources to deal with an economic recession or social crisis and ensure that it does not degenerate into political crisis.

What Can Divide the Regime and Make It Change?

Xi himself is the first and most immediate source of division within the party leadership, as are his unprecedented accumulation of power, fierce and selective anticorruption drive, move to bolster the state economy, unyielding hostility to any political (including intraparty) reforms, and his realized ambition to perpetuate his reign. Behind the façade of unanimity and brazen flattery of Xi courtiers, the CCP nomenklatura is far from approving of all these changes. Witness the tardy implementation of some reforms announced in previous years and the Sun Zhengcai affair (see chapter 1). However, the October 2017 19th Party Congress only boosted Xi's powers and those of his allies, raising the probability of a continuation of the current state of affairs and further marginalization of the few liberal and reformist forces at all levels and especially at the top. The revision of the state constitution in March 2018 and the extension without limit of Xi's presidency have confirmed this trend.

This does not mean Xi will not be forced to make some concessions to his detractors, such as lowering the anticorruption drive's intensity, if only to be able to introduce economic reforms he considers a priority (such as consolidation of big state enterprises) and likely to stimulate the economy. In early 2019 Xi and his advisers, including Liu He, also accepted making concessions to the Trump administration in order to put a provisional end to the trade war with the United States. When it comes to political control, a temporary relaxation of surveillance over activists cannot be ruled out either. The party has always alternated periods of tightening (*shou*) and loosening (*fang*), of both economic and political restrictions.[44]

But trade-offs negotiated and compromises arrived at only buttress the consensus within the leadership, and this pushes further into the future any possibility of a political dispute being able to engender real change. Similarly, contrary to what some observers think, the alternating of *shou* and *fang* has never endangered the regime's basis; it has always known how to overcome systemic rigidities by cyclically introducing some flexibility.

Each period of relaxation of controls allows CCP liberals, loyal to the legacy of reformers Hu Yaobang or Zhao Ziyang, and other activists to raise their heads. But such episodes have never been high profile, except in 1989, precisely the reason Deng and the majority of the nomenklatura cite when defending the Tiananmen bloodletting. Jiang Zemin and Hu

Jintao were hardly more political reform minded than Xi Jinping. The differences between Xi and Li Keqiang are minor. And perfectly weighing the risks attached to any real political reform, Xi's successor will no doubt quickly adopt a path close to that trod by his predecessors.

Consequently, as Shambaugh and others have predicted, a possible turn toward a looser authoritarianism will not constitute, in my view, the first step toward real political change. It will rather be a long or short lull before a new tightening overtakes it, and so on. And this will occur as long as the regime is not pushed to take a long, hard look at the way it governs society.

What then could lead the party-state's leadership to change?

In a previous book I have offered several possible political change scenarios,[45] and I return to them in this book when describing longer term changes. Suffice it to note here that in the foreseeable future, a regime transformation imposed by economic and intellectual elites, and more generally by civil society, remains improbable. Similarly, a regime change caused by armed forces that refuse to suppress protestors is difficult to envisage. For one thing, it is hard to see how a large social, or even more a political, movement could rise to the point where the Armed Police and PLA would be incapable of dealing with them; for another, the party's tight hold over the military and the professionalization of generals and their loyalty to the regime make such a scenario unlikely. As in 1989, some generals might refuse to act, but most will obey.

It is not impossible that in case of serious trouble, PLA top brass could see their political influence grow and some of them could develop political ambitions. Regular campaigns against the PLA's "nationalization" (*guojiahua*) suggest that some in uniform resent the party's tutelage and favor another type of state-army relationship and perhaps political system. But these hypotheses seem far removed from the daily functioning of state institutions and from most Chinese officers' state of mind.

There remains the possibility of a top-down transformation. Some people set great store by a generational change in the party leadership. The current generation, the fifth, or Xi's, grew up during the Cultural Revolution. Traumatized by that period of political chaos and economic stagnation, it is obsessed with order and modernization. Having studied rather late, it knows little of the world. Being nationalistic, it distrusts the West.

What of coming generations of leaders? Some members of the 1960s-born sixth generation, now part of the Politburo, hardly augur well for a greater opening, being mere sycophants of Xi, whether former Hu Jintao protégés, like Hu Chunhua, or of Xi himself, such as Chen Min'er. We may have to wait for the seventh generation, consisting of many educated abroad in the 1990s, and onward for any evolution. Then again, this "generations" theory has its limits, given that the ideology in which leading young cadres are socialized remains dominated by Leninism, the New Left, authoritarian Confucianism, and nationalism, unlike, say, in the 1980s in Taiwan. In sum, the ideology of the seventh generation basically goes against any idea of democracy.[46]

Nothing therefore will force the party-state in the coming five to ten years to plan for anything other than modernizing and perfecting the government system it has gradually transformed since 1979, without however destroying its 1949 foundations. Its present and future divisions have little chance of forcing a fundamental change in its functioning, knowing too well—inspired by Alexis de Tocqueville's formulation, set out in his *L'ancien régime et la révolution* (*The Ancien Régime and the French Revolution*)—that it is the introduction of real political reforms that will lead China into treacherous terrain. Wang Qishan's intra-CCP popularization of de Tocqueville's book in late 2012 was in fact intended to help Xi block not only any exit from the one-party system but any destabilizing political reform.

INTERNATIONAL CRISIS

Finally, let's turn to the possible effects of an international crisis on China's political regime: Such an impact is unlikely, as the regime and the country are strong and the authorities avoid taking too many risks in the global arena. But such a scenario needs to be considered because a crisis could well be imposed from outside, and the government will then be forced to try to contain it and prevent any lasting internal repercussions.

With its rising economic and military might, nationalism, and regional muscle-flexing, the PRC could be more tempted than in the past by a military adventure. Since 2012 it has not hesitated to enforce its domination on the maritime space it claims in the East China Sea and the South China Sea, impinging on its neighbors' own claims, multiplying frictions with Japan, some Southeast Asian countries such as Vietnam and the

Philippines, and the US Navy. Similar ambitions around the disputed Himalayan border have stoked tensions with India in recent years.[47] Anyone watching Chinese television channels would be struck by numerous programs extolling the technical prowess of PLA-acquired modern armaments and even speculating on their use in war contexts. Xi's speech to the 19th Party Congress only confirmed this tendency on Beijing's part to assert its international might through military force.

But at the same time the Chinese government has until now avoided any armed conflict over these disputes. In the South China Sea, in April 2012 it took control of the Scarborough shoals, which the Philippines had previously abandoned, and built a number of artificial islands that are now militarized, but did not seek to dislodge the Vietnamese or Filipinos—or the Malaysians or Taiwanese—from atolls they occupied. Similarly, it has tested New Delhi's patience many times, for instance in August 2017 at Doklam, an area also claimed by Bhutan, but has taken care to avoid armed conflict. China has also been careful on the issue of the Senkaku (Diaoyu) islands, under Japanese administration since 1895 but claimed by the PRC since 1971; despite several incursions by its coast guards, fishing boats, and fighter jets in the area, Beijing knows that the Japanese-US security treaty would apply if the PLA sought to take control; Washington has given the PRC several reminders. In Taiwan's case too, China cannot ignore the US security engagement despite its ambiguity. It escalates intimidations when the political majority on the island seems too independence-minded but continues to pursue economic integration under the "United Front" slogan, a strategy aimed at winning over the elites and then Taiwanese society at large.

More generally, the PRC intends to maintain stable and close relations with the United States and to manage all its differences with this country peacefully. On the whole it wants to avoid any irreparable deterioration externally. Beijing prefers to keep pushing its advantage by relying on its economic and commercial stranglehold and by multiplying diplomatic-strategic initiatives that serve its increasing might, new Silk Roads (Belt and Road Initiative) and the creation of the Asian Infrastructure Investment Bank (AIIB) being recent examples. It is also boosting its soft power to the extent possible, relying on increasingly sophisticated propaganda and United Front techniques.

North Korea remains a major instability factor. A war in the Korean peninsula or the collapse of Kim Jong-un's regime could force China to intervene, if only to neutralize North Korean nuclear weaponry and block any advance of US and South Korean troops north of the 38th Parallel. In such a situation, China cannot remain disinterested over the peninsula's future: no more than during the Ming era or in 1950, when Mao decided against the advice of most of his comrades to send in the PLA to save Kim Il-sung's regime. In other words, the peninsula is intimately linked to Chinese security interests.

But the Pyongyang regime is more solid than is generally believed. It has invested in nuclear arms in order to transfer a part of its defense spending to the civil economy, has undertaken tentative economic reforms, and has gradually opened up to the outside world, especially through tourism, from which it earns hard currency. United Nations sanctions can upset but not subdue it. Moreover, the current improvement of relations with China and the United States is likely to persuade North Korea of the rightness of its strategy and to help it defend itself with its limited but internationally contested nuclear arsenal.

Nevertheless, let us imagine a military crisis provoked by, for instance, the US Trump administration, a regime collapse in Pyongyang, or a gradual democratization of the peninsula's north. The impact of such a scenario on the Chinese political regime is difficult to assess. On the one hand, any militarization of the conflict will affect China's northeast. It could also reactivate discussion on the nature and prospects of the Beijing regime itself. But on the other hand, the PRC is too strong to be directly shaken by a political transformation of one of its neighbors, even the closest of them. The democratization of South Korea and Taiwan, and more recently Burma's political changes, have not really affected the balance of power within the Chinese political elites or even intellectuals. Why then would a regime change in Pyongyang destabilize the PRC's political regime? In such conditions North Korea's democratization is likely to be as slow and gradual as the peninsula's political reunification, thus presenting Beijing with an entirely manageable threat.

Only a military adventure initiated by Beijing that turned out bad, that is, with a loss of face for China, could pose a real threat. Such an eventuality could hurt the CCP's credibility, possibly turn the nationalists against it, and plunge the country into political crisis. Among the most often advanced scenarios is a failed attempt to invade Taiwan or take control of the Senkaku islands. In order to avoid such outcomes, in the first case the PLA would have to act fast to force Taiwan's regime to capitulate before the United States, possibly backed by Japan, could intervene militarily. In the second case, the PLA navy would have to prevail over Japan's navy, which is today much smaller but more modern and better trained than China's. In both cases, it would be a risky wager, even though the possibility of a gradual decoupling between US security and that of its two allies should not be neglected. That would be all the more risky because the nuclearization of a possible Sino-US military confrontation cannot be ruled out. [48]

This is why the Chinese government has managed until now to stop short of resorting to military force, limiting its pressures to the gestures described previously. Be that as it may, the issue of a political crisis unleashed by a military defeat necessarily remains uncertain. The party-state will probably have the political, ideological, and security means to take charge of the situation. Further, barring major changes (see chapter 5), nationalist elites could demand that heads roll but on the whole would back retaining a strong regime. In brief, it is difficult to envisage an external failure leading to democratization.

One can, however, imagine China's government being tempted by a possible short and decisive war against a weaker enemy, such as Vietnam or the Philippines in the South China Sea, or an operation to rescue its nationals in an African country descending into chaos, as in the 2017 propaganda film *Wolf Warrior 2* (*Langzhan er*), but perhaps in a less anti-West vein (see chapter 4). The CCP regime would then emerge crowned with reinforced nationalist legitimacy.

Conversely, could internal threats provoke an external adventure? Considering the armed conflicts in which China has been embroiled thus far, the answer is no. In 1950 it was fear of US (and UN) forces crossing the Yalu River frontier with Korea that led Mao to intervene in support of Kim Il-sung. The 1962 Sino-Indian border conflict was not without internal causes—the PLA overhaul and need for a military victory after the disastrous Great Leap Forward—but mainly had international objectives; Mao was signaling his independence from Soviet influence and targeting other Kremlin allies. Deng's 1979 "lesson" to "Asia's Cuba," Vietnam, was meant to contain the latter's ambitions in the former French Indochina.

Circumstances have changed vastly, and the PLA has greatly modernized since the 1990s. Moreover, unlike Western and mainly US militaries, China's has not seen action for forty years (thirty if the PLA navy's 1988 conquest of some Vietnamese islands in the South China Sea is included). This new reality could persuade Beijing to continue to be extra-cautious before getting into a hot war or, conversely, to test its new military hardware. However, there again, it is likely that stability and regime survival will take priority over an external war whose outcome is not guaranteed. Therefore, thinking that a foreign military adventure could be a spillway for internal threats goes against not only the motivations of previous conflicts but also CCP strategic culture. When it is divided or challenged by sections of Chinese society as in 1989, the party tends to close in on itself, focus attention on regaining control of the internal situation with possible PLA help, and avoid any foreign armed conflict.

WHAT OF THE LONGER TERM?

In the long run, the range of possibilities widens exponentially, as do the numerous factors that could transform the regime or destroy it. The Chinese political system's shape twenty or thirty years from now is especially difficult to imagine, and any hypothesis would be even more speculative. Looking beyond the forces at work now, which will likely continue to dominate, it cannot be assumed that the political system's adaptation will in the longer term overcome a tendency to atrophy. In other words, the CCP's adaptation efforts have gradually helped it transform and distort its original design, directly facilitating also its progressive decline. This is what Bruce Dickson calls the "dictator's dilemma" in his book, which as already noted, underpins my own reflections. But what will result from this metamorphosis and decay? A Taiwan-style democratization? Differences between China and Taiwan are too vast to render such an evolution probable. Adoption of a Singapore-inspired semidemocratic system? Again, difficulties abound. There remains an evolution toward a more specific political model, sui generis and no doubt less and less communist, but still largely authoritarian and nationalistic and increasingly neotraditionalist and imperial.

Adaptation and Atrophy

It should be admitted that the PRC regime's adaptation to a new economic, social, and international environment remains incomplete. As Andrew Nathan, Minxin Pei, David Shambaugh, and others have pointed out, fatigue, ossification, and atrophy have overtaken the party-state and are condemning it to change in the short or longer term.

Among signs of this atrophy may be mentioned limits to any measures taken by the CCP against corruption or privileges accumulated by leaders. The nomenklatura's corruption and privileges are fundamentally systemic. Xi's campaign has forced leading cadres to be more discreet. It has probably reduced petty corruption but has also raised the costs of transactions that implicate the bureaucracy (see chapter 1). But there is little prospect of an end to the collusion between political and economic powers. As long as it is in power, the party will probably refuse to make public the extent of the country's leaders' wealth as well as its own. No doubt "princelings" will continue to form an essential part of political elites, so deep-rooted is nepotism in the entire hierarchy, and not only at the top. And the nomenklatura will keep globalizing, transferring part of its assets abroad and sending its children to study overseas with increasing frequency. That much privilege, corruption, and rents can only fuel social tensions and boost antiregime forces, particularly among the growing number of taxpayers who are more and more interested in knowing where their money goes.

Linked to the foregoing, the second sign of atrophy stems from the increasingly flagrant gap between party ideals and its members' state of mind, between its formal organization and its real functioning. Rare are those who believe in communism or even socialism. Violating rules, a growing number of members practice one or more religions: Buddhism, a form of Daoism, and to a lesser extent, Christianity. Procedures are ignored: the collective leadership principle is rarely respected; elections and consultations are simple formalities; boring and ritualized meetings are rarely paid attention to and party fees irregularly paid; and inner-party democracy is a mere slogan. Party schools are business clubs where trainees exchange get-rich-quick tips. The only active communists are leading cadres or those with a personal interest, more often immediate economic or financial. In brief, the CCP has few idealists, many careerists, and even more cynics, who see in it the best and surest social launching pad. In such circumstances, can the party and its leaders remain role models for society? How can the political elite correct this state of affairs without challenging the CCP's leading role and thus unleashing a democratization process?

A third manifestation of regime atrophy is the ever-growing distance between party political discourse—still steeped in Marxism-Leninism, ideological jargon with abstruse slogans—and China's economic and social reality. We have seen the extent to which the party has tried to rework its propaganda and remain relevant to society. However, fewer and fewer Chinese people speak the "communist" language used by the apparatus, its websites, electronic media, and press organs. Even if inner-party democracy were to become reality—rather improbable under Xi—it cannot by definition bridge the gap, as less than 7 percent of the population is involved, unless it is conceived as reform prefiguring democratization of party and government officials' elections with all Chinese citizens participating, something that is even more improbable.

The fourth factor in growing regime decay is the widening distance between the CCP's proclaimed socialism and the cut-throat capitalism governing much of social exchange. We have seen how insidiously the CCP's ideology has closed in on the KMT's. But communism or statism remains its final objective, whereas the increase in private initiatives and private capitalism have been the main factors of China's economic development. How long will this ideological and structural gap last?

Another often-neglected weakness is the CCP's persistent inability to promote women to key posts in a still largely male-dominated political system. Women's status in China is ambiguous and changing; since 1949, they have been said to "hold up half the sky," in Mao's worn-out expression. But as in all socialist countries, it means they have been called on to "take part in production" while remaining the only ones confined to household tasks traditionally theirs, with no increase whatsoever in their political role. Reforms have had contradictory impacts on women, leading to a return to more conservative values governing relations with men and at the same time freeing them from Confucian-inspired conventions that the CCP and socialist morality have perpetuated. Without going into gender theories, it could be said that greater participation by women in politics, including within the party, could have major consequences for the regime's future. The noteworthy political role women have played in Taiwan and even Hong Kong is an interesting element of comparison, although feminization of politics, especially in Taiwan, is more the result of democratization than its cause.

The last and in my view essential factor for regime erosion is the slow emergence of democratic values within society and among economic and intellectual elites, a process to which the CCP contributes despite itself through formal political norms such as the constitution and even regularly invoked catchwords such as "human rights protection," "justice," and "democracy." At the same time, one has to be wary of the apparent domination of CCP official discourse or New Left ideas. As noted previously, they are played out in advance. However, it is worth paying attention to the influence the Taiwanese and Hong Kong societies and the diaspora—that is, other ways of being Chinese—can have on the PRC and its political values. Over time, pressure from the society and some of the more liberal segments of elites could grow stronger. In other words, the well-known eighteenth-century American slogan "no taxation without representation" may very well also take root in China.

This growing distance between the political model sought and reality on the ground is pregnant with changes and ruptures in the long run. The question arises of whether concentration of power in Xi's hands is not a response to this gradual atrophying of the political and institutional model created in 1949. In other words, is the emergence of what seems increasingly like a personal dictatorship a desperate attempt to halt systemic decay and any decisive change in the party-state/society relationship?

But is it really a personal dictatorship? Is the party teetering on the brink? Xi is not Mao, and like his immediate predecessors, he depends on a nomenklatura and a military he can to some extent manipulate but whose backing is crucial to succeed in reforms he intends to introduce. As noted previously, the CCP and the PLA are solid and resisting institutions if only thanks to inertia. Therefore, party architecture as we know it today will probably be the last political system construction to fall. Further, the state apparatus's modernization and its attentive steering of economic development will continue delaying such a collapse. Then again, various signs of atrophy noted previously will gradually eat away the system from within. However, only an accumulation of exceptional circumstances, unforeseeable by definition, can precipitate an exit from the current regime. Will an economic crisis turn into a social one and spark a political crisis? Or will political divisions at the top lead to dramatic changes with support from social forces activated and mobilized for that purpose?

Previous chapters and developments point even in the long run toward top-down political change under the party's leadership. But will it be gradual and peaceful? Won't any political transformation lead to a rupture?

Before speculating on such scenarios, I consider the difficulties China would face in embracing a Taiwan-style democratization or even introducing a Singapore-inspired semidemocracy.

An Improbable Taiwan-Style, Top-Down Democratization

The first difficulty arises from the CCP's fierce ideological and political opposition to any democratization, whereas the ideologically liberal KMT only put off democracy until after 1986–1987 under the pretext of continuing civil war between the mainland and Taiwan, where it took refuge in 1949. For many Chinese liberals and dissidents, Taiwan's experience is a precedent showing the compatibility between Chinese culture and democracy as well as the path to take in terms of orderly and peaceful evolution toward greater political freedoms. But a real ideological rupture will have to occur among the CCP leadership and nomenklatura before such a reform can be envisaged.

The points of departure between the two regimes make for the second obstacle. Right from 1950 in Taiwan, partial and local elections were regularly held, despite martial law and severe limitations imposed by the KMT. Its opponents could stand for elections as nonparty candidates (*dangwai*). It was these politicians who organized the opposition group — the Democratic Progressive Party — as soon as president Chiang Ching-kuo decided to let them do so in 1986. Nothing of the sort exists in China: village elections are under tight party control, more so for the grassroots people's congresses. Really independent candidates are not allowed, and even less is the appearance of any organized opposition. Electoral practice is in its infancy, and despite promises by some leaders, there is no chance of its being extended to higher levels of the government pyramid.

The third difference is linked to the two political systems' geostrategic environment. Even after Washington's "derecognition" in 1979, the de facto alliance with the United States put Taiwan in an awkward situation, its growing diplomatic isolation adding external pressure for democratization. In China, on the other hand, ideological, strategic, and economic rivalry with the United States has militated against introduction of a pluralistic multiparty system. Moreover, the PRC has become so powerful that even major democratic countries have stopped pushing it on human rights and political reforms.[49]

In Taiwan, the personal role of Chiang Ching-kuo, Chang Kai-shek's son, was decisive. With his charisma, he succeeded in imposing the beginnings of democratization—legalizing opposition parties and lifting of martial law in 1987—on a KMT leadership mostly hostile to such measures. However, it is doubtful whether the CCP's top leader, even one as powerful as Xi, could embark on such a process without his peers' backing. Of course, if a Politburo majority backs the general secretary, force of habitus and traditional obedience would see the party accepting the reform. But resistance from all levels of the hierarchy is likely if cadres' powers and privileges are threatened. Much more integrated in the state, with tentacles everywhere while being more decentralized, the CCP's machine will have more means than the KMT's to oppose such a process,[50] unless reformer-leaders decide to involve society at large and especially civil society in the process, which would not only be totally against the CCP's political culture but risk opening a Pandora's box that it intends to keep firmly shut.[51]

This brings me to the last difference: the obvious difference in geographic and population sizes between the two political entities. The large physical size and population of the PRC will render any top-down democratization slower, unequal, and fragmented; once begun, the process could even favor local opposition groups and raise the risk of local rebellions which, should they spread, might lead to civil war. Democratization of a big country is more risky if not supported and extended on the ground by local elites.

Toward a Singapore-Style Semidemocracy?

Ever since Deng's trip to Singapore in 1978, the CCP has evinced great admiration for the city-state's economic success and political stability. Many Chinese leaders and intellectuals continue to view Singapore as a model to emulate. For long ruled with an iron hand by Lee Kuan Yew (1923–2015), father of its separation from the Malaysian federation and independence in 1965, Singapore presents major differences with the PRC. Also, it is doubtful whether Beijing really intends to draw inspiration to a great extent from this political model.[52]

Singapore, unlike China, has always had a kind of multiparty system, with elections, of course, held under well-known constraints. The PAP (People's Action Party), founded by Lee, father of current prime minister Lee Hsien-Loong, has long dominated the legislature (holding eighty-three of eighty-nine seats since 2015), and chances of the opposition winning a majority are almost nil. But any election reverse for the PAP, such as in 2011, when the main opposition Workers' Party got six seats, is interpreted as a signal for the government to take serious note of.

As a former British colony, Singapore inherited a common law system close to Hong Kong's, which Lee Kuan Yew, himself once a left-leaning lawyer, worked assiduously to retain. Although Singapore's rule of law has real limits when it comes to political opponents, its courts ensure legal safeguards more reliable than those in the PRC, attracting many multinational groups and personnel to move there.

Singapore also inherited from the British an antigraft institution, the Corrupt Practices Investigation Bureau. Set up in 1952, its independence—it reports directly to the prime minister—is the basis of its efficiency.[53] Another factor in Singaporean officials' probity is their high salaries.

Clearly Singapore's authorities are almost as obsessed with stability and control of society as Chinese ones. However, the city-state's print and electronic media, Internet, and social media have much more elbow room. And although the closer security ties developed with the United States in recent years in order to balance China's growing might have not affected Singapore's internal politics much, they do place it in a somewhat more liberal environment.[54]

Finally, the difference in territorial size between China and Singapore is even greater than in the case of Taiwan, so there is no point addressing it here. Consequently, while borrowing some recipes from Singapore's success, the CCP cannot, and has no desire to, copy the model.

CONCLUSION: CONSOLIDATION OF AN AUTHORITARIAN, ELITIST, PATERNALISTIC, AND IMPERIAL REGIME

Differences with Taiwan and Singapore, like all the other forces at work previously discussed, render improbable any evolution toward democracy of China's regime. Rather, while continuing to move away from its initial socialist project, adapting and modernizing itself, the CCP will doubtless retain its monopolistic hold over the political system. Without changing the name or questioning the PRC's foundational myths (1949 "liberation," People's Republic, Mao), it could in its own way give a greater place to state Confucianism, retaining useful aspects of it, particularly its authoritarian, elitist, paternalist, and imperial dimensions. But as the guarantor of national unity and stability, the CCP will remain the supreme organizer of the Chinese economy's and society's modernization, claiming a key role in this endeavor. The better equipped and more powerful armed forces will continue to support it. The increasingly more competent administration will pursue its task of institutional modernization and economic management. More professional and autonomous courts will offer better legal safeguards to society, particularly its economic actors and its middle classes. Authorities will be more inclined in the future to consult society, elites above all, perhaps setting up more formal mechanisms of representation without, however, taking the risk of democratizing or liberalizing local elections. Presenting itself as society's protector, the CCP will have the last word: government for the people but certainly not by the people.[55]

Externally, the PRC will probably continue seeking not only to regain its unquestioned place in Asia but globally to counterbalance and weaken US might and Western influence, without entering into a major armed conflict with the United States, as the CCP's priority will continue to be pursuit of development and internal stability as well as the political regime's long-term survival.

Should destabilizing political events, even attempts at democratic transition, intervene, the size of China's population and of its territory, the urban-rural chasm, the immensity of the economic and social needs to satisfy, its aging population, its long bureaucratic tradition, and its political values that still dominate the society are many hurdles that contribute to perpetuating an authoritarian regime. This is the case despite the numerous social and potentially political challenges the CCP must face in the coming years: pollution, deepening inequalities, and the rudimentary nature of procedures for questioning the authorities.

Briefly stated, China has greater chances of evolving into a regime that will still be largely authoritarian, elitist, paternalist, and imperial. The CCP will keep alternating periods of political toughness and relaxation but countenance no exit from the current system. Rather, using its cultural otherness, the PRC could continue being the main political challenge to not only Western democracies but all democrats seeking to understand politics and political life.

NOTES

1. Bruce J. Dickson, *The Dictator's Dilemma: The Chinese Communist Party's Strategy for Survival* (Oxford: Oxford University Press, 2016), 222–225.

2. David Shambaugh, *China's Future* (Cambridge, UK, and Malden, MA: Polity, 2016), 22.

3. Wayne M. Morrison, *China's Economic Rise: History, Trends, Challenges, and Implications for the United States* (Washington, DC: Congressional Research Service, 2017).

4. Daniel C. Lynch, *China's Futures: PRC Elites Debate Economics, Politics, and Foreign Policy* (Stanford, CA: Stanford University Press, 2015), 55–67.

5. And 28 percent of assets, if wealth managements products of commercial banks and financial institutions are included. See Chao Xi and Le Xia, "Shadow Banking in China: Then and Now," *Journal of Banking and Finance Law and Practice* 28, no. 2 (June 2, 2017): 146–157.

6. International Monetary Fund, "IMF Executive Board Concludes 2017 Article IV Consultation with the People's Republic of China," press release 17/326, August 15, 2017, http://www.imf.org/en/News/Articles/2017/08/15/pr17326-china-imf-executive-board-concludes-2017-article-iv-consultation.

7. "China Private Consumption: % of GDP," CEIC, https://www.ceicdata.com/en/indicator/china/private-consumption--of-nominal-gdp.

8. "What's Next for China?," McKinsey & Company, n.d., https://www.mckinsey.com/global-themes/asia-pacific/whats-next-for-china.

9. "China: Distribution of Gross Domestic Product (GDP) across Economic Sectors from 2007 to 2017," Statista, n.d., https://www.statista.com/statistics/270325/distribution-of-gross-domestic-product-gdp-across-economic-sectors-in-china/; and Prableen Bajpai, "China's GDP Examined: A Service-Sector Surge," October 31, 2014, http://www.investopedia.com/articles/investing/103114/chinas-gdp-examined-servicesector-surge.asp.

10. Victor Shih, "Financial Instability in China: Possible Pathways and Their Likelihood," *Merics China Monitor*, Mercator Institute for China Studies, October 20, 2017.

11. Don Weinland, "Alibaba and Tencent among Investors in China Unicom," *Financial Times*, August 16, 2017, https://www.ft.com/content/cf5d76ca-8276-11e7-94e2-c5b903247afd.

12. In mid-2018 shadow banking amounted to $10 trillion, representing 70 percent of GDP. "A Guide to China's $10 Trillion Shadow-Banking Maze," *Bloomberg*, June 7, 2018, https://www.bloomberg.com/news/articles/2018-06-07/a-guide-to-china-s-10-trillion-shadow-banking-maze-quicktake.

13. Colbertism is an economic and political doctrine created in the seventeenth century by Jean-Baptiste Colbert, minister to French king Louis XIV. It promotes the role of the state in the economy in stimulating the development of new industries as well as adopting an offensive protectionism. Today, Colbertism characterizes a government's inclination to carry out a proactive industrial policy, in which it plays a key role in investing in the industries of the future. Influenced by Colbertism and initiated in the 1960s by French president Charles de Gaulle, Gaullism articulated a similar approach to economic development based on state intervention, a certain degree of planification, the creation of national champions, and financial stability. However, being in favor of the European construction, Gaullism does not promote protectionism.

14. Jost Wübekke et al., "Made in China 2025: The Making of a High-Tech Superpower and Consequences for Industrial Countries," *Merics Papers on China*, no. 2 (December 2016), https://www.merics.org/sites/default/files/2017-09/MPOC_No.2_Made inChina2025.pdf.

15. Dennis Normile, "Science Suffers as China's Internet Censors Plug Holes in Great Firewall," *Science*, August 30, 2017, http://www.sciencemag.org/news/2017/08/science-suffers-china-s-internet-censors-plug-holes-great-firewall.

16. Samm Sacks, *Disruptors, Innovators, and Thieves: Assessing Innovation in China's Digital Economy* (Washington, DC: CSIS, 2018), https://csis-prod.s3.amazonaws.com/s3fs-public/publication/180108_Sacks_DisruptorsInnovatorsThieves_Web.pdf?22jQM v.fUUhvJsneUUmP767drezraCXy.

17. "SIPO Releases Patent Statistics of China for 2016," https://s3.amazonaws.com/documents.lexology.com/e57eecda-979e-4a57-ae6d-46461dbd37a7.pdf; and "SIPO Releases Patent Statistics of China for 2017," http://www.cpahkltd.com/EN/info.aspx?n=20180308160701100381.

18. Scott Kennedy, *The Fat Tech Dragon: Benchmarking China's Innovation Drive* (Washington, DC: CSIS, 2017), https://csis-prod.s3.amazonaws.com/s3fs-public/publication/170829_Kennedy_FatTechDragon_Web.pdf.

19. Barry Eichengreen, "Escaping the Middle-Income Trap," in *Proceedings of the Economic Policy Symposium, Jackson Hole*, 2011, 409–419, https://www.kansascityfed.org/publicat/sympos/2011/Eichengreen_final.pdf. See also George Magnus, *Red Flags: Why Xi's China Is in Jeopardy* (New Haven, CT: Yale University Press, 2018).

20. Shambaugh has analyzed this very well in *China's Future*, 56.

21. Isabelle Thireau and Wang Hansheng, eds., *Disputes au village chinois: Formes du juste et recompositions locales des espaces normatifs* [Disputes in a Chinese village: Local forms of justice and reconstructions of normative situations] (Paris: Editions de la Maison des sciences de l'homme, 2001).

22. Some studies put China's Gini at 0.61. Gabriel Wildau and Tom Mitchell, "China Income Inequality among World's Worst," *Financial Times*, January 14, 2016, https://www.ft.com/content/3c521faa-baa6-11e5-a7cc-280dfe875e28.

23. "China's New Approach to Beating Poverty," *The Economist*, April 29, 2017, 21. The 2017 report by Hurun, a Chinese institution that evaluates private entrepreneurs' fortunes, said the number of those possessing capital of over $300 million was 2,130 (compared to 2,056 in 2016); Phila Siu, "Tales from Beijing and Hong Kong Show Challenge of Fighting Poverty, Especially among Working Poor," *SCMP*, November 26, 2017, https://www.scmp.com/news/hong-kong/economy/article/2121613/tales-beijing-and-hong-kong-show-challenge-fighting-poverty.

24. Martin King Whyte, *Myth of Social Volcano: Perceptions of Inequality and Distributive Injustice in Contemporary China* (Stanford, CA: Stanford University Press, 2010); and Dickson, *The Dictator's Dilemma*, 255–257.

25. Thireau and Hua, *Les ruses de la démocratie*.

26. Hsiao Hsin-huang, ed., *The Changing Faces of the Middle Classes in Asia-Pacific* (Taipei: Academia Sinica, 2006); David M. Jones, "Democratization, Civil Society and Illiberal Middle Class Culture in Pacific Asia," *Comparative Politics* 30, no. 2 (January 1998): 147–169; and Jeremy L. Wallace, *Cities and Stability: Urbanization, Redistribution, and Regime Survival in China* (New York: Oxford University Press, 2014). See also Andrew Nathan, "The Puzzle of the Chinese Middle Class," *Journal of Democracy* 27, no. 2 (April 2016): 5–19.

27. But not always, as shown by some Beijing residents' support for migrants expelled from the Daxing area in late 2017; see also Dickson, *The Dictator's Dilemma*, 199–200.

28. Wallace, *Cities and Stability*.

29. He Qinglian, "Zhongguo weihe bu hui chuxian duanyashi bengkui" [Why China is not on the edge of an abyss], *Voice of America*, June 26–27, 2017, http://heqinglian.net/2017/06/27/china-future/.

30. Kevin J. O'Brien and Lianjiang Li, *Rightful Resistance in Rural China* (Cambridge, UK: Cambridge University Press, 2006); and Thireau and Wang, *Disputes au village chinois*.

31. Graeme Smith, "The Hollow State: Rural Governance in China," *The China Quarterly*, no. 203 (2010): 601–618.

32. Wu Zhihong, *Juyingguo* [A nation of giant infants] (Hangzhou: Zhejiang renmin chubanshe, 2016).

33. Zeng Yuli, "Turn Off, Drop Out: Why Young Chinese Are Abandoning Ambition," *Sixth Tone*, June 27, 2017, http://www.sixthtone.com/news/1000407/turn-off%2C-drop-out-why-young-chinese-are-abandoning-ambition.

34. Gene Sharp, *From Dictatorship to Democracy: A Conceptual Framework for Liberation* (Boston: The Albert Einstein Institution, 1993); and Gene Sharp, *Cong ducai dao minzhu: Jiefang yundong de gainian kuangjia*, 2nd Chinese ed. (Bangkok: Huifu Miandian minzhu weiyuanhui & *Xinshidai* [The New Era Journal], 2003).

35. Hong Kong's chief executive is chosen by an electoral committee of twelve hundred members, mostly pro-Beijing figures. The Legislative Council consists of seventy members, forty of them elected through universal suffrage and thirty by "functional constituencies" in which the city's proestablishment elites are overrepresented.

36. See the debate provoked by John Pomfret's article, "Chinese Cash at American Colleges Is a Massive Problem," *Supchina*, August 23, 2017, http://supchina.com/2017/08/23/john-pomfret-chinese-cash-american-colleges-massive-problem/; and Lawrence Kuok's response, "Lawrence Kuok: The Real Chinese Student Story—a Response to John Pomfret," *Supchina*, September 5, 2017, http://supchina.com/2017/09/05/lawrence-kuok-real-chinese-student-story-response-john-pomfret/.

37. At the end of 2017, among CYL's 81.24 million members, 57.95 million were students; *Zhongguo Gongqingtuan wang*, May 31, 2018, http://qnzz.youth.cn/gzdt/201805/t20180531_11632923.htm.

38. Diandian Guo, "Chinese Communist Youth League Joins Bilibili—Where Official Discourse Meets Online Subculture," What's on Weibo, January 3, 2017, http://www.whatsonweibo.com/chinese-communist-youth-league-joins-bilibili-official-discourse-meets-online-subculture/.

39. In order to influence young Chinese living abroad, especially students, the League opened a Twitter account in September 2017, although this online forum is banned in China. Minnie Chan, "China's Communist Youth League Opens Twitter Account amid Crackdown on Internet Access," *SCMP*, September 17, 2017, https://www.scmp.com/news/china/policies-politics/article/2111566/chinas-communist-youth-league-opens-twitter-account.

40. See Isabelle Attané and Baocheng Gu, eds., *Analysing China's Population: Social Change in a New Demographic Era* (Dordrecht, Netherlands: Ined, Springer, 2014).

41. For a Marxist-Sunyatsenist interpretation of *minsheng*, see Dan Xiaohong, "Lun Zhongguo gongchandangren de 'minsheng guang'" [On the conception of "people's

livelihood" developed by CCP members], *Beijing Ribao* [Beijing Daily], October 10, 2009, http://dangshi.people.com.cn/GB/85041/10167089.html.

42. Dickson, *The Dictator's Dilemma*, 243–245.

43. Teresa Wright, *Accepting Authoritarianism: State-Society Relations in China's Reform Era* (Stanford, CA: Stanford University Press, 2006).

44. Shambaugh, *China's Future*, 98; and Dickson, *The Dictator's Dilemma*, 39–45.

45. Jean-Pierre Cabestan, *Le système politique chinois: Un nouvel équilibre autoritaire* [The Chinese political system: A new authoritarian equilibrium] (Paris: Presses de Sciences-Po, 2014), 606–613.

46. Cheng Li, *Chinese Politics in the Xi Jinping Era: Reassessing Collective Leadership* (Washington, DC: Brookings Institution, 2016).

47. See Jean-Pierre Cabestan, *La politique internationale de la Chine: Entre intégration et volonté de puissance* [China's international policies: Between integration and pursuit of power], 2nd ed. (Paris: Presses de Sciences Po, 2015).

48. On the ever-present risk of a possible invasion of Taiwan, see Michael Beckley, "The Emerging Military Balance in East Asia: How China's Neighbors Can Check Chinese Naval Expansion," *International Security* 42, no. 2 (Autumn 2017): 78–119; and Denny Roy, "Prospects for Taiwan Maintaining Its Autonomy under Chinese Pressure," *Asian Survey* 57, no. 6 (November–December 2017): 1135–1158.

49. This is very well analyzed by He Qinglian, "Zhongguo weihe buhui."

50. Yongshun Cai, "Power Structure and Regime Resilience: Contentious Politics in China," *British Journal of Political Science*, no. 38 (May 2008): 411–432.

51. Dickson, *The Dictator's Dilemma*, 305.

52. Cherian George, *Singapore, Incomplete: Reflections on a First World Nation's Arrested Political Development* (Singapore: Woodsville News, 2017).

53. Hong Kong set up a similar institution in 1974, the Independent Commission Against Corruption.

54. On the differences between Singapore and China, see Mark R. Thompson, "How Deng and His Heirs Misunderstood Singapore," *New Mandala*, February 1, 2019, https://www.newmandala.org/how-deng-and-his-heirs-misunderstood-singapore/. See also Mark R. Thomson, *Authoritarian Modernism in East Asia* (London and New York: Palgrave Macmillan, 2019).

55. These conclusions are quite close to those of Bruce Dickson in *The Dictator's Dilemma* (301–321) but differ greatly from predictions by Bruce Gilley, who in 2004 had said only democratization could ensure CCP elites remain in power. Bruce Gilley, *China's Democratic Future: How It Will Happen and Where It Will Lead* (New York: Columbia University Press, 2004).

Conclusion

A Regime on Extended Reprieve

Some countries have trouble reforming and are finally driven to revolution. It seems China, somewhat like eighteenth-century France or early twentieth-century Russia, is among them. During the late Qing era, the regime got rid of elites who sought to introduce modest reforms. By stalling all land redistribution and democratization, Chiang Kai-shek facilitated CCP victory, although it was the Sino-Japanese War and Soviet aid that helped it militarily defeat the KMT in 1948–1949. Today CCP elites think they can indefinitely postpone political reforms, perpetuating the one-party rule founded in 1949. Proud of China's newfound might, they are increasingly inclined to promote their model of authoritarian development abroad. But are they assured of victory? How should democracies in Europe, North America, Asia, and elsewhere face up to these ambitions?

THE PRC IS CONDEMNED . . . IN THE LONG TERM

I think that in the end Fukuyama's arguments will prevail, at least in China: good governance is important, but so is democracy. China's one-party system persists because of economic growth and repression but mostly for want of democrats, to paraphrase Fukuyama.[1] But clearly China's political regime is decadent and debauched, having long replaced its communist or even socialist illusions with a nationalist dream of power without democracy, grandeur without freedom, and prosperity without equity. Such are the failings of strong states. In this sense, I join Shambaugh, Minxin Pei, and Nathan, but over the long run, and not for the reasons they cite (see the introduction). Lack of freedoms will not affect the economy, elites' corruption will not precipitate regime collapse, and it is rather improbable that society will rise up first against authoritarianism and the political system.

171

My reasoning is that Chinese intellectual and even political elites are divided on the final policy outcome of the ongoing modernization process. Some clearly have Singapore in mind without fully being inspired by it. Others, fewer in number, think China will democratize eventually, taking the path Taiwan has. But most believe this will take time, perhaps a century or at least half that long, and they are ready to wait for society's "quality" to improve before engaging with the process or rather let their children or grandchildren push it. Between these two groups, opinions oscillate, some wanting to embrace the Singapore model fully and others preferring a form of elite-run and elitist semidemocratic regime close to Hong Kong's semicorporatist formula. But in general, the idea that Chinese culture and in particular Confucianism are incompatible with democracy is gradually receding. Of course academics like Lucien Pye have always thought (and still think) the opposite.[2] Others, such as Shaohua Hu, talk of a variable neutral ground, holding that Chinese political culture is more "a-democratic" than antidemocratic.[3] Despite the skewed interpretations that may be advanced, the democratic idea has gradually taken hold in China since the late nineteenth century. As in Taiwan or South Korea earlier, China's liberal intellectuals are now showcasing the "seeds of democracy," to borrow Pierre-Etienne Will's expression, stemming from imperial political tradition such as the power of remonstrance, selection of officials through competitions, moral duties of the educated, or even the right to rebellion.[4] Liberal ideas (also feminist ideas or at least of male-female parity) diffused from Taiwan, Hong Kong, and the Chinese diaspora are continuously spreading and influencing elites and society at large gradually. More Chinese taxpayers want to be represented and question the Communist Party's sources of funding. Debates invoked in this book show there is no more cause to deplore, with Bo Yang, Chinese people's inability to enter modernity. As in Taiwan when Bo wrote his famous pamphlet (1985), in China now it is more the dangers faced by reformers than "slave mentality" that dissuade most Chinese from working toward a democratic society.[5]

Meanwhile, hypotheses of gradual evolution toward a less authoritarian but ill-defined regime are of limited value, because once a political reform process is unleashed, it is difficult to block its path. Should the regime engage in it early—that is, before civil society pressure becomes too strong—the democratization process has chances of being gradual and controlled, letting the PRC evolve toward a Singapore-style or even

Hong Kong–style semidemocracy. In this regard, the conservative political culture that still dominates Chinese society could prove an asset.[6]

But there is no guarantee of success for such a slow and peaceful evolution toward democracy. History shows that gradualism has limits; once underway, regime liberalization leads almost mechanically to its democratization, except if it is negated and authoritarianism is restored — a costly process.[7] If tomorrow or rather the day after, a majority of China's society demands democracy, or it is conceded by reform-minded elites, China will not for long retain CCP tutelage or a parliament elected only in part by its citizens. Poland's political evolution in 1989 best illustrates this. Once the "one person-one vote" principle is introduced, all other democratic demands arise whether reforming elites wish them to or not: freedom of opinion, press, assembly, and association; an independent judiciary; separation of powers; and many other fundamental transformations, such as freeing of political prisoners and an end to harassment of dissidents. The CCP's leadership is fully aware of this and hence offers mere superficial reforms, guarding tooth and nail its ruling one-party status.

But by indefinitely postponing any real political reform, Xi Jinping and his colleagues risk incurring a higher cost of democratic transition. Instead of being peaceful, it could be violent. Rather than being directed and channeled, it could be erratic and disorderly. It could end up neither reconciling nor facilitating a new political consensus but be divisive, even precipitate a civil war, forcing the army to arbitrate and intervene to restore order or national unity. Or perhaps the armed forces themselves will stand divided between the CCP's defenders and democracy's partisans, fighting each other and leading China to the abyss.

Therefore the party's seventh- or eighth-generation leaders—at least some among them—could themselves be inclined to initiate the political reform process. Moving China closer to other civilized nations' ranks and improving their country's international image may motivate them. But before undertaking such an adventure and braving resistance from conservatives, the CCP apparatus, and regime beneficiaries, they have to win support from outside the party-state, among civil society and especially intellectual and economic elites, including counter-elites. Thus, they have to engage in a process both perilous and slow, one that will remain dangerous even if led from above.

Will they be courageous enough to take such risks? Will they definitely engage in a democratization process when, as Robert Dahl says, they realize the cost of repression has become prohibitive?[8] What exogenous event may divide elites in power and provoke democratization?[9] Nobody knows.

I have wished to show in this book that in the long run, the Chinese regime is doomed, not as much for economic reasons as for political and human ones. It will end when taxpayers want to be politically represented, and when elites and society find it unacceptable to jail people for their ideas, have had enough of being ruled by a secret society—the CPC—and conclude that only a democratic China can become a respected great power and full member of the international community.

In other words, no historic determinism condemns China to remain authoritarian forever. However, what I have also sought to highlight is the multiplicity of obstacles that can slow the country's march toward democracy and the perils any democratization process presents. I believe these dangers are greater than often thought of, as the process will certainly bring out profound divisions, as already noted, among both elites and society. These dangers fuel the determination of the CCP's leadership and the intellectuals who support it to refuse any political opening.

Therefore—and this is quite important in the foreseeable future—the PRC will pursue its fight against what it calls "Western democracy," that is, *against us*, and continue backing all regimes that help it to highlight deficiencies in our political systems and the qualities of its own. How should we face this challenge? It is this difficult question that I now briefly consider.

WHAT SHOULD DEMOCRACIES DO?

Faced with the consolidation of an authoritarian regime in China and its rising power internationally, what should democracies do? What can they do? How can they face the challenge? What common strategy should not only Europeans and Northern Americans but also all democracies adopt to defend their interests, contain the return and reinforcement of political authoritarianism, and instead steer the global trend toward democracy and freedom?[10]

These questions lie way beyond this book's scope. Their answers depend on global economic, social, political, and military-strategic changes implicating multiple actors and forces at work: from the US retreat internationally under Donald Trump to the rise of populism, from the Arab Spring's failure to Islamic terrorism's persistence, from the unprecedented rise of China and other newly emerging nations to the repeated failures of African development strategies, and from Western economies' relative stagnation to governance crises in the European Union (EU) and more generally in quite a number of democracies. It is impossible to ignore that the increasing assaults against democracy as widely understood are closely related to a relative weakening of the West globally and especially the perception of such weakening.[11] It is also impossible to ignore that this unfavorable context weighs on relations with the PRC, now the world's number 2 economy and a great power with ambitions—and increasingly the means—not only to question some of the most fundamental and universal norms established after World War II, but to overtake the United States as world leading superpower.

As for China's future political transformation, I think we should be modest and realistic. By we, I mean all democracies, and particularly those, such as the United States and to some extent the EU, that pretend and hope to influence China's political future. Of course we must first put our own house in order. In other words, we need to improve our own political systems, in particular better resist the populist trap, guarantee our liberties, and enhance our rulers' accountability to make our democracies more attractive, not only in the eyes of the Chinese but to any people living under authoritarian regimes. Reining in populism and more important the economic and social causes of its emergence—deindustrialization, growing income inequalities and regional disparities, and mismanaged migrations, to name a few—should become a priority, since populism often opens the door not only to anti-elite sentiments but also to forces that favor strongmen regimes and jeopardize the principle of elections, political representation, judicial independence, and democratic order.

We must also try to put our differences aside to focus on the defense of liberal democracy and reach a consensus on the best ways to fulfill this objective. Clearly Trump's election and the way the current US administration has run its trade war with China, scrapped the Iran nuclear deal, turned its back on the Paris agreement on climate change, and more generally jeopardized multilateral international institutions have not helped. Obvious structural discrepancies in terms of geostrategic responsibilities and interests also complicate the game: while the United States and its Asia-Pacific allies have good reason to be concerned about China's rapid military modernization and ambitions, particularly in the maritime domain that it claims, European nations have less reason to get involved. For example, although the British and the French navies now regularly sail through the South China Sea to remind Beijing of its obligations vis-à-vis the international law of the sea, they are not willing or able to conduct there, contrary to the US Navy, more robust "freedom of navigation operations" that directly confront the status of China's newly created artificial islands in the Spratly. Yet the EU cannot ignore the growing bipolar strategic rivalry as well as risks of cold if not hot war between China and the United States. As US allies, most European nations, but also Japan, South Korea, Australia, and others, are affected by this new reality and will be forced to make often more difficult choices down the road.

More generally, the EU (particularly its major member states, such as France, Germany, Italy, Spain, and Poland), the United States, and other like-minded countries (such as Australia, Canada, New Zealand, and the United Kingdom) should try to think beyond the Trump era and work harder on defining common objectives and probably also more similar strategies regarding our relationships with China. Among these common objectives, the promotion of a rule-based international order and of the universality of human rights, especially civil and political rights, should remain a common priority. Although not directly related to the defense of democracy, the protection of sensitive and key technologies, the reform of the WTO, and increasing pressure on China to open its market, scrap its nontrade barriers, reduce the power of its state-owned enterprises, and submit them to market mechanisms — in other words introduce a more even playing field to foreign economic actors — are also conducive to consolidating the liberal international order that underpins the survival of our democracies. And a US ratification of the United Nations Convention on the Law of the Sea would strengthen our hand vis-à-vis China's behavior in the South China Sea.

We must finally continue to engage not only the Chinese party-state (see below) but also, and as much as possible, the Chinese society, training its future elites and providing scholarships to its students, as well as multiplying channels of intellectual, cultural, and religious interactions and dialogues with it.

Of course China's eventual democratization depends not on us but the Chinese themselves, especially endogenous forces which, barring international conflict, will continue confronting each other on economic, social, cultural, judicial, and political grounds. Our opening to Chinese society and availability can help. But one should not harbor illusions about the capacity of foreign powers, including the United States, to shape China's future. In that respect, rereading James Mann's prescient book *The Chinese Fantasy* may be useful.[12] And although it is partly based on incorrect assumptions, the current debate unfolding in the United States about the failure of past engagement policies toward China, all the way back to Richard Nixon and Henry Kissinger, is welcome. While it will be unable to kill America's legendary missionary zeal, it may contribute to convincing a growing number of US policy makers and scholars to propose and adopt more realistic, feasible, and pragmatic policies toward China and, more important, to manage their expectations.

Having said that, I think that we can and need to better protect ourselves against any Chinese influence that hurts our interests. It is therefore essential that we take stock of the ideological and strategic rivalry we are engaged in with China. The CCP never ceases to denounce the "pernicious influence" of the Enlightenment and of liberal political ideas generally. Although in international forums Chinese diplomats sound more ambiguous, one would have to be blind not to notice that the CCP is at war against us, our values, and our ideals.

Some believe that this hostility to "Western democracy" is defensive and that there is no intention to promote the Chinese model or "Beijing consensus" worldwide. That had long been true but is not anymore since 2008, when the PRC began more clearly asserting its might. Xi has only amplified this tendency.[13] China's economic globalization and greater international ambitions have led it to indulge in muscle-flexing abroad. The Chinese society is still made to learn of the superiority of "socialist democracy" over "bourgeois democracy" that Karl Marx denounced. On the international stage, China is busy weakening the universal democratic idea as democracies conceive it and boosting authoritarian ideology's camp globally. In this battle, China does not lack allies: other authoritarian countries, or what the Americans call "illiberal democracies," such as Putin's Russia, Belarus, and the Central Asian states, of course, but also Rwanda, Turkey, Venezuela, and many other developing countries. Disturbingly, some EU members heavily dependent on China economically,

such as the Czech Republic, Greece, and Hungary, have become coopera-
tive and fallen silent on contentious issues (human rights, Xinjiang, Tibet
and the Dalai Lama). Even more worryingly, sections of Western political
and economic elites filled with admiration for China's economic success,
and seeing the growing asymmetry in our relations with the world's
number 2 economy or because of personal interests, such as their financial dependence on the Chinese government or Chinese companies, have
abandoned the defense of our values. Weakening the cause of democracies, since Trump came to office the US administration has until very
recently largely ignored the Chinese government's increasing infringe-
ments of its citizens' political rights.

This problem is not new. But it has become much more acute due for
the reasons already noted. China has become clearly more aggressive
ideologically, and democracy is in crisis, ill served by populist movements seeking strongmen and radical solutions, often antidemocratic.[14]
This relatively new state of affairs will certainly change in the future. But
can it change in our favor if we do nothing, if we give up the fight?

Given China's rising power, this struggle has evidently become
tougher. There is no question whatsoever of freezing ties with the PRC.
Because of the innumerable links democracies have forged with China
since its opening to the outside world, that would be totally impossible.
There is no question either of stopping cooperation where interests con-
verge, be it in matters economic, diplomatic, environmental, cultural, or
security related. The current US-China trade war and growing geostrategic rivalry have obviously contributed to reducing these common interests but are unlikely to completely sideline them. While the US and EU
economic integration with China may be questioned in the sectors that
are perceived as too strategic or security related, a total economic decoupling between the West (not to mention US Asian allies such as Japan,
Taiwan, and South Korea) and China remains in my view highly unlikely. Similarly, US-China military tensions have increased, particularly in
the South China Sea, increasing the risk of incidents and even crisis between the two countries. Nonetheless, a hot war between these two nuclear powers—or a fall in what some, with Graham Allison, have called
Thucydides's trap—remains unlikely precisely because of the Armaged-
don it would trigger.[15]

Since 2018 the previous US administrations' "engagement" policy toward China has been increasingly criticized in the United States, convinc-

ing a growing number of politicians and experts to adopt instead a "confrontational policy" or at the very least a "conditional engagement policy" toward this country.[16] As James Mann has more recently reminded us, "engagement policy" has two different meanings. The first is well accepted and should not be questioned: stop ignoring or isolating the PRC; rather, interact and dialogue with it as much as possible in order to find common ground when and where possible or put pressure on it when we disagree. The second, introduced by the Bill Clinton administration and around the same time the EU, was more ambitious and in retrospect unrealistic: engage China with the expectation that its political regime and economic system will move closer to ours.[17] This latter form of engagement clearly needs to be abandoned; as this book has tried to demonstrate, the CCP is willing neither to open up its political system nor to fully liberalize its economic structures. Actually, it can be argued that a more conditional engagement policy toward China has already been implemented for some time by the United States, the EU, and other democracies. And I strongly recommend that all democracies attach more conditions and limits to their China policy, not only to better promote their values but also to better protect them. Consequently, democracies should, I believe, be more vigilant, prudent, selective, combative, and confident. I also recommend that they try as much as possible to put their differences aside, enhance their discussions and coordination about China, and adopt common policies and strategies toward this country. While adopting a selective engagement policy on issues where we can make progress, we should not hesitate to confront China on issues on which we are unable to find common ground.

MORE VIGILANT

First of all, we should be more careful about all Chinese initiatives aimed at boosting its position and weakening ours. Its initiatives include maritime and territorial claims in the South China Sea; the construction of militarized artificial islands there; the Belt and Road Initiative (BRI); and its proposals on the North Korean nuclear issue, which place the recalcitrant Pyongyang regime on a par with democratic South Korea and the United States.[18]

On issues with a clear ideological dimension, such as human rights, dialogue is of course preferable to its absence. But perpetuation of unproductive dialogues is particularly harmful. Dialogue should be undertaken under result-oriented conditions, facilitating the freeing of political prisoners and opponents.

On Tibet, the political and economic cost of any official and even semiofficial meeting with the Dalai Lama has become extremely high. But is capitulation the answer? I personally think democratic countries' political leaders should not only continue meeting the Tibetan spiritual leader (or his successor) according to an appropriate format but should also more openly support the greater political autonomy within the boundaries of the PRC he has demanded for Tibet since 1988.

On Xinjiang, in view of the long-standing but growing repression unleashed by the Chinese authorities of any Islam-related activities, democracies should not only speak up but also develop a dialogue with Uyghur and other groups' democratic organizations in exile to promote a political settlement within the PRC's boundaries.

Greater vigilance is also needed regarding Hong Kong politics. When some prospective candidates for legislative elections in September 2016 were barred by the territory's administration because they were suspected of favoring independence, the EU kept completely silent. And in Washington, it was less the Obama administration than the US-China Economic and Security Review Commission that rang the alarm bell.[19] That move by Hong Kong authorities presaged other more disturbing ones, including the jailing in August 2017 of three leaders of the 2014 Umbrella Movement and the banning in September 2018 of the proindependence Hong Kong National Party. Threats to Hong Kong's autonomy and political freedoms have become too numerous not to be more loudly denounced by democracies. These repeated threats have only drawn mild reactions in Brussels, Berlin, Paris, or even Washington. Let us not forget that a part of the struggle over China's political future plays out in this Special Administrative Region of the PRC.

While democracies' semiofficial relations with Taiwan have notably developed since the island democratized in the early 1990s, their solidarity with Taiwanese democracy should be more clearly affirmed: against PLA intimidations and in support of unconditional cross-Strait talks; against Beijing's interference in Taiwan's domestic politics and elections; and through a deepening of exchanges between Taiwanese and democratic countries' government officials and political leaders. Adopted by the US Congress in February 2018, the Taiwan Travel Act is part of this growing awareness and need to engage in normal relations with Taiwan and its elected leaders. While other democracies may refrain from adopting specific legislation on the matter, they can easily enhance to cabinet level their delegations to Taiwan. And more generally, democracies have a clear interest in protecting Taiwan's political autonomy and promoting its democratic experience; Taiwan's peaceful democratization is the most vivid demonstration of Confucian societies' compatibility with liberal democracy.

We should also be more vigilant regarding apparently cultural initiatives that are in fact political ones launched by China. An example is the Confucius Institutes or language centers funded by the Hanban (Office of Chinese Language Council International) under the Ministry of Education; again, it is not about blocking these institutes from being established or giving them advantages identical to those received by Alliance Françaises or Goethe Institutes in China, but Confucius Institutes are part of the CCP's United Front strategy, whose official aim is to boost China's "soft power." In these circumstances, letting our universities welcome them is a political error, as they only add to these universities' dependence on China, curbing their freedom of speech regarding that country. It is not surprising that under these circumstances, a growing number of American universities have discontinued their cooperation with the Confucius Institute that they hosted. Other democracies' universities should do the same. Welcome Confucius Institutes, but let them operate within their own walls.[20]

Finally, we should be more vigilant about the PRC's and its embassies' methods for watching Chinese students in foreign universities, controlling old and new diasporas worldwide and influencing elections through subsidies.[21] The 2017 scandals in Canada, Australia, and New Zealand should be borne in mind.[22]

MORE PRUDENT AND SELECTIVE

While continuing cooperation and dialogue with China, particularly its society, democracies should be more prudent and selective in their actions, raising political, economic, and military pressure on a regime whose ideological and imperial ambitions are increasingly evident. Above all, we should avoid using the word "friendship." Part of undiluted Soviet jargon, any expression including the idea (friends, friendly relations) is meant to disarm foreign partners facing the Chinese government's demands. Once such relations have been established, all negotiations become arduous, caught up in a web of obligations unfavorable to us and that we don't need.[23] Moreover, by definition, it is impossible to develop friendly ties with a state (I am referring to the party-state, not Chinese society) that does not share our political values. The same holds true for the trite term "trust." Let us not seek "trust" from a partner that fundamentally distrusts us, as it sees in democracies a threat to its own system. Let us instead protect our interests, a concept that China understands very well and much better than in the past, including as far as its own interests are concerned.

Democracies have already partly decentralized their cooperation with China. But we should go further in this direction, forging more frequent direct relations and projects not only with local governments but also to the extent possible with private companies, NGOs, and civil society as a whole. Of course, in China the state and its foreign affairs officials (security, diplomatic) are omnipresent. But bear in mind that any cooperation is more substantial and beneficial to the extent that it limits Chinese state intermediation.

Meanwhile, we are becoming aware that some Chinese investments in Europe, North America, and other democracies have the objective of mastering our cutting-edge technologies. Prudence and selectivity in this domain are essential not only for economic reasons — retaining our firms' competitiveness — but also for strategic ones, as many high technologies are dual use and thus have military implications.

An embargo on EU arms sales to China has been in force since Tiananmen (1989), as efforts to find a consensus on lifting it have failed, notably in 2003. A similar embargo has been imposed by the United States. But these embargos apply only to lethal arms, not to transfer of dual-use technologies. Again, greater prudence and selectivity are recommended and have started to be observed. The reason is that Chinese companies now increasingly have the means to acquire sensitive and high technologies by buying the foreign companies that possess them. Hence the decision of the Trump administration made in August 2018 to introduce a new law, the Foreign Investment Risk Review Modernization Act (FIRRMA), in order to strengthen the Committee on Foreign Investment in the United States (CFIUS) review process. European nations have also started to react, particularly after the German government was unable to prevent the sale of Kuka, a leading German robotics firm, to Midea, a Chinese company, in 2016. Since then, more restrictive vetting mechanisms on the grounds of national security have been introduced, at least in major European economies such as Germany and France. However, at the end of 2018 less than half of EU countries had adopted stricter legislation. Actually, weaker European economies, such as Italy, Portugal, and Greece, are reluctant to not only adopt similar vetting mechanisms but also endorse the EU Commission's plan, initiated in November 2018, aimed at stepping up cooperation and information exchange on non-member states' investments in the EU. As a result, it remains unlikely that the EU as such will introduce a CFIUS-like review process for Chinese investments, complicating to some extent transatlantic relations. While this battle is far from being over, key European economies and companies are today more aware of the choices they need to make to protect their technologies and secure their activities on the US market.[24]

Finally, prudence and selectivity are needed over China's international initiatives. One example is the BRI. Launched by Xi in 2013, the BRI testifies to not only China's economic interests but also its diplomatic-strategic ones. But does it benefit us really? Should we not be critical of this initiative? Again, this does not mean that on the ground some cooperation projects now part of this plan cannot be developed, provided the Chinese side is fully transparent about their status, funding, and intentions. But if BRI attracts less affluent states in Central and Southern Europe to the Chinese orbit and divides the EU, with the help of the so-called 16 + 1 initiative, we cannot but distance ourselves from and try to thwart it.[25] In fact, Brussels recommends this approach. I can only add my worry over the negative consequences of any BRI-stimulated rapprochement with Beijing for the future of young and not-so-young European democracies as well as for a growing number of developing countries. A positive development is that in 2018 both the United States and the EU introduced plans to support private investments in the developing countries targeted by the BRI, particularly in Asia and Africa. In October 2018 the US Congress adopted a BUILD Act, which establishes a new agency—the US International Development Finance Corporation—aimed at boosting the US role in fighting against poverty and supporting US companies abroad, doubling the envelope of the previous organization to US$60 billion. In the same month the EU adopted a new strategy to connect Europe and Asia, putting "people's interests and rights . . . at the core of any policy" and committing an additional 60 billion euros to support investments in connectivity. More will need to be accomplished to counter China's BRI. But ironically, Xi's BRI has forced both the United States and the EU (as well as other democracies, such as Japan) to adjust and commit more investments to the Global South. These new developments should be an opportunity for both Americans and Europeans to enhance their dialogue on the BRI and its economic and political impacts in the targeted countries.[26]

MORE COMBATIVE AND CONFIDENT

In our relations with China, the most important dispute today is over international norms, in principle backed by all UN member states and, on economic relations, by the WTO. These norms have a bearing on international security as well as territorial issues and economic, social, civil, and political rights.

Quite logically given its rising power, China seeks greater say in international multilateral organizations and to influence current norms in its favor. In late 2015 it demanded and got an upward revision of its financial participation (6 percent, up from 3.8 percent) and thus its voting power in the International Monetary Fund. Similarly, albeit nonconvertible, the yuan is now part of the basket of currencies on the basis of which Special Drawing Rights are calculated.

The problem is that the nature of its political system drives the PRC to contest a number of norms the previous Chinese government (KMT) had contributed to drafting and approved during the UN's founding in 1945. Such is the case with the 1948 Universal Declaration of Human Rights, whose principles Beijing largely ignores. This is also the case with the International Covenant on Economic, Social and Cultural Rights, which China ratified in 2001 but with a crucial reservation concerning trade union rights. It also signed the International Covenant on Civil and Political Rights in 1998 but has not ratified it, for understandable reasons: despite its abolishing in 2013 of reeducation through labor (*laojiao*), an administrative detention system run by Public Security officials and outside judicial review, various forms of such detention continue to be used, particularly but not only in Xinjiang.

Such selective application of international norms also shows up in its handling of maritime and territorial disputes. China rejects international mediation; it vehemently denounced the July 12, 2016, verdict of the Permanent Court of Arbitration, based in The Hague, on its maritime conflict with the Philippines in a case the latter initiated.

Just as important, China has been using WTO rules to its advantage, invoking the right to recourse in settlement matters that the institution offers while maintaining its own protectionism in all sectors where it wishes to support its "national champions." European, American, and Japanese complaints about Chinese market access have therefore multiplied. But they also need to go beyond the WTO framework and revisit the concessions made to China in 2001 in terms of subsidies, forced technology transfers, and nontrade barriers. Again, the strategy privileged by the Trump administration and its obsession with the trade deficit are not supported by the EU, Japan, or others such as Canada. Moreover, these economies have their own trade disputes with the United States. Nonetheless, they all face the same obstacles, concerns, and objectives as far as their economic relations with China are concerned. And ironically, Trump's heavy-handed strategy has been more efficient than the patient negotiations preferred by the Europeans. This new situation should therefore favor a closer transatlantic cooperation on trade issue vis-à-vis China and hopefully convince the EU Commission, which is clearly empowered to negotiate in the name of all EU member states, to adopt a more combative approach. The EU Commission has actually started to move in that direction in issuing on March 12, 2019, a robust 10-point action plan, for the first time qualifying China as a "systemic rival promoting alternative models of governance."[27]

China has also begun setting up its own international multilateral organizations, such as the Shanghai Cooperation Organisation (2001) and more recently the AIIB, in which, quite logically, it tries to retain a key role. Thus, in AIIB it enjoys veto power and wields decisive influence despite denials. My advice is to remain critical and cautious toward these initiatives, as they are aimed at enhancing the influence of China and weakening ours.

How should we manage these divergent values and interests? It is not for me to propose concrete methods but simply to draw attention to the link between the position China takes on these issues and the nature of its political system. China is not the only emerging power to contest the US-dominated post–World War II world order. But it is the most virulent, and its revisionism serves ideological and political interests totally in contradiction to ours. It is therefore dangerous to offer such revisionism even the least support.[28] At the end of 2017, the Trump administration officially acknowledged that China (and Russia) were "revisionist powers" trying to change the global status quo and engaged in a strategic competition with the United States. On this issue, I think that Trump is right, the EU is moving in the right direction, and it is time now for other like-minded countries to follow suit. Likewise, contrary to what Beijing keeps claiming, it is not democracies that have declared a "cold war" on China, it is China that has forced it on us, in trying to impose on the international community, particularly the UN system, a negation of the universality of human rights, especially civil and political rights.

For all these reasons, we should not only be more combative but also more confident in ourselves. We should be more combative in imposing wherever possible the reciprocity principle in our dealings with China and more precisely the CCP, as well as in invoking our values and rejecting Beijing's increasingly arrogant lectures. We should also be more combative in strengthening dialogues and coordination among democracies, especially the United States, the EU, Australia, Canada, Japan, and India, on the best way to deal with China. We should be more confident because we know many Chinese are rather split or even schizophrenic, defending their government in public due to nationalistic pressure but being critical in private over lack of democracy and freedoms and acting in their personal interests. We should also be more confident because China's economy is and will remain for a long time on the whole semideveloped, with an average standard of living lower than ours. And finally, we should be more confident because Chinese society is fast changing, and the distance between it and ours has a good chance of gradually becoming narrower than that between it and the party-state that rules and controls it.[29]

Of course China's democratization would not resolve all our differences or our disputes with it. It would be naïve to imagine that a democratic and powerful China would cease to be Confucian, nationalistic, and even imperial, arduously defending its interests. It is even probable that it will continue to challenge aspects of the current international order that go against its own interests. However, like India and Japan, such a China would be both closer to us and more integrated globally, starting with the United Nations, wherein it has been seeking to play a bigger role.

There are many reasons to stay the course, have self-confidence in our values, and keep up our fight for democracy while at the same time working more assiduously to improve our own democratic systems and inform people of China's current political reality: a strong China led by an authoritarian political system that is strong, arrogant, and popular, a party-state that will remain for long in power but will eventually be doomed.

NOTES

1. He said in 1989: "There is no democracy without democrats," quoted in *The End of History and the Last Man* (New York: Free Press, 2006), 134–135.

2. Lucian Pye, *Dynamics of Chinese Politics* (Cambridge, MA: Oelgeschlage, Gunn & Hain, 1981); and Lucian Pye, *The Spirit of Chinese Politics* (Cambridge, MA: Harvard University Press, 1992). Lucian Pye died in 2008.

3. Shaohua Hu, "Confucianism and Western Democracy," in *China and Democracy : Reconsidering the Prospect for a Democratic China*, ed. Suisheng Zhao (New York and London: Routledge, 2000), 55–72.

4. Pierre-Etienne Will, Introduction to *China, Democracy and Law: A Historical and Contemporary Approach*, ed. Mireille Delmas-Marty and Pierre-Etienne Will (Leiden, Netherlands: Brill, 2012), 31–32.

5. Bo Yang, *Choulou de Zhongguoren* (Taipei: Linbai chubanshe, 1985); and Bo Yang, *The Ugly Chinaman and the Crisis of Chinese Culture*, trans. and ed. Don J. Cohn and Jing Qing (St. Leonards, NSW: Allen and Unwin, 1992).

6. For a good discussion of the range of nondemocratic regimes, see Paul Brooker, *Non-Democratic Regimes* (New York: Palgrave Macmillan, 2014).

7. Guillermo O'Donnell and Philippe C. Schmitter, *Transitions from Authoritarian Rule: Tentative Conclusions about Uncertain Democracies* (Baltimore, MD: Johns Hopkins University Press, 1986); and Juan Linz and Alfred Stepan, *Problems of Democratic Transition and Consolidation* (Washington, DC: Johns Hopkins University Press, 1996).

8. Robert A. Dahl, *Polyarchy: Participation and Opposition* (New Haven, CT: Yale University Press, 1971), 15.

9. Barbara Geddes, "What Do We Know About Democratization After Twenty Years?," *Annual Review of Political Science*, no. 2 (June 1999): 115–144.

10. According to Larry Diamond, "democratic recession" began around 2006; "Facing Up to the Democratic Recession," *Journal of Democracy* 26, no. 1 (January 2015): 141–155.

11. For a discussion of this correlation, see the highly controversial book by its equally controversial Singaporean author of Indian origin, Kishore Mahbubani, *Has the West Lost It?* (London: Penguin, 2017).

12. James Mann, *The Chinese Fantasy: How Our Leaders Explain Away Chinese Repression* (New York: Viking, 2007).

13. See Jean-Pierre Cabestan, *La politique internationale de la Chine : Entre intégration et volonté de puissance* [China's international policies: Between integration and pursuit of power], 2nd ed. (Paris: Presses de Sciences Po, 2015); and James McGregor, "Xi

Jinping's New Era of Global Leadership," *Diplomatic Courier*, December 7, 2017, https:/
/www.diplomaticourier.com/xi-jinpings-new-era-global-leadership/.

14. Fareed Zakaria, *The Future of Freedom: Illiberal Democracy at Home and Abroad* (New York: Norton, 2004).

15. Graham Allison, *Destined for War: Can America and China Escape Thucydides's Trap?* (Boston and New York: Houghton Mifflin Harcourt, 2017); Jean-Pierre Cabestan, "Le piège de Thucydide vu de Pékin: Comment la Chine affirme son leadership tout en évitant la guerre" [Thucydides's trap seen from Beijing: How China assets its leadership while avoiding war], *Le Débat*, December 2018, 4–15.

16. Kurt M. Campbell and Ely Ratner, "The China Reckoning. How Beijing Defied American Expectations," *Foreign Affairs* (March/April 2018), https://www.foreign affairs.com/articles/china/2018-02-13/china-reckoning; and Jeffrey Bader, "U.S.-China Relations: Is It Time to End the Engagement?," *Brooking Policy Brief*, September 2018, https://www.brookings.edu/wp-content/uploads/2018/09/FP_20180925_us_china_rela tions.pdf. For a good discussion of the major fault lines among US China experts, see Elizabeth C. Economy, *The Third Revolution: Xi Jinping and the New Chinese State* (New York: Oxford University Press, 2018), 233–236.

17. "Jim Mann Details Why 'Engagement' with China Failed," *Bill Bishop of Sinocism*, December 15, 2018, https://www.axios.com/interview-james-mann-us-china-engagement-trade-8477691b-e353-41cd-8c8b-30ff9e48bd88.html?utm_source=newslet ter&utm_medium=email&utm_campaign=newsletter_axioschina&stream=top; see also Stewart Paterson, *China, Trade and Power: Why the West's Economic Engagement Has Failed* (London: London Publishing Partnership, 2018). In her latest book, Elizabeth Economy has developed a view that is close to Jim Mann's as well as my own; see *The Third Revolution*, 237–250.

18. For a study partly along these lines, see Mikko Huotari, Jan Gaspers, Thomas Eder, Helena Legarda, and Sabine Mokry, "China's Emergence as a Global Security Actor: Strategies for Europe," *Merics Papers on China*, no. 4 (July 2017), https://www. merics.org/en/papers-on-china/chinas-emergence-global-security-actor-1.

19. "Section 3: China and Hong Kong," in *2016 Annual Report to Congress* (Washington, DC: 2016), 407–408, https://www.uscc.gov/sites/default/files/Annual_Report/ Chapters/Chapter%203%2C%20Section%203%20-%20China%20and%20Hong%20 Kong.pdf.

20. See Marshall Shahlins, *Confucius Institutes: Academic Malfare* (Chicago: Prickly Paradigm Press, 2014); and Christopher R. Hughes, "Confucius Institutes and the University: Distinguishing the Political Mission from the Cultural," *Issues and Studies* 50, no. 4 (2014): 45–83.

21. See James Jiann Hua To, *Qiaowu: Extra-Territorial Policies for the Overseas Chinese* (Leiden, Netherlands, and Boston: Brill, 2014).

22. Anne-Marie Brady, "Magic Weapons: China's Political Influence Activities under Xi Jinping," Wilson Center, September 18, 2017, https://www.wilsoncenter.org/ article/magic-weapons-chinas-political-influence-activities-under-xi-jinping.

23. The China Association for International Friendly Contact (Zhongguo guoji youhao lianluo hui) functions under the CCP's United Front Work Department.

24. John Seaman, Mikko Huotari, and Miguel Otero-Iglesias, eds., *Chinese Investment in Europe: A Country-Level Approach*, ETNC Report (Paris: IFRI, 2017), https:// www.ifri.org/sites/default/files/atoms/files/etnc_reports_2017_final_20dec2017.pdf; and Ashley Feng and Sagatom Saha, "Emerging EU Policies Take a Harder Look at

Chinese Investments," *China Brief* 19, no. 2 (January 18, 2019), https://jamestown.org/program/emerging-eu-policies-take-a-harder-look-at-chinese-investments/.

25. François Godement and Abigaël Vasselier, *China at the Gates: A New Power Audit of EU-China Relations* (London: European Council on Foreign Relations, 2017).

26. Erik Brattberg and Etienne Soula, *Europe's Emerging Approach to China's Belt and Road Initiative* (Washington, DC: Carnegie Endowment for International Peace, 2018), https://carnegieendowment.org/2018/10/19/europe-s-emerging-approach-to-china-s-belt-and-road-initiative-pub-77536.

27. European Commission and HR/VP Contribution to the European Council, "Joint Communication to the European Parliament, the European Council and the Council. EU-China Strategic Outlook," Brussels, March 12, 2019, https://ec.europa.eu/commission/sites/beta-political/files/communication-eu-china-a-strategic-outlook.pdf.

28. See "What Kind of International Order Does China Want? Between Reformism and Revisionism," special feature, *China Perspectives*, no. 2 (2016): 3–35.

29. On pluralism in Chinese society, see Kristin Shi-Kupfer, Mareike Ohlberg, Simon Lang, and Bertram Lang, "Ideas and Ideologies Competing for China's Political Future: How Online Pluralism Challenges Official Orthodoxy," *Merics Papers on China*, no. 5 (October 2017), https://www.merics.org/en/papers-on-china/ideas-and-ideologies-competing-chinas-political-future.

Index

191

government officials (*guan erdai*), 16,
148. *See also* Chinese Communist
Party; family; "little emperors";
one-child policy; youth
China. *See* People's Republic of China;
Republic of China
China Aid Associations, 91
China Democratic Party, 32
Chinese Academy of Sciences, 117
Chinese Academy of Social Sciences
(CASS), 126
Chinese Air Force. *See* People's
Liberation Army
Chinese Communist Party (CCP), 2–3,
8, 13, 14, 14–15, 16, 24, 26, 33, 39, 50,
60, 63, 65, 67, 75, 95, 137, 138, 144,
171; adaptation, 6, 7, 13, 26, 141, 159;
atrophy, 5, 8, 160–162; cadres
(*ganbu*), 5, 15–16, 19, 23, 30, 31, 153;
centenary, 27; collective leadership,
42, 160; conservatives, 64, 65, 173;
Constitution, 100; co-optation,
20–21; divisions, 116, 137, 150, 153,
164; election, 24; factions, 21;
funding, 172; future, 8, 165–166;
general secretary, 19, 30; growth
model, 4; ideology, 7, 13–14, 14, 15,
26–27, 35, 44, 47, 48, 49, 53, 66, 68,
95, 98–99, 123, 124, 125, 155, 161;
and imperial tradition, 39, 40, 41, 42,
44–45, 45–46, 47, 48–49, 56;
institutionalization (or lack of), 7,
19, 21; intraparty democracy, 20, 94,
111n45, 160–161; leaders'
generations, 154–155, 173;
leadership, 4, 19, 20–21, 23, 27, 33,
35, 59, 91, 92, 100, 114, 115, 116, 118,
128, 150, 153, 154, 162, 163, 173;
leading cadres (*lingdao ganbu*), 15,
16, 18, 19, 20–21, 22, 23, 24, 25, 26,
48, 83, 95, 160; legitimacy, 7, 62–63,
143, 151; mafia-ization, 13, 16, 19, 30,
38n34; members, membership, 16,
22, 24, 25, 29, 30, 35, 63, 92–93,
94–96, 107, 111n47, 160; modus
operandi, 23, 114, 153;
nomenklatura, 15, 20, 30, 48, 100,
116, 122, 132, 153, 160, 162, 163;
objectives, 26, 47; opacity, 19, 22;

and opposition, 32; organization, 20,
22–23, 23, 162; political discipline,
31; and political reform, 33, 150, 155,
173, 178; reformers, 153; and
reforms, 4, 15, 178; repressive
power, 171; resilience (*see*
adaptation); as a ruling party, 26; as
a secret society, 22; support for, 63,
136n40, 152; United Front strategy,
152, 156, 181. *See also* Chinese
Communist Party Congresses and
Plenums; Chinese Communist Party
Central and Local Organs; Chinese
government; Chinese People's
Political Consultative Conferences;
corruption; National People's
Congress; nationalism; People's
Republic of China; propaganda
Chinese Communist Party Congresses
and Plenums: 18th Congress, 30;
19th Congress, 5, 20–21, 27, 31, 47,
86, 111n45, 116, 153, 156; 3rd
plenum of the 18th Central
Committee, 15; 4th Plenum of the
18th Central Committee, 86;
Congress, 20, 45
Chinese Communist Party Central and
Local Organs: Central Committee,
15, 19, 20–21, 30, 45; central
departments, 19; Central Discipline
Inspection Commission, 29, 31, 119,
122; Central Military Commission,
19, 20, 27; commissions, 46, 80;
Control commissions, 45; discipline
inspection commissions, 29, 30, 31,
34, 45; leading small groups, 19, 46,
80; local party organizations, 3, 16,
24, 25, 65, 147; National Security
Commission, 32, 96; Organization
Department, 20; Politburo, 11n12,
20, 34; Politburo Standing
Committee, 19, 20, 34, 115; political
and legal affairs commissions
(*zhengfa weiyuanhui*), 17, 86; United
Front Work Department, 88, 188n23
Chinese Dream, 27, 99, 101, 119, 171
Chinese government, 2, 4, 6, 16–17, 18,
19, 28, 29, 30, 32, 42, 46, 48, 60, 61,
61–62, 69, 78, 79, 87, 97, 98, 100, 105,

About the Author

Jean-Pierre Cabestan is professor in the Department of Government and International Studies, Hong Kong Baptist University. He is associate researcher at the Asia Centre, Paris, and at the French Centre for Research on Contemporary China (CEFC) in Hong Kong. He is also senior research fellow at the French National Centre for Scientific Research. From 1998 to 2003, he was director of the CEFC and chief editor of *China Perspectives*. From 1994 to 1998, he was director of the Taipei Office of the CEFC. In 1990–1991, he was lecturer at the Politics Department of the School of Oriental and African Studies. He has been researching contemporary China for more than forty years and has published extensively in English and in French on China's domestic politics and institutions, foreign and security policy, Taiwanese politics, relations across the Taiwan Strait, and more recently, China-Africa relations. His most recent publications include *La politique internationale de la Chine: Entre intégration et volonté de puissance*, 2nd ed. (2015); *China and the Global Financial Crisis: A Comparison with Europe* (2012) (coedited with Jean-François Di Meglio and Xavier Richet); *Secessionism and Separatism in Europe and Asia: To Have a State of One's Own* (2013) (coedited with Aleksandar Pavkovic); *Le système politique chinois: Un nouvel équilibre autoritaire* (The Chinese political system: A new authoritarian equilibrium) (2014); *Political Changes in Taiwan Under Ma Ying-jeou: Partisan Conflict, Policy Choices, External Constraints and Security Challenges* (2014; coedited with Jacques deLisle); *Tanzania-China All-Weather Friendship in the Era of Multipolarity* (2017; with Jean-Raphaël Chaponnière); and *Demain la Chine: Démocratie ou dictature?* (China tomorrow: Democracy or dictatorship?) (2018). He received his PhD from the University of Paris 1 (Panthéon-Sorbonne).